"Train Time" at Bala summer station, 1919.
The S.S. "Cherokee" is connecting with the northbound train from Toronto.
Courtesy, *Public Archives of Canada* PA 83885

THE STEAMBOAT ERA

in the

MUSKOKAS

VOLUME II — *The Golden Years to the Present*

in the
MUSKOKAS

VOLUME II — *The Golden Years to the Present*

Richard Tatley

A History of Steam Navigation
in the districts of
Muskoka and Parry Sound
1906 to Present

Stoddart

A BOSTON MILLS PRESS BOOK

JAMES S. PLAYFAIR, President

HUGH C. MACLEAN, Vice-Preside

THE MUSKOKA LAKES NAVIGATION AND HOTEL COMPANY, LIMITED

Operating the Royal Muskoka Hotel
and a fleet of Ten Modern Steamers

W. F. Wasley.   L.W. Maxson.
Manager Transportation.   Manager Royal Muskoka.

Canadian Cataloguing in Publication Data

Tatley, Richard
  The steamboat era in the Muskokas

Contents: v. 1. To the golden years — v. 2. The ships we remember.
Bibliography: v.
Includes index.
ISBN 0-919822-50-9 (v. 1). — 0-919783-10-4 (v. 2).

1. Steam-navigation — Ontario — Muskoka — History
2. Steamboats — Ontario — Muskoka — History. 3.
Inland water transportation — Ontario — Muskoka —
History.   I. Title.

VM627.05T37 1983   386'.5'0971316   C83-098606-5

Published by
Stoddart Publishing Co. Limited
34 Lesmill Road
Toronto, Ontario
M3B 2T6
(416) 445-3333

A BOSTON MILLS PRESS BOOK
The Boston Mills Press
132 Main Street
Erin, Ontario
N0B 1T0

4th printing 1995

Typeset by Linotext, Toronto, Ontario
Printed in Canada

The publisher gratefully acknowledges the support of the
Canada Council, Ministry of Culture, Tourism and Recreation,
Ontario Arts Council and Ontario Publishing Centre in the
development of writing and publishing in Canada.

Steamers at Port Carling, 1907.
In this scene are the yachts "Rambler" (left) and "Shamrock", with the Navigation Company steamers "Kenozha", "Oriole" and "Medora".
Courtesy, *Ontario Archives* S.3631

CONTENTS

A summer holiday just wasn't complete without a cruise on the mighty "Sagamo".
Painting by Thomas Sinclair of Sharon, Ontario—1984.

Thomas Sinclair is an illustrator of historical transportation machinery, having for many years painted aircraft and automobiles as well as railway scenes. His work has been exhibited in a number of Ontario galleries.

A commercial artist by profession, he lives in the country north of Toronto.

FOREWORD

This writer's interest in steamboats, and in particular those on the Muskoka Lakes, began in 1952 at the highly impressionable age of ten, when his family obtained a cottage on Lake Muskoka and began summering there. That same season he took his first of many 100 Mile Cruises aboard the lordly *Sagamo*, which was then nearing the end of her dignified career. To the author, the "Sag" seemed like a miniature ocean liner—and sounded like one too! His imagination was fired from that day on. It became a part of every summer day during those years to watch for the black plume of smoke among the islands, announcing that "The steamboat's coming!" Whenever possible, it was customary to hop into one's motorboat and scuttle out to meet the big ships on their runs, and to chase them as far as possible. Thus the writer was privileged to witness the last remnants of a gracious, charming era. We cherished the lake steamers because they were haughty, graceful and large, and because we realized that they were a vanishing breed whose days were numbered. We missed them very much when they were gone.

It did not take long for the writer to sense that the lake steamers had a long history behind them. Having a passion for history generally, he soon began to delve into the past; trying to find out more about the boats. Little did he imagine that it would turn into a 30-year search, eventually involving thousands of hours of wading through pictures, books, manuscripts, newspapers and documents. Best of all were the scores of interviews, many with people no longer with us, in an effort to piece together a gigantic mosaic of a million inlays, of which at least 950,000 were missing. In spite of the enormous complexity of the subject matter, however, it has been an exciting quest; an attempt to salvage some of the lore of the past. This book, and its counterpart, are the results of those efforts.

The author wishes to thank all those who, in diverse ways, have helped to make this book possible, and to apologize for any errors or omissions which will inevitably be found in it. For these and all other defects he assumes full responsibility. If the text seems too long and cumbersome, the writer can only shrug helplessly and beg to remind the reader that it would have been much longer still, had a lot more information not been deleted from it. If at times the author has plagiarized a bit from some of his earlier writings, he can only reply that sometimes he was unable to think of a better way to express his ideas. And if perceptive readers notice discrepancies between this book and any others by this writer, let him freely admit that additional research has sometimes thrown a new light on things and induced him to alter some of his earlier impressions. At the very least, he hopes and believes that most of his information and conclusions are correct. As to his biases, which may become obvious to the reader, the author is proud to acknowledge them. What could be more monotonous than unbiased history?

If this book and its previous partner (Volume I) prove to be of some interest, and help to arouse a deeper awareness and appreciation of the lake steamers of old, the author will consider his efforts amply rewarded.

"Train Time" at Bala summer station.
The S.S. "Cherokee" awaits her passengers at the left.
Courtesy, *Canadian Pacific Corporate Archives*, No. 21723

Wooding up on the S.S. "Oriole".
Courtesy, *Mr. Alldyn Clark*, Bracebridge

Bridge of the S.S. "Sagamo", around 1907.
In this view, the pilothouse does not yet have its two side wings. Commodore Bailey stands beside the engine room telegraph.
Courtesy, *Public Archives of Canada* PA 132136

CHAPTER 1
The Golden Age of the Muskoka Steamers
(1905-1920)

By the year 1906, Canada was in the middle of the fashionable, prosperous interval commonly called the Edwardian Era. Bluff, good-humoured King Edward VII was on the throne, the British Empire was at its height, and in Ottawa, Sir Wilfrid Laurier was proclaiming that the 20th century belonged to Canada. Despite the occasional lapse, the country was prospering as never before. Capital flowed freely from the London money markets; settlers from all over Europe were pouring into the prairies; the riches of the Canadian Shield were being tapped, and the factories and foundries of the East were rushing to turn out the machinery, equipment and rails needed in the West. The picture was not entirely rosy, of course. Wages were generally low. Many lived in squalor. Industries polluted the air and covered the cities in grime, while towns and mills dumped raw sewage and untreated wastes into the lakes and rivers. Roads were bad, working hours long, and parochialism rampant. Every small village considered itself the centre of the universe.

Yet every age has its faults, and this one, despite its defects, was essentially a confident, dynamic decade, full of exciting opportunities. Communities were starting to generate electricity. Telephones and talking machines were appearing. The first horseless carriages were stirring up dust on the roads, while a few daredevils were experimenting with flying machines. On all fronts, civilization seemed to be making rapid strides. Progress was taken for granted, war seemed to be disappearing, and strife, if it existed, was always remote and far away: in any case, Canadians had a country to build. For the successful, and the well-to-do generally, this was an era of vigorous optimism. It was an era of top hats, frock coats and hoopskirts; of reserved manners and elegant social teas; of intensive business activity in the cities alternating with leisurely weekends in the country. For many fashionable Canadians, and Americans, summertime in the country meant Muskoka. By 1909, the resorts on the Muskoka Lakes were advertising that they could, collectively, house over 4,983 guests. So great was the annual influx, additional resorts had to be opened in adjoining regions, such as Sparrow Lake, the Huntsville lakes and the Magnetawan.

Right in the middle of this comfortable, satisfied world was the Muskoka Lakes Navigation and Hotel Company, now the largest inland waterway steamboat line in the country. Its capital stock in 1905 came to about $173,600, and it owned the palatial Royal Muskoka Hotel on Lake Rosseau as well as eight steamships. Its founder, A. P. Cockburn, passed away in June of 1905, but his place on the Board of Directors was briefly taken by his son, J. Roy Cockburn, until 1907 when he was followed by James Playfair of Midland, a son of J. S. Playfair, the President. (James Playfair himself became President shortly afterwards.) Another newcomer to the Board in 1905 was Major Hugh Cameron MacLean of Winnipeg, already one of Canada's leading newspapermen, having founded the MacLean Publishing Company in 1886; a connection that would later prove invaluable to the Navigation Company. Within seven years Major MacLean would buy out both of the Playfairs and become President of the Line himself.

C. H. Nicholson, the anticipated heir to A. P. Cockburn, never did assume the position of Manager of the boat division. For some reason he was judged unsuitable or untrustworthy, and the post went instead to William Franklin Wasley of Gravenhurst, who also emerged as Secretary and Treasurer.

W. F. Wasley was the only son of Frank Wasley, who founded and ran the Albion Hotel in Gravenhurst. Born near Newmarket in 1873, young Wasley came with his parents to Muskoka at the age of four. In his youth he sometimes helped run the Albion. After leaving the local schools, he graduated with honours from the Ontario Business College at Belleville in 1892, before returning home to serve as bookkeeper with the firm of Mowry and Sons, who ran an iron foundry in Gravenhurst. Within a year, he joined the Navigation Company, broadening his

William Franklin Wasley, Manager of the Muskoka Navigation Company, 1906-1941.

experience by serving as a crew member on the boats and ultimately obtaining his own Master's ticket. After two seasons as purser on the *Nipissing*, he went to work on the Magnetawan division, virtually as Regional Manager, until his return in 1901, when he succeeded Daniel McKinnon as bookkeeper. Soon he was recognized as the logical successor to A.P. Cockburn. A Presbyterian turned Anglican in religion and an active sportsman, Mr. Wasley managed the Gravenhurst Hockey Club for a year and established the Wasley Prize for curling, of which he was a great enthusiast. He also became a founder of the Gravenhurst Rotary Club and Master of the local Masonic Lodge. For many years he was active on the Gravenhurst Light and Water Commission, the Gravenhurst Board of Trade and the Muskoka Tourist Development Association, constantly exhorting them never to rest on their laurels and always to upgrade their facilities and advertise Muskoka. As Manager, Wasley proved strict, efficient and autocratic. He was a veritable martinet to his staff, who for the most part were rather afraid of him, but those who knew him well respected and even venerated him for his honesty, integrity and total dedication to his work. As with A. P. Cockburn, the well-being of the Navigation Company became an obsession with Wasley. It would be his tragedy that his long tenure in office extended well past the best days of the Company, into the grim years of the thirties and forties, when the very survival of the Line sometimes hung in the balance.

All that was far in the future when Wasley assumed the mantle of A. P. Cockburn in 1905. That autumn the Company sold all its assets on the Magnetawan and henceforth confined itself solely to the Muskoka Lakes. At the same time it was putting the finishing touches on plans for a mammoth new palace steamer capable of carrying as many passengers as any two existing ships in the fleet.

The new flagship was indeed a masterpiece, and a description of her will help illustrate the impressive strides made in steamboating over the years. First of all, she was designed by the noted naval architect Arendt Engstrom of Cleveland, who had just finished plans for the S.S. *Cayuga*, soon to enter service on the Toronto to Niagara run. The new Muskoka steamship was in many respects a copy of the *Cayuga*, though much smaller: she was 146 feet in length from the bow to the rudder post and 152 feet overall, with a beam of 29 feet and a hold depth of 9 feet. She had a rivetted steel hull constructed in nine sections by the Canadian Ship Building Company in Toronto, but was assembled at Muskoka Wharf. Her upper deck framework was also steel, though the superstructure was built of wood. She was fitted out with two ultramodern triple expansion steam engines, with cylinder diameters of ten, sixteen and twenty-six inches respectively, plus four Scotch marine boilers, each seven feet in diameter and eleven feet in length and good for 175 lbs. pressure: two stokers, working on alternate shifts, were needed to tend them. The two forward boilers were set with their fireboxes facing aft, while the latter two faced forward. The total horsepower delivered was officially 68.8, giving the new vessel speeds of eighteen miles per hour or more. Except for the *Waubamik* (1869) and the *Muskoka*, the new steamer was the first twin-screw ship in the fleet. She was also the first to have steam steering and electric lighting, and the first to burn coal. She may also have been the first to carry a septic tank. Her upper works were impressive. Designed as a day-observation-type vessel, she had two full-length decks plus two partial decks above. The main deck featured washrooms, a roomy galley, and an elegant dining room finished in weathered oak and burlap, filling the entire fantail and seating 90 patrons. The promenade deck overhead had a large forward lounge and a ladies' lounge aft, also panelled with oak and burlap, while the deck above that was provided with a smoking room. When completed, the new ship was reckoned to gross 744 tons, although the register tonnage was only 420.27: even so, that was nearly equivalent to the *Medora* and *Nipissing* combined. Her colour scheme, like that of her sister ships at this time, was red at the waterline, black up to the main deck, white above with green trim, and a red and black stack. She could carry 800 passengers, complete with trunks and baggage, and required a crew of twenty-six.

While still only partially completed, the new ship was launched at Muskoka Wharf on July 25, 1906, a few minutes past 3:00 p.m. For hours that morning, the work crews were busy removing all superfluous blocking and shoring, while a big crowd assembled from miles around. Every ship in the fleet except the *Kenozha* took the day off for the grand event, as did countless yachts and innumerable dignitaries. Finally the brief ceremony began. Miss Jessie Alexander, granddaughter of President Playfair, broke the customary bottle of champagne, while a pennant ran up the mast and unfurled the name SAGAMO ("big chief") to the breeze. The crowd gave a resounding cheer. Then the lines were cut, and the *Sagamo* slid gracefully backwards into the bay amid the applause of the throng and a crescendo of whistle blasts from the other steamers.

The *Sagamo* was afterwards towed over to the Navigation Company shipyards to be completed. Captain George Bailey, her commander-to-be, must have found it hard to restrain his excitement, but as it turned out he was kept waiting all summer for his new charge. The engines of the *Sagamo* were finally tested in October, but she did not complete a trip until June 15, 1907. Once in service, she proved to have plenty of power, could reverse easily, and handled more efficiently than any other steamer in the fleet. Her weakness was her lofty silhouette, which, combined with her rather shallow draft, allowed her to drift sideways in a crosswind. Nevertheless she was loved by her crews and the public alike, and became a veritable institution on the Muskoka Lakes.

The *Sagamo* was the largest passenger steamer on any of the minor lakes of Ontario. In fact, she was so big that many of the local wharves were too small to receive her. She had barely a foot of clearance when locking through the chamber at Port Carling, and required a line attached to the wharf above the locks on the port side to spring her around the bend in the Indian River: on the rudder alone she would have piled up on the opposite shore. The lock master always cast off the line in response to a toot from the whistle, while the deckhands whipped the line aboard

S.S. "Sagamo", under construction, 1906.

S.S. "Sagamo", starting up in 1907.
Courtesy *Mrs. Irene Dickson*, Willowdale

S.S. "Sagamo", around 1910.
The new flagship now has a canvas tarpaulin sheltering the auxiliary helm, and a buff coloured stack.

Courtesy *Mrs. Irene Dickson*, Willowdale

quickly before it got caught in the propellers. Her size also prevented her from entering Bala Bay or ascending the Muskoka River. She is said to have visited Bala just once, around 1942, to collect a huge throng of passengers, but she scraped against the railway bridge at Bala Park both ways and never repeated the episode. At least one of her captains volunteered to try to bring her to Bracebridge, but Mr. Wasley adamantly refused to take the risk. The new flagship always conducted the main run north from Gravenhurst early in the morning, following the arrival of the Muskoka Midnight Special from Toronto and Buffalo. Initially, she plied daily to Port Cockburn and back, making connections with some of the smaller steamers at such places as Beaumaris, Port Carling, Windermere and the Royal Muskoka, and returning at 7:45 p.m. The smaller ships in turn acted as feeders to the flagship, servicing the lesser ports of call.

The first season of the *Sagamo* also proved to be the last active season for the steamer *Muskoka*. By the year 1907 the *Muskoka* was 26 years old, and despite the addition of 12,000 board feet of new lumber in her hull, the old vessel was growing leaky, so leaky that near the end she was known to take two or three feet of water every night and had to be pumped out daily to remain afloat. The Company was already planning a replacement for her, but the new ship, like the *Sagamo*, was not ready on schedule, and the old *Muskoka* had to struggle through the entire 1907 season, still on the Bala run.

One evening after returning to Bala for the night, the men left the ship to visit the local hotel. Last to leave was one of the firemen, who banked the boiler fires, as usual, before heading uptown. Apparently he left a "little too much steam up," because, just a few minutes later, she "blew off" all the water in the boiler. Hurrying back, the men found the wharf soaking wet, the ladies of the dining room staff much alarmed, and scarcely any water visible in the gauge-glass. The boiler was now in grave danger of overheating and exploding, and the hands lost no time refilling it and putting out the fires. The boiler did not blow up, and the *Muskoka* and her crew were spared to finish the season. The following year, however, the old ship was officially condemned, but luckily by that time the new steamer was ready. For the next five years the *Muskoka* was left idle at the Gravenhurst dockyards, growing steadily more decrepit, until finally she was dismantled in 1912 and stroked off the registry. Her massive timbers proved too much for the wreckers, though, and the hulk was left at the dockyard for years, gradually falling to pieces. Parts of it were still visible in the 1920s.

Her successor was under construction in 1906 and was, essentially, a smaller edition of the *Sagamo*. Like the *Sagamo*, she had a steel hull built by the Canadian Ship Building Company in Toronto and assembled at Muskoka Wharf. She also had twin triple expansion engines, twin propellers, steel framework, steam steering, electric lights and wooden superstructure. Also like the flagship, she was a coal-burner, and, though she had only a single boiler, she could generate 41 hp. and carry about 400 people. Her interior appointments were almost as luxurious as the *Sagamo*'s. She was, however, only 120 feet in length at the keel and 23 feet in beam and registered just 159.60 tons.

The new steamer was largely completed by July 17, 1907, the date set for her launching. This time the daughter of Frank Phillips, Vice-President of the Company, performed the honours, christening the ship the *Cherokee*. Unlike the *Sagamo*, the *Cherokee* was launched sideways, quite smoothly, after which the Mickle tug *Grace M.* towed her over to the shipyards for the finishing touches. At best, however, she managed only a few shakedown cruises late in the fall of 1907. Her first paying trip took place on June 12, 1908, when she sailed triumphantly to Bracebridge under the command of Captain John Henry, who, next to Bailey, was senior officer of the Line. Captain Henry adored the *Cherokee*, and refused to let anyone else take her wheel. For that matter, she was not exactly unpopular with the public either. Bracebridge residents, when chartering a steamer for a cruise, always demanded the *Cherokee*, and complained bitterly if one of the older ships was substituted. In every sense the *Cherokee* was a lovely ship. If she had a fault, it was primarily that her boiler and engines were set rather far forward, making her light in the stern and heavy at the bow, and giving her a tendency to plough her way through the water.

Meanwhile the other steamers were not neglected. By 1907, the piping systems on all the older ships had been rebuilt and modernized, with holding tanks added. One by one, the boats exchanged their old coal oil lamps for electric lights: the *Medora* and *Islander* were converted in 1911. The Muskoka 'Herald' commented approvingly that "The Company seems to spare no

S.S. "Muskoka" (Final Version).
Courtesy, Bracebridge *Herald-Gazette*

S.S. "Muskoka", derelict at Gravenhurst.

S.S. "Cherokee", newly built.
The new palace steamer appears on the marine railway at Gravenhurst. Her predecessor, the "Muskoka", can be seen at the left.
Courtesy, *Mr. Gerald Leeder*, Kearney

S.S. "Cherokee", on a Y.W.C.A. cruise, 1909.
Courtesy, *Mrs. Irene Dickson*, Willowdale

expense to provide for the wants of the passenger and freight business of the entire territory, both as to equipment and favourable rates, and we wish them every success." The captains in 1907 were as follows: Commodore Bailey/*Sagamo*; John Henry/*Cherokee*; Edward McAlpine/*Medora*; C.E. Jackson/*Nipissing*; Ross Hansen/*Kenozha*; William Elder/*Islander*; Ralph Lee/*Muskoka*; John Bibby of Gravenhurst/*Ahmic*; Bert Campbell of Rosseau/*Oriole*; and A.P. Larson/*Charlie M.*.

With the Navigation Company so solidly entrenched on the Muskoka Lakes, it seems rather startling that anyone would seriously have considered competing with it, yet efforts were made to do exactly that. There had always been the local workboats or "tramps" trying to cut in on the freighting business and A.P. Cockburn noted as early as 1902, "that some of them were becoming more aggressive and were no longer content with just the crumbs of the trade."

An even more direct challenge was the appearance of rival passenger steamers, all of which were owned and operated by local residents and their families. The first of these boats after A.T. Lowe's *Lady of the Lake* (1886) was the steamer *Florence Main*, built by Captain Alfred Mortimer and his sons at Mortimer's Point in 1901. Named after the captain's wife, the *Florence Main* was the fourth of his boats and the second that he built himself. She was a good 82.4 feet in length and 13.2 in beam and registered 52.46 tons. Her keel was built in three sections and the massive ribs hewn with adzes and broadaxes from solid white oak, a technique reminiscent of the *Wenonah* in 1866. She had twin engines but only a single deck, with a bank of cabins surmounted by a pilot house. This rather limited her carrying capacity, but Captain Mortimer was apparently nervous about high winds on Lake Muskoka.

The *Florence Main* was launched in 1901, and on her maiden voyage to Bracebridge she was received with whistle salutes from every steamer she encountered. Captain Mortimer intended to use her to ply regularly from Mortimer's Point, which still had no road to connect it with "civilization", to such centres as Bala, Whiteside, Beaumaris, Bracebridge and Port Carling, and perhaps, to do a little towing in the off-season. It has been claimed that she could outrace

S.S. "Florence Main" (Original Version).
A reconstruction sketch by the Author, based on registry information plus two photographs showing glimpses of the vessel. Some of the aft detail is conjectural.

Steamers at Bracebridge old wharf, around 1904.
Gathered for the Fair are the "Florence Main" (left), "City of Bala", "Kenozha" and "Islander".

the *Islander* on a straight course, and no doubt residents of Mortimer's Point were very pleased to have a new passenger boat to take them to town.

The *Florence Main* had scarcely entered service when the Strouds of Milford Bay decided to get in on the act. Like many other families around the lake, the Strouds had tried their hand at nearly everything, including farming, sawmilling and towing, using a succession of tugs, the *Jennie Willson*, *Comet* and *Wawonaissa*. During the 1880s, Robert Stroud, the head of the family, also built the Milford Bay Temperance Hotel, often called the "Stroud House", which by 1903 was large enough to take 100 guests. In 1902, Mr. Stroud's son, Robert J. Stroud, built the steamer *Nymph*, a 20 ton vessel with a length of 72 feet, as an added attraction for the hotel. It was advertised that the *Nymph* would tow or scow at the lowest rates for six months of the year, and that she had a covered scow for perishable goods. She was chartered for excursions; running a moonlight cruise to Gravenhurst for the Sons of Scotland in July 1904, attending the Water Carnivals at Port Carling with the *Ahmic*, and shuttling picnickers to Browning Island, along with the *Islander*, always using a palace scow. Captain Ben Dewey of Gravenhurst was running the *Nymph* in 1905-06, and Captain Andy Corbett in 1907. In the latter year, she was advertising regular trips from Bracebridge to Rosseau on Mondays, Bracebridge to Bala on Tuesdays, and Bracebridge to the American House hotel at Whiteside on Thursdays and Saturdays. On other days, she was available for private charters. The following year she was sailing regularly to Torrance and Port Sandfield. Also, in 1905, Hubert C. Minett built a 51 foot steam yacht called the *Mineta* (7.35 tons), which he used to run charter cruises on the two upper lakes, adding further to the competition.

Steamers such as these had a certain advantage, in that they could call at remote docking places more frequently and flexibly than the big ships, which were bound to very tight schedules. Obviously it was impossible for the Navigation Company steamers to call at every cape and cottage on the lakes several times a day. However, with eight and then nine vessels plying on regular schedules every summer, the Navigation Company was able to offer fairly comprehensive and reliable service. So strong was its position that local competitors never stood a chance on any of the important routes. As an example, in 1902, both the Strouds and Captain Mortimer

Milford Bay House, Milford Bay.
This temperance hotel, often called "Stroud House",
survived until the 1930s, when it was destroyed by
fire.

Steamer "Nymph".
Courtesy, *Mr. Peter B. Campbell*, Campbell's Landing

Steam Yacht "Mineta", of Clevelands House.
Courtesy, *Public Archives of Canada* PA 132118

received a severe setback when they applied for berths at Muskoka Wharf. Both were politely denied that privilege by the Grand Trunk, which chose to remain loyal to its old partner. Thus it is not surprising that Captain Mortimer decided to sell the *Florence Main* in the fall of 1904: she went to Charles Orlando Shaw of the Huntsville tannery, and soon became part of the Huntsville Navigation Company fleet. In 1908 the *Nymph* was also sold, to Captain Peter Campbell of west Muskoka Township, whose sons used her as a tug and scow for the next sixteen years (she had had a boiler retube in 1907 and at the same time was extensively rebuilt). In 1910, the *Mineta* also changed hands and was moved to other waters. The failure of these competing services simply reaffirmed the tendency of any long-lasting boat service on a given waterway to be a monopolistic one, under one direction and management. Any competition was likely to be small-scale, on a local basis, subsisting perhaps on routes judged by the large company to be unprofitable.

However, one individual was willing to try operating on this basis and he managed to do it successfully. This was Captain Charles Wesley Archer. The son of an English settler at Stephen's Bay on Lake Muskoka, Wes Archer went to work at Bracebridge, before taking up residence on the east side of Browning Island, where he had often gone on canoe trips. Part of the island is arable, and had once been used by the Boyd brothers of Bracebridge for raising hay and pasturing draft horses engaged in the lumber camps. Hence Mr. Archer was able to make a living selling firewood, ice and hay, and also milk, eggs and vegetables from the family farm. He also became a contractor and built docks and cottages. Ever an avid boatman, Archer greatly admired the lake steamers and decided he must have one of his own.

In the spring of 1905, Wes Archer purchased the *Eagle*, a small 20 foot launch, from a local cottager and soon found work for her, running to and from Browning Island, taking small parties on cruises, and towing scowloads of commodities for his customers. Sometimes Mrs. Archer used to steer the vessel while her husband handled the engine controls. In time Browning Island became a popular place for picnics, and also the unofficial headquarters of the Sayawa Canoe Club, whose members liked to pitch their tents there. All this was good for the water-taxi business, and soon Captain Archer decided that he needed a larger boat. He also dreamed of expanding his home into a regular tourist resort, but never got around to it.

In 1907, the *Eagle* was sold to a Bracebridge man, while Captain Archer bought the *Shamrock* (3 tons), a handsome big launch built originally at Kingston in 1903 and previously owned by a Port Carling gentleman. By 1910, Archer was advertising that the *Shamrock* would ply between Bracebridge and Camp Sayawa every Saturday and Monday for the benefit of his guests, free of charge. He also conducted charter cruises anywhere on the lakes, and frequently made a point of being at Muskoka Wharf just as the ice was breaking up in the spring, to meet commercial travellers eager to see the resort proprietors and secure orders for wines and tobacco before their competitors did. Captain Archer's main difficulty was with logs on the Muskoka River, which sometimes made for bumpy and adventurous trips. On the night of August 10, 1912 the *Shamrock* lost her rudder amid the logs near Bracebridge wharf, but her plucky owner had her repaired in time for the return trip early the following Monday.

Business remained promising, and in April 1914, Captain Archer sold the *Shamrock* to a resident of Milford Bay and bought the steamer *Algoma* (3.20 tons) a 36.6 foot launch with a ten horsepower engine, also built at Kingston (in 1901) and previously berthed at Fairholme Island, near Beaumaris. Capable of carrying 30 passengers at the speed of fourteen miles per hour, the trim little *Algoma* was also used as a water-taxi to Browning Island, and for special outings. Captain Archer now scored a major coup. Having arranged for a summer post office at Browning Island, he secured the contract to deliver the mail both to the island and to St. Elmo, near the mouth of the river, where many prosperous people from Bracebridge were erecting cottages. The *Algoma* also ran a weekly market trip into town so that the cottagers could do their shopping.

Captain Archer continued operating the *Algoma* until 1918, when he sold her to Bill Campbell of Shanty Bay, Lake Muskoka, (a son of Captain Campbell) who used her as a workboat, scowing earth, stone and lumber for new cottages around Beaumaris. A succession of later owners used her in much the same way, until 1929. Captain Archer meanwhile bought the steamer *Llano* from the Irwin estate and continued carrying passengers. We shall return to him later.

Steam Launch "Eagle".

Steam Launch "Shamrock".
Courtesy, *Public Archives of Canada* PA 132101

Steam Launch "Algoma".

Shortly after the turn of the century, Muskoka's railway facilities were suddenly tripled, as two of Canada's expanding transcontinentals decided to build new lines from Toronto through to the Sudbury basin, skirting the west side of the Muskoka Lakes. One of the newcomers was incorporated as the James Bay Junction Railway, running up the east side of Lake Simcoe, passing through Washago and Port Stanton on Sparrow Lake, and thence through Torrance and across the length of Bala Park Island, and then to the west side of Lake Joseph at Barnesdale and Gordon Bay. By 1905, all of these hamlets were 'booming', often literally, as dynamite charges echoed through the woods as the railway construction crews proceeded northward. Local tugs such as Captain Campbell's *Gravenhurst* won some very lucrative contracts scowing supplies to Barnesdale for the railway crews. On October 10, 1906, the new line was officially opened, but already it had been absorbed into the Canadian Northern Railway system. At the same time, the Canadian Pacific was laying its own tracks north from Toronto, but the C.P. line crossed Simcoe County west of Barrie and Orillia, bridged the Severn, swung through Bala, and ran almost side-by-side with the Canadian Northern right through to Parry Sound. On July 23, 1907, this line was declared open as far as Bala, and the remainder soon after. Neither of the two railways seemed to have had much inherent interest in Muskoka, but both were quick to realize the possible revenues they could derive by wooing the tourist traffic in competition with the Grand Trunk. Both accordingly built lakeside stations (used only in summertime), where their respective trains could connect with the lake steamers; the C.P.R. at Bala, complete with customs agents for the convenience of American tourists, and the Canadian Northern at both Bala Park and Barnesdale.

The new lines brought considerable prosperity to some of the places on their routes. Bala, hitherto no more than a minor sawmill centre, noted only for its falls and fishing, now began to expand rapidly. Old Thomas Burgess, the "Laird of Bala", died just a few years before the iron horse arrived, but his sons were soon busy subdividing his lands into lots, and before long the population swelled from 40 in 1900 to about 300 in 1914. In that year, Bala's official status jumped from that of a rural post office to a fully incorporated town. It had two stations; one for regular use, and the other a wharf station for summer tourists. At the latter, passengers could detrain and walk down a ramp to the wharf below, where a steamer would be waiting for them. On June 30, 1907, the *Islander* was on hand to greet the first train at Bala; the station looking very trim with its red roof and its fresh green and buff paint. By 1910, Bala could boast several new shops, improved recreation facilities, and four summer resorts. It also had hopes of becoming a division point, but the railway chose instead to locate it about ten miles up the line beside Stewart Lake in Freeman Township, probably because this spot offered far more level land for sidings. Thus was born the railway village of MacTier.

Other Muskoka communities benefitted as well, but not to the same extent as Bala. Torrance, on the Canadian Northern, coalesced from a scattered rural settlement into a small village in its own right. Nearby, on Bala Park Island, the railway built Bala Park Station, which, as at Bala, was really two stations; one on the main line, and the other a wharf station at the end of a "wye". This also became an important rendezvous point for the Navigation Company steamers. Problems, however, surfaced as a result of rail construction. On July 8, 1905, the *Islander* struck a rock no one had ever encountered before near Wallace's Cut, at one end of Bala Park Island, and later the same day the Beaumont steamer *Nymoca* holed her bow on the same rock and had to race for nearby Whiteside to unload her cargo, before sinking in shallow water. (She was raised and repaired within a few days.) The rock in question was suspected of being there as a result of railway dynamiting.

However, this was not the worst. During construction, the railway navvies allowed one of the three channels into Bala Bay to become clogged with broken rock. Besides cutting off a navigating channel, this led to flooding, waterlogged lands, ice damage to wharves, and generally cooler area temperatures. Presently, James J. Beaumont of Alport, one of the principal sufferers, backed by many of the local farmers and the Council of Monck, launched appeals to make the railway clear the channel. All these efforts failed, as cynics said they would, until the matter was finally referred to the Board of Railway Commissioners in 1909. The Board listened to the case, and decided in favour of Mr. Beaumont. The Canadian Northern was ordered to remove the rocks, and it did so.

The railways meanwhile developed stations on Lake Joseph, hitherto the remotest of the three lakes. The C.P.R. opened a station at Barnesdale, while the Canadian Northern, which came closer to the water, built two; one opposite the C.P.R. station, and the other on a spur running down to the lake, forming another wharf station. The Canadian Northern's depots at Barnesdale were originally called "Muskoka Station", but this was soon changed to "Lake Joseph Station" to avoid confusion with Muskoka Wharf. Barnesdale now became the cardinal distribution centre on Lake Joseph, supplanting Port Cockburn, which was bypassed by the railways, though some of the steamers continued to dock for the night at the Summit House. The Canadian Northern also opened summer stations at Gordon Bay on Lake Joseph, and Parkside on Bala Bay.

What effect did the new lines have on the lake trade? Apparently they caused little or no diminution in business for the Navigation Company, except that there were now perhaps fewer tourists going to Bala by boat. Any losses here, though, were more than offset by the new inflow of tourists through Bala and Barnesdale. In 1907, the C.P.R. announced that it would run four trains a day from Toronto to MacTier during the summer months. Had either the C.P.R. or the Canadian Northern chosen to build through Gravenhurst as well as Bala, the Navigation Company would most certainly have lost a lot of traffic, but since they did not, people still found it far more convenient to go from Gravenhurst to Bala by boat than south to Washago to wait for

"Train Time" at Bala summer station.
The ramp down to the wharf can be seen at the right. The train is southbound.
Courtesy, *Public Archives of Canada* A83858

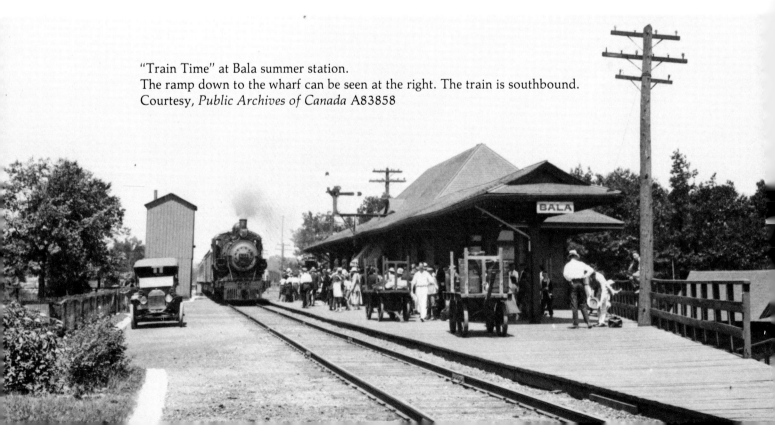

C.P.R. summer station at Bala, from the wharf.
Courtesy, *Canadian Pacific Corporate Archives*, No. 14944

C.N.O. Station, Bala Park, Muskoka Lakes, Canada

C.N.R. wharfside station at Bala Park.

Canadian Northern wharf station, Lake Joseph, under construction (around 1907).
Note the stairway up to the main line depot.
Courtesy, *Public Archives of Canada* PA 132105

Steamers at Lake Joseph station.
In the foreground are the yacht "Kacymo" (left), the S.S. "Ahmic" and the supply boat "Constance".
The S.S. "Sagamo" is behind the train.
Courtesy, *Public Archives of Canada* PA 129964   J. Micklethwaite Collection.

a train to Torrance. There were, of course, some changes resulting from the new lines. The mail for Port Carling, for example, now arrived on the Bala steamer rather than from Muskoka Wharf, and the schedules had to be adjusted to allow for connections at Bala, Barnesdale and Bala Park. The new lines were, in fact, one of the main influences behind the construction of the *Cherokee*, since both railways wanted better ships to connect with their trains. Usually it was the *Cherokee* that met the trains at Bala, making two round trips a day to Beaumaris to meet the *Sagamo* and the other main line boats. One of the small auxiliary steamers, usually the *Ahmic* or the *Charlie M.*, would handle the local calls around Bala Bay. Later, as the boats began converting to coal, some of them would refill their bunkers at Barnesdale and Bala Park. The *Sagamo* meanwhile took on coal at Muskoka Wharf.

The Grand Trunk Railway was not very happy about this double-barreled invasion of its private fiefdom in Muskoka, although it continued to enjoy the lion's share of the traffic. In 1907, Muskoka Wharf was lengthened considerably to provide additional space for the trains and steamers, and about the same time a persistent rumour was afoot that the G.T.R. was planning to build a spur from Bracebridge or Falkenburg to Port Carling, though nothing ever came of it. That same year, the three railways agreed to set comparable tariffs on their runs to Muskoka, to avoid the consequences of ruinous rate wars.

While the railways and the Navigation Company were beefing up their facilities and services, the government lent a hand by rebuilding some of the local dams and docks. After the usual bureaucratic delays, the Bracebridge wharf was rebuilt in 1905 at its present location, somewhat closer to the falls, but there was no proper road to the new wharf, until 1906. In the spring of 1905, the old tug *Ontario* went aground on a sandbar trying to approach the new wharf, yet it wasn't until 1907 that the Dominion Government agreed to redredge the river, which was now the central artery of the Bracebridge tourist trade. By 1912, so many boats were coming to town that the wharf could not accommodate them, and the Town Council was soon after the government to have it extended. That same year, Ottawa voted monies to rebuild the steamer docks at Severn Bridge, Huntsville, Windermere and Beaumaris.

Another major improvement undertaken in 1905 was the construction of a lighthouse at the all-important Gravenhurst Narrows. The first navigating aid at this strategic spot was a coal oil lantern, erected in 1885 on a mast on the small island guarding the entrance to the channel. A small shed had also been built to house supplies, while a local settler acted as lightkeeper. In 1905, Mr. George Brown of Bracebridge was awarded the contract to replace the mast with a lighthouse on the same spot. Supplies were ferried in by the tug *Gypsy* and a scow. The lighthouse is an attractive white square tower, built of wood, on a masonry foundation, with sloping sides and a red light set 28 feet above the water, visible in some directions for eight miles. It still stands today, a faithful sentinel and a great boon to boatmen. It was electrified early in the 1950s.

In the meantime, steam yachts were proliferating with bewildering rapidity. Approximately 70 yachts are known to have arrived between 1904 and 1918, and even this list is not complete. Very little is known today about some of the boats nor is it always certain when they were brought to Muskoka. All we can attempt here is a brief summary, in the approximate order they appeared.

Starting in 1904, we note the *Morinus* (6.52 tons), possibly used in connection with the Morinus Hotel on Lake Rosseau until she was sold to take passengers on Georgian Bay in 1908; the *Iagara* (5.05 tons), built in 1901 and used by the Forman family of Cliff Island, Lake Joseph, until the 1920s; the *Naniwa* (7.45 tons), owned by Frank J. Phillips of Wistowe Island, Vice-President of the Navigation Company (this vessel apparently burned in a boat-house fire around 1913); the *Oriska* (3.95 tons), usually used around Port Carling; the *Rulo* (5.87 tons), which belonged to J.H. Willmott of Beaumaris until 1906, when she went to Lake Rosseau to replace the *Fidelia*, only to burn near Gravenhurst on November 22, 1913; and the *Willoudee* (8.92 tons), ordered from Kingston by Sir Wilfred Hepton, a wealthy Englishman who owned Loon Island, Lake Joseph. The vessel arrived by rail and was found to be damaged. Hepton, dissatisfied with it, sold it in 1908 to Mrs. Gratwick of Craigie Lea, who renamed it the *Pukwana*. Hepton meanwhile imported a larger yacht, the second *Willoudee* (17 tons), which he retained until 1910. The vessel was then sold to Dr. C.S. Winslow, inventor of Winslow's Soothing Syrup for coughs, whose cottage stood at St. Helen's Island, Lake Joseph. Winslow intended the second *Willoudee* as a replacement for his old yacht, the *Scudder*, which was sold to another

S.S. "Islander", at Bracebridge new wharf.
Courtesy, *Ontario Archives*, Acc. 9939, Roll 8, #9

New wharf at Beaumaris, under construction, 1912.
The S.S. "Islander" is in attendance.

Steam Yacht "Morinus".
Courtesy, *Port Carling Pioneer Museum*

Steam Yacht "Oriska".
Collection of the late Mr. Lester Turnbull

Steam Yacht "Iagara".
Courtesy, *Public Archives of Canada* PA 132156

Steam Yacht "Fidelia".
Courtesy, *Mr. Arthur Blachford*

Steam Yacht "Willoudee".
Collection of the late *Mr. Lester Turnbull*

Steam Yacht "Anchora", of Anchor Island, Lake Joseph.
Courtesy, *Public Archives of Canada* PA 132157

Steam Yacht "Helena".
Collection of the late *Mr. Lester Turnbull*

Steam Yacht "Lotus".
Collection of the late *Mr. Lester Turnbull*

Steam Yacht "Ida" at Cinderwood Island.

31

Steam Yacht "Elsa".
Collection of the late *Mr. Lester Turnbull*

Steam Yacht "Adjie".
Collection of the late *Mr. Lester Turnbull*

Steam Yacht "Kacymo".
Courtesy, *Mrs. Barbara Mills*, Georgetown

cottager on Lake Joseph. Both vessels survived for several decades, but the *Willoudee* was dieselized around 1934. On August 24, 1938, she burned in a boat-house fire.

Aside from the aforementioned *Mineta*, the year 1905 saw few new steam yachts on the Muskoka Lakes. An exception was the *Wanda II* (32.62 tons), a lovely 94 foot craft built in Toronto for Timothy Eaton, the department store tycoon, after his original *Wanda* lost a race. Equipped with a triple expansion Doty engine, the *Wanda II* could go 21 miles per hour, which was more than sufficient to leave any other boats behind! She lasted until the morning of August 7, 1914, when she was destroyed in another boat-house fire at "Ravenscrag", Mrs. Eaton's summer home at Windermere, along with several canoes and sailboats and a gas launch: the ex-steamer *Wapenao* was damaged in the same blaze. The original *Wanda* meanwhile went to Northern Ontario, and became known as the *Temagami*.

Several new yachts arrived in 1906. Among them were the *Puritan*; the *Helena* (10 tons), used around Beaumaris; the *Lotus* (26 tons), also owned by cottagers from Beaumaris; and the *Ida* (17 tons) owned by the Borntraeger family of Cinderwood Island, Lake Muskoka. Dissatisfied with her appearance, the Borntraegers soon sold the *Ida* to Bill Campbell, who used her as a tug and supply boat, peddling farm produce to the local cottagers until 1918, when he obtained the *Algoma* from Captain Archer. The *Ida* carried on as a workboat until 1940. Meanwhile the Borntraegers bought the second *Ida* (11 tons), a much prettier craft built at Kingston in 1906: she later changed hands and was renamed the *Elsa*. The *Elsa* remained on the Muskoka Lakes until 1927. Also in 1906, the yacht *Kacymo*, soon renamed the *Wawa*, was imported by the O'Grady family of Toronto and berthed near Craigie Lea.

The year 1907 brought a bumper crop of new steam yachts. One was the *Adjie* (11.29 tons), also from Kingston and owned by C. O. Scull of Beaumaris, who was president of a trust company in Baltimore. Used primarily for fishing and picnics, the *Adjie* served the Scull family until 1929. She still survives today, fully restored as a motor launch. Other yachts introduced around 1907 were the *Lena*, the *Mattie*, the *Sunbeam* and the *Thelma*, plus the second *Shamrock* (3.91 tons), imported from Kingston by Robert Hardcastle Johnston of Port Carling to carry passengers after he sold the original *Shamrock* to Captain Archer. We also find the *Iona* (14 tons), a very speedy big launch with a 14.7 hp. engine, owned by John A. C. Stevenson of Sharon, Pa. and Beaumaris and used until 1918, after which she, like the *Wanda*, was eventually sold to take passengers on Lake Temagami; the *Swastika* (9 tons) owned by American cottagers near Beaumaris; and the *Phoebe* (11 tons) which was given as a gift by Andrew Carnegie to Professor J. A. Brashear, the American astronomer, after the latter's earlier boat, the *Alleghania*, was gutted by fire at her winter berth near Beaumaris. Named for Mr. Brashear's wife, the *Phoebe* was essentially a copy of the *Adjie*. She ran many a fishing trip, to say nothing of market trips to town for the neighbours, until November of 1913, when she, too, fell victim to fire. As a gesture of their esteem, the professor's wealthy neighbours passed the hat, and bought him a new *Phoebe* (9 tons) from Kingston. After Professor Brashear's death in 1920, the *Phoebe II* eventually went to the Huntsville lakes, and afterwards to the Finger Lakes region of New York State. Today, she is back where she was built, at Kingston, where she still takes the occasional cruise, under steam power.

By this time steam launches were giving way to gasoline motorboats, which in the early days were notoriously balky and unreliable (which is hardly surprising, since they ran on unprocessed fuel). One evening in June of 1905, the *Nymoca* had to come to the rescue of six couples stranded in a gas boat near the mouth of the Muskoka River. About three years later Captain Fraser, commanding the tug *Linden*, did the same for some of the members of the Sharon Fishing Club on Lake Muskoka. In August 1906, a tremendous uproar resulted when an inspector for the Federal Government suddenly seized over 60 launches on Lake Rosseau, both steam and gasoline, because the owners had not employed licensed captains and engineers for them. Apparently this was quite legal, but it seems likely that the official in question was advised to be a little less zealous in future!

As motorboats gained in popularity, the influx of steam yachts began to slow down. None are definitely known to have appeared in 1908 or 1909, though at least four arrived in 1910. One was the *Ella Mary* (24.64 tons), a 66 foot Polson cruiser with a triple expansion engine, berthed at Belle Island, north of Beaumaris. She went to the Lake of Bays in 1925 to serve as a ferry to

Steam Yacht "Iona".
Courtesy, of the late *Captain Ted Guppy*,
Temagami

Steam Yacht "Phoebe II."

Steam Yacht "Ilderim".
Collection of the late *Mr. Lester Turnbull*

Steam Yacht "Osso".
Collection of the late *Mr. Lester Turnbull*

Steam Yacht "Spray".

Steam Yacht "Nishka", at a regatta at Port Sandfield.
Courtesy, *Public Archives of Canada*, PA 132133

Bigwin Island. Another was the *Ilderim* (12 tons), used near Port Keewaydin for over 35 years. A third was the *Tokolo*, which seems to have been replaced by a namesake boat in 1912. A fourth was called the *Amanda*, built apparently to replace an earlier launch of the same name. In September 1910, the steamer *Osso* burned with her boat-house behind Beaumaris, along with another launch, the *Kola*. A second *Osso* (15 tons) was ordered from Kingston to replace the first. The second *Osso* is said to have lasted until 1931, when she was sold and removed from the lakes. Other steamers dating from this period include the *Bonita*, the *Beaver* (formerly the *Scudder*), the *Juanita*, the *Margaret* (from Mortimer's Point), the *Ptarmigan*, the *Rhoda* (said to have been a former police boat from the Thames in England and capable of doing 18 miles per hour), and the *Spray*. An elegant big launch first imported from Toronto early in the century, the *Spray* was used variously as a pleasure boat, then as a water-taxi and laundry boat from Orgill's Point, and finally (around 1910) becoming a hotel yacht for the Gordon House at Gordon Bay, Lake Joseph. She went to pieces there during the 1920s.

Few private steam launches can be dated after 1910. In 1914 the steamer *Minga* (13.43 tons) arrived from New York City for a six year stay around Port Carling. In 1920, she was sold to a lumberman from the Timmins area. In 1915, Mrs. Eaton imported the *Wanda III* (37.54 tons), from Toronto to replace the ill-fated *Wanda II*. With a length of 94 feet and a beam of only twelve, the *Wanda III* has a composite frame, a torpedo stern, an oak-panelled hull below the waterline, and a steel hull above it. She was powered by a triple expansion engine, and, like her predecessor, could go 20 miles per hour. She plied to the Eaton estate at Kawandag, near Rosseau, for many years, but despite her speed she failed, tragically, to save the life of a little girl who suddenly developed acute appendicitis at Rosseau around 1927: the child died on the boat while being taken to the hospital at Bracebridge. Lady Eaton (daughter-in-law of Mrs. Eaton) never forgave the yacht for this failure, and shortly afterwards the *Wanda III* was sold and taken to the Lake of Bays. She still plies periodically on that lake to this day. In 1914 we also hear of three small yachts on the Moon River below Bala: the *Minnie C.* (7 tons), the *Harvey* (7 tons) and the *Louisa Lee*. Since the First World War, however, motorboats have been the norm on the Muskoka Lakes, and it has only been within the last twenty years that any new steam launches have been seen on the lakes; usually fitted out by buffs with a passion for steam.

Steam Yacht "Wanda III".

Though steam yachts were on the decline after 1907, the supply steamers were not. Several new supply boats, either built or adapted for the purpose, appeared after the turn of the century. The Hanna Company steamer *Mink*, rebuilt after the fire of 1898, carried on until 1908. The following spring the Bracebridge 'Gazette' reported that the Company was building a new supply boat, larger than either the *Mink* or the *Constance*, as a successor. The new steamer was 84 feet in keel by 16.5 feet in beam, and was registered at 81 tons. She was the largest supply boat ever to appear in Muskoka. She had the usual fore-and-aft compound engine (13.5 hp.), and, since she was expected to carry a few passengers as well as provisions, she was fitted with a hurricane deck for shelter. As the replacement for the *Mink*, which was retired, the new steamer was christened the *Newminko*.

The *Newminko* began making her rounds on the upper lakes in 1909, and soon proved a faster vessel than her predecessor. In the spring and fall she was often engaged to help the local stores stock up with bulk provisions, such as flour and feed, from the railway depots at Bala and Barnesdale. Occasionally she was chartered for special cruises. Then on the evening of May 13, 1915, she caught fire at Port Carling and was pushed out into the river, where she burned to the waterline, lighting up the whole area and finally grounding at Beverley Lodge. The loss was reckoned at about $12,000, but fortunately the vessel was fairly well insured and before long she was rebuilt and put back in service.

In the meantime, the Hannas already had another supply steamer in commission to relieve pressure on the *Newminko*. This craft was the second *Mink*, built at Gravenhurst in 1912. Somewhat smaller than the *Newminko*, but larger than her namesake, the second *Mink* was 78 feet in keel and registered 60.18 tons. Unlike her running mate, she had a steel frame and two engines, giving her speeds estimated at 10 knots. Nothing of the old *Mink* was incorporated into the new one, except one grocery counter. She completed her first trip to Bracebridge in July of 1912, under the command of Captain William McCulley of Port Carling, whose brother James usually commanded the *Newminko*. During the war years, the two steamers used to tour Lake Rosseau twice a week, one proceeding up each side until they met near Rosseau; on two alternate

Supply Steamers "Mink" (II) and "Newminko".
The two vessels are moored together at Port Carling for the winter. The "Mink" (left) is in her second version, with a hurricane deck.

days they would tour Lake Joseph, and once a week one or both would ply to Bala. In 1915, following the *Newminko* fire, the *Mink* had to do the work of two vessels.

The daily routine on the supply boats was monotonously predictable. At 4:30 every morning the steamers were freshly stocked, primarily with groceries. Hardware was carried only on special order, aside from a few staples such as nails. The same applied to clothing, boots and shoes. Meats were supplied from McCulley's Meat Market, founded by George McCulley of Port Carling, a brother of James and William. The iceboxes were located in the bows of both steamers, followed by the grocery sections, then the boilers and engineers. Usually each vessel carried a crew of four: a captain, engineer, butcher and grocer, with extra help on busy days. The grocery department was also responsible for wooding or coaling up the boats and handling the lines. Passengers were permitted, provided that they remained on the upper deck and did not interfere with the schedules. They also had to supply their own lunches.

At 7:00 a.m. the lines would be cast off, and the *Mink* and the *Newminko* would set off on their rounds. As their chimed, three-toned whistles were heard in the distance, people would run up a white flag, signalling them to call; if at half-mast the message meant "we don't need anything today." As the supply boat hove into view a small crowd would gather at the wharf, including youngsters clutching nickels and dimes to be converted into candies; housewives anxiously scanning their shopping lists; boys with empty cans to be replenished with coal oil, vinegar or maple syrup; local farmers with produce of their own to sell and curious cottagers waiting to join the fun. As soon as the lines were secured, the crowd would surge aboard, resulting in perfect pandemonium as people babbled their orders, and money and merchandise crossed over the counters. Meanwhile, the butcher would be cutting up meat as if his very life depended on it. The merchants generally maintained a jovial disposition, but they wasted no words as they transacted business: after all, there might easily be 60 calls in a single day, and sometimes the boats did not get back to Port Carling until 10:00 or 11:00 p.m. Even then they were not finished, since all the unsold foodstuffs had to be unloaded until the following morning. No doubt Sundays were always exceedingly welcome!

Supply Steamer "Newminko" (Original Version).

Supply Steamer "Newminko" (Second Version) at Port Carling.

Except for the *Constance*, the Hanna boats had Lakes Rosseau and Joseph more or less to themselves. On Lake Muskoka, the main operators were the Packer family of Torrance, who were then running the *Onaganoh*, the Mills family of Milford Bay, and the Beaumonts of Alport. As a result, the various supply boats did not call simultaneously at the same wharves. Each knew the others' schedules, and contrived to call on different days.

As noted in Volume I, the Beaumont family had been in the supply boat business since 1893 with the steamer *Nymoca*. In 1911, like the Hannas, they proposed to run a second boat, and purchased the steamer *City of Bala* for that purpose, only to find her rotting out in the ribs and no longer fit for service. This meant that another vessel was needed, and in 1912 they had the steamer *Alporto* built, utilizing the steel frame of a former Great Lakes yacht and the engine from the *City of Bala*. The *Alporto* was 85.15 feet in keel and registered 78.88 tons, which made her almost as large as the *Newminko*. Along with the smaller *Nymoca*, the *Alporto* began distributing meat and produce to the hotels and cottages, as well as taking church parties, farmers' conventions and other outings. She was usually commanded by Captain Frank Beaumont, whose brother William now took charge of the *Nymoca*.

On July 27, 1912, tragedy struck while the *Alporto* was making her rounds near Beaumaris. On board was Frank Beaumont's lively little nephew Jackie, then eight years of age, who was visiting with his parents from Toronto. The lad was sitting on the meatblock near the gangway, which had not been closed after the previous stop. Around 5:00 p.m., the boat gave a sudden lurch and both the boy and the block fell overboard. Without a moment's pause, Frank Beaumont dived in after him, and soon had the youngster on his back as he made for a nearby rock. The men on the steamer reversed engines, but it took agonizingly long for the vessel to respond and come back to help. Even so, they almost reached the pair when Frank suddenly stopped swimming and went under. The boy splashed around for a few more seconds . . . . then he too disappeared. Word of the calamity spread quickly. The passing steamer *Islander* passed the news on to the *Nymoca*, which went to the scene to help. By the next morning dozens of boats were out looking, and soon the bodies were recovered. There was no water in Frank Beaumont's lungs, from which it was judged that heart failure had been the actual cause of death. A few days later the *Alporto*, her flag at half-mast and heading a solemn procession of boats, brought the two bodies to Bracebridge, where a large, subdued crowd was waiting at the wharf. For days afterwards there was general gloom in Bracebridge.

Supply Steamer "Alporto".
Courtesy, *Mr. Fred Mills*, Milford Bay

Interior view of Str. "Alporto".
Courtesy, *Mr. Fred Mills*, Milford Bay

Another boating misfortune struck the Beaumont family only a few weeks later. On the morning of August 19th., the *Nymoca* backed onto a shelving rock off Browning Island, canted over, filled with water, and sank. The crew were rescued by two passing motor launches, and two days later the steamer was refloated, using the *Mink* and some other boats. Local cottagers helped effect repairs, allowing the *Nymoca* to return home under her own power.

The Beaumonts did not carry on with the supply boat business very long afterwards. Not only was the death of Frank Beaumont a serious loss, but the War broke out just two years later. Fewer cottagers were coming now, and engineers and crew members became scarce. Before long the *Nymoca* disappeared, apparently scrapped at Mortimer's Point around 1919. The *Alporto* was tied up around 1915, and never sailed for the Beaumonts again. During the War, the *Onaganoh* was left to go to pieces in East Bay. The *Newminko*, too, was tied up for the duration, for much the same reasons. Henceforth it was the Hanna and Mills families who dominated the supply boat business on Lake Muskoka.

"Captain" Frederick Mills was also an old hand at supply boating, having started in 1903 with the little steamer *Manolia*, acquired from Clevelands House to distribute produce from his farm at Milford Bay. In 1908, Mills replaced the *Manolia* with a new and larger vessel called the *Awahwanna II*, (pronounced Arawana) which registered 41.03 tons. The *Awahwanna II* was a stubby, odd-looking craft, only 44 feet in keel by 12.3 in beam, yet she had two decks. Mr. Mills used her for eleven seasons, sometimes as a towboat and excursion vessel to the local regattas, but he did not find her very satisfactory. She was cramped, awkward and hard to steer. In 1918, he discussed the idea of lengthening the vessel with his friend John Walker of Pittsburgh and Buck Island, but Walker, an engineer by training, advised against it. The *Awahwanna* was scrapped and the machinery sold. In 1919, Mr. Walker put up the money to help Mills acquire the *Alporto*, which had been idle for several years, from the Beaumonts. Under the Mills family, the *Alporto* continued as a supply boat in the summertime, and a towboat in the spring and fall, hauling tanbark, pulpwood and timber from all around the lakes, especially from distant Gordon Bay. The only real competition during the 1900s came from the *Mink*, operating from Port Carling, but generally relations between the two were friendly, since each vessel had its own customers. Occasionally the *Mink* and the *Alporto* were known to race each other if they met on the open lake. In 1930 the *Alporto* also came to the rescue of the *Newminko*, which had grounded on a shoal in Bala Bay during foggy weather.

Pileup on Bala Bay!
The "Alporto" (right) and the oil tanker "Muskokalite" (left) are rescuing the "Newminko", grounded on a shoal in foggy weather, 1930.

S.S. "City of Bala" at Bracebridge New Tannery.
Courtesy, *Mrs. Barbara Mills*, Georgetown

Str. "Onaganoh", abandoned in East Bay.

Supply Steamer "Nymoca".

Captain Wesley Hill sometimes commanded the *Alporto* during this period, usually on scowing trips. On one of these, he nearly met with disaster. He was taking a scow to Rosseau one dark night, when a thunderstorm began. Unable to see through the driving rain, Hill decided to set his course by the Rosseau lighthouse, which stands astride a shoal at the entrance to the harbour. But the lighthouse keeper had neglected to set the lanterns that night, so the captain mistook the adjacent light at Kawandag (the Eaton family estate) for the safety beacon. This took him straight towards the lighthouse shoal. He was just on the verge of piling his vessel up on the rocks when a flash of lightning suddenly lit up the skies; Hill was shocked to behold the tower, without a light, directly in his path. The captain had just enough time to swing the wheel and bypass the shoal, but by the time he got into Rosseau he wasn't feeling very good. No action was taken against the chastened lighthouse keeper, who was never again derelict in his duties.

The little *Alporto* continued to tow and scow and carry foodstuffs until 1935, but by then the Depression was on and some of Mr. Mills' sons were moving away, making it more difficult to maintain the gardens or crew the steamer. The boat was ultimately converted into a floating workshop, while the store was transferred to a shed on the wharf at south Milford Bay. The end came on November 26, 1936, when the steamer burned at her dock, apparently as a result of defective wiring. She had had a long and useful career on the Muskoka Lakes.

Three more short-lived supply boat operations from the 1910s should be noted. One of these was conducted by David Owens, a farmer from East Bay, near Torrance, who used a launch called the *Mary Caroline* to sell apples, fruit and vegetables around the lake, until about 1919. In 1911, the William Davies Company of Toronto, a noted meat packing firm, having already opened a branch store in Bracebridge, also imported the steamer *Ada Alice* (36 tons) from Toronto Harbour to serve as a floating food store, delivering fresh and cooked meats to their customers. First built at Port Dalhousie in 1879 and rebuilt in 1900, the *Ada Alice* was 66.5 feet in keel and powered by a 3.33 hp. non-condensing engine. In 1912, the Company also took over a butcher shop in Port Carling, and was soon selling meats, butter, eggs and vegetables even to the Hannas. But it came at a bad time. The prosperity of the Laurier era came to an end in 1912, leading to a slump in the tourist trade. Apparently the *Ada Alice* failed to make money. Worse still, the vessel caught fire at the wharf at Port Carling on the night of June 18th. and was badly

Str. "Ada Alice", collecting tanbark at Bala, June 30, 1917.
Courtesy, *Public Archives of Canada* PA 70913

43

damaged, though prompt action by the villagers prevented a total loss. Afterwards she was put up for sale—cheap. But no buyers stepped forward until March 18, 1915, when the Navigation Company somehow ended up with her. Since the *Ada Alice* was repaired, it may be conjectured that her owners hired the Navigation Company to do the work, only to find themselves unable to pay for it. For its part, the Navigation Company never used the vessel, and promptly resold it to Captain Fraser, who wanted a new tug to replace the *Southwood*. Fraser seems to have kept the *Ada Alice* until 1919, but after that she was allowed to sink at the Gravenhurst dockyards alongside the remains of the old *Muskoka*.

The last major supply boat of this period was the steamer *Ina* (10 tons), a 56 foot yacht built in Toronto in 1901 and used near Beaumaris until 1914. About that time, she was purchased by Rosario Lazzaro, an amiable Bracebridge fruit dealer who personally ran the vessel to deliver fresh produce to his customers. Mr. Lazzaro kept the *Ina* as late as 1940, but finally sold her to the owner of a Bracebridge service station, who in turn converted the craft into a gas-powered oil tanker, known as the *Peerless*. The *Peerless* delivered petroleum products around the Muskoka Lakes until she blew up in the Muskoka River in 1959, with the loss of one life. Her steel-plated successor, the *Peerless II*, is still in service today.

Now we must leave the supply boats for a time and return to steamboating in general.

Str. "Ina" at Port Carling.

Diesel Oil Tanker "Peerless", formerly the Str. "Ina".

The greatest nuisance to all the boats until the 1920s was, of course, the log drives. Small craft, both steam and motor powered, had the worst trouble, since the lumbermen never bothered to leave a passage clear for them, as they sometimes did for the passenger ships. Frequently the only way little boats could get to Bracebridge or Port Carling was by directly following the big ships. But even the large steamers sometimes had problems. In May of 1905, the *Kenozha* broke two propeller blades on a log while approaching Muskoka Wharf. Three years later she also went aground in the Indian River while trying to avoid a sea of logs. The *Charlie M.* came to the rescue, only to get stuck as well. (Both vessels were eventually pulled off by the *Southwood*.) The *Islander*, too, was a frequent victim of the logs, and all too often her trips to Bracebridge, which normally took one hour, were turned into all day affairs as she tried to cope with the drives. Nor were the rivers the only problem areas. Early in June 1907, the *Islander* broke her propeller on a log about a mile north of Beaumaris and had to be towed back to Gravenhurst for repairs. One evening the following August, she struck a deadhead in the Muskoka River and got it caught under the propeller. The log lifted the boat and shook it from side to side like a terrier with a rabbit; passengers lost their balance and screamed. The steamer remained immobilized for hours, and some of the people asked to be put ashore. Eventually the log came loose, but the propeller no longer worked, and the disabled ship could only whistle for help. The *Oriole*, then at Bracebridge, finally answered the call and picked up the remaining passengers, but for the *Islander* it meant another trip under tow to the Gravenhurst drydock.

The *Cherokee* also had the occasional trouble. In August 1909, she too was held up by logs and failed to connect on time with the train at Bala; her patrons were none too pleased to find themselves stranded. Twice that season, she was chartered to run cruises from Bracebridge, but on both days Mr. Mickle was running some of his logs downriver, and consequently W.F. Wasley, unwilling to risk damage to one of his finest ships, sent the older, plainer *Kenozha* in her place, much to the annoyance of the excursionists.

The year 1909 was especially troublesome for owners of small craft trying to reach Bracebridge to do their shopping. Complaints about the logs grew so loud that the Town Council again decided to lay charges in Magistrate's Court against Mr. Mickle and the drive foreman for obstructing navigation and delaying the Royal Mail. Ample evidence was presented by the plaintiffs, none at all by the defendants. The second charge was dismissed, but both Mickle and his foreman were committed for trial at the higher court and meanwhile released on $100 bail. The problem made headlines again in 1912, when the Federal Government, in response to further complaints, issued an Order-in-Council prohibiting the lumbermen from driving loose logs down the river after July 10th: after that date all logs were to be bagged in booms. The lumbermen ignored the order and ran their logs as usual, and the Government Engineer seemed powerless to do anything about it. In 1913, in a further attempt to resolve the problem, the provincial Deputy Minister of Lands and Forests, Aubrey White—the same Aubrey White who had pioneered at Bracebridge and captained A.P. Cockburn's *Waubamik* in 1869—reaffirmed that all logs in the river must be bagged below Bracebridge, but granted Mr. Mickle permission to conduct drives until the end of July. To meet that deadline, Mickle hired extra hands and paid them a bonus to have the river cleared on time; they managed it with a scant fifteen minutes to spare. Gradually the problem solved itself, as the timber limits finally gave out, and sawmill after sawmill closed its doors for lack of logs. By the mid-1920s the great drives were a thing of the past.

As the lumber trade busily wrought its own extinction, the tugs that served the industry also disappeared, and were not replaced. A list compiled by Captain Rogers, the Port Sandfield hydrographer, mentions about eleven tugs or part-time tugs on the Muskoka Lakes in 1915, of which only three were still in commission in 1927. In fact, very few new tugs appeared on the lakes after 1904. One exception was the *Hiawatha* (18.12 tons), a 49 foot craft built in 1905 at Port Carling by Thomas and Alfred Croucher of Craigie Lea to replace their earlier steamer, the *Linnia*. The Crouchers carried on with the *Hiawatha* until she wore out and sank about 1917. She was then replaced by the *Shamrock*, hitherto used by her owner, R.H. Johnston, for pleasure cruises. Under the Crouchers, this second *Shamrock* became a scowboat: unlike the original *Shamrock*, she lasted into the 1940s and proved the second-last steam tug to disappear from the lakes. In 1906, a lumberman named Charles J.H. Ames of Gregory built a small 33 foot steamer called the *Rosena* (4.29 tons) to tow for his mill. After his death in 1908, his sons enlarged the

S.S. "Islander", amid logs on the Muskoka River.

boat to 40 feet and 5.74 tons and used her mostly for charter cruises, at least until 1915. The *Rosena* subsequently went to pieces on the Joseph River. Also in 1906, Captain Fraser decided to become a freelance boatman and imported a little steamer called the *Linden* (3 tons), a 40 foot craft built at Magnetawan four years earlier. He used the *Linden* for only a few years before scrapping her and chartering the *Allena May* from Walter Fowler. Then, in 1910, he acquired the *Southwood*, which he had earlier commanded for Andrew Boyd of Bracebridge, and operated her until 1914. Captain Fraser seldom, if ever, sold his boats, and the fact that he was running another vessel in 1915 probably means that the hardy little *Southwood*, after 27 years of good service, had finally worn out. Shortly afterwards, she was broken up near the Rathbun Company "red mill" at Gravenhurst.

Fraser's next steamer was the *Ada Alice*, until lately the Davies Company floating meat marketeria. He had barely taken charge of her when she almost met the same fate as the old tug *Lake Joseph*. In May of 1915, near the mouth of the Indian River, she was taking a scow alongside, loaded with frames for a new extension to the Elgin House plus some cordwood for fuel, when sparks from the stack set the load on fire. Within seconds, the scow was ablaze from one end to the other, and the steamer too, on the side next to the scow. The captain rang for "stop engines" and swung around so that the wind would carry the flames the other way; then he and his three crew members began battling the blaze. The tug was soon out of danger, but nothing, it seemed, could save the scow. After a desperate fifteen minute fight, however, a man in a motorboat came alongside to lend a hand, and with his timely assistance, the fire was soon out. The motorboat owner then left before anyone had a chance to thank him.

Fraser's next vessel was the lovely *Queen of the Isles*, which he bought on March 12, 1925, from the Bracebridge "old tannery" (which had just lately shut down). This splendid craft was now 40 years old and still seaworthy. Captain Fraser used her for another nine years, and like everyone before him, found her the fastest, most comfortable and most useful boat he ever owned.

Very few additional Muskoka Lakes tugs remain to be recorded. The little *Jennie Willson*, which first arrived in 1879, survived a total of 30 years and served a succession of owners, starting with the Beardmore tannery, and afterwards the Strouds of Milford Bay, the Snider Lumber Company of Gravenhurst, and finally David Schell of Barlochan, before she finally fell to pieces at what is now Campbell's Landing Marina, near Gravenhurst. Schell replaced her in 1909 with a new tug, the *Maggie Main* (15.90 tons), which inherited the engine from the *Jennie*.

Str. "Queen of the Isles", on a Tannery excursion cruise.
Courtesy, Bracebridge *Herald-Gazette*

Named in part after Mr. Schell's daughter, who later married Captain Hill, the *Maggie Main* was a 40 foot craft with a deep draft, used primarily for scowing. Schell used her until the War years, afterwards selling her to a consortium engaged in salvaging sunken logs on Muskoka Bay. She disappeared during the 1920s. In 1918, Mr. Schell obtained the aging yacht *Kestrel* to bring in scows of cordwood for the Navigation Company steamers at Muskoka Wharf. Utilizing two scows at a time, the *Kestrel* could deliver 2,000 cords per trip, valued at $1.00 per cord. She was used until 1926, when Schell tried transferring her boiler and engine to a pointed flat-bottomed scow he called the *Huckleberry*. It didn't work because the scow never stopped leaking, and in the meantime David Schell died in January 1927.

Another late-arriving tug was the *Nubertha* (17 tons), the fifth and last vessel owned by Captain Harper Walker of Walker's Point. He built the craft in 1914 to replace the *Bertha May*, hence the name, and fitted her out with the engines from the old tug. Unluckily, the *Nubertha* was damaged by fire in July of her maiden season, and served no more that year. Based at a rural community that had no roads to the outside world until the 1930s, the *Nubertha*, along with the rebuilt *Bertha May*, were very busy boats; sometimes taking families to church and housewives to town to do their shopping, in addition to scowing. In the fall of 1930, the *Bertha May* was finally dismantled and sunk at Barlochan, while a year or so later the *Nubertha* was sold and removed to Georgian Bay. Finally, we must acknowledge the *Animay* (4.57 tons), another of Charles Woodroffe's tugs. Built near Foot's Bay in 1912 to replace the second *Ethel May*, the *Animay* ran until 1925, and was followed by the *Voyageur*. The grimy little *Voyageur* towed logs to Mr. Woodroffe's mill, and later hauled drums of gasoline from the railway depot at Bala, until she was finally cut up with blowtorches at Muskoka Wharf. One more steam workboat would be imported from the Huntsville lakes as late as 1938, but otherwise the day of the steam tug was coming to an end in Muskoka.

One by one the older tugs were disappearing. A few, like the *Nubertha*, were sold off the lakes. The *Theresa*, owned by the Mutchenbakers of Rosseau Falls, went to the Magnetawan in 1904, and in 1908, the *Gravenhurst* followed; both shipped on railway flatcars. Captain

Steam Tug "Nubertha", at Walker's Point.
Courtesy, *Mrs. Joyce Schell*, Barlochan

Steam Tug "Bertha May" (Original Version).
Photograph taken during the vessel's service with the Mickle Company, 1886-1908.
Miss Bertha May Mickle is among the passengers.
Courtesy, *Mr. Charles Mickle Cane*, Toronto

Steam Tug "Animay", at Port Carling.
Collection of the late *Mr. Lester Turnbull*

Campbell replaced the latter boat with the *Nymph*, hitherto owned by the Strouds; after his death in 1912, the vessel went to his sons, George and James. The Campbells towed logs and scowed every type of cargo up the lakes, including drums of gasoline for the Ditchburn Motorboat Company of Gravenhurst. One night, according to a family story, Jim Campbell fell asleep at the wheel of the *Nymph* and piled her up on a small island, spilling several 90 gallon drums into Lake Muskoka. No damage was done except to Jim Campbell's pride, but the drums had to be rolled up onto the island before they could be reloaded onto the tug. The *Nymph* worked until 1925, and was then scrapped at Muskoka Wharf. Campbell then took charge of the old Mickle tug *Grace M.* for a season, then acquired the former supply boat *Constance* in 1927. She became his charge for the next seven years.

Quietly, and unobtrusively, the other old veterans went to their rest. The *Comet* was beached at Milford Bay around 1914, the old *Ontario* finished up in the Indian River near Port Carling about 1916, and the *Algoma* and *Siesta* both fell to pieces near Gravenhurst during the late 1920s. A similar fate overtook the aging steamer *Rosseau*, which had been plying the lakes since 1879; first for A.P. Cockburn, afterwards for the Beardmore tannery, then (1899) for the Snider Lumber Company, which had mills at both Gravenhurst and Rosseau Falls. In 1907, the *Rosseau* went to Charles William Henshaw, a Gravenhurst tug captain, and in 1909, to Captain Mortimer of Mortimer's Point. The vessel was still listed in 1915, but was no longer running. Shortly afterwards she was dismantled, and stroked off the registry on April 10, 1924. All that remains today are her running lights, in the possession of the Mortimer family.

Though towing was manifestly in decline, the Navigation Company ships were showing no signs of slackening. By the turn of the century the tourist industry was definitely supreme in Muskoka and the resorts were booming. Roads were still a thing to be avoided if possible, except in winter, and automobiles were scarce. The first resident motor car in Bracebridge appeared only in 1911, and it is said that the first automobile to reach Rosseau came, not by road, but on the freight deck of the *Sagamo*. Motor launches were becoming commoner; Captain Rogers counted 506 gas boats by 1915, compared with only 51 steamers. The motorboats were little faster than the steamers, but they had the enormous advantage of being free of cumbersome boilers that had to be fired up in advance of sailings. They were already driving the classic steam yachts to the verge of extinction, and their rapid proliferation was an ominous sign for the passenger ships as well.

Str. "Nymph", during her days with the Campbell Family, 1907.

Steam Tug "Grace M".
Courtesy, *Public Archives of Canada*, PA 132158

Str. "Rosseau" at Port Sandfield.

Despite these signs, the passenger steamers were in their prime during the Edwardian era. Nine were in service after 1906, besides those on the Huntsville lakes; ranging from the haughty *Sagamo* to the natty little *Charlie M.*

According to the timetable of 1913, the *Sagamo* was assigned the main route up the lakes from Gravenhurst, starting at 7:30 a.m., with calls at Beaumaris, Port Carling, Windermere, the Royal Muskoka, Minett and Port Sandfield; connecting with the trains at Lake Joseph Station at 12:30 and reaching Port Cockburn by 1:00 p.m. At 1:30, she would begin her return trip and be back, hopefully, by 7:50 p.m. The *Medora* meanwhile left Rosseau at 7:30 a.m., calling at several points on the way to Port Carling, and then proceeded directly to Muskoka Wharf with no intervening stops, arriving at 11:55. She would leave again at 4:00 p.m., following the arrival of the afternoon trains, and be back at Rosseau by 8:00. The *Cherokee*, a faster ship, handled the southbound Lake Joseph route, leaving Port Cockburn at 6:30 a.m. for Hamill's Point, Elgin House and Pinelands and calling at the local stops on western Lake Rosseau before joining the other steamers at Port Carling. At 10:00, she would leave for Beaumaris, and then head for Bala; arriving at 12:30 and leaving again at 3:50. In reverse procedure, the *Kenozha* would dock overnight at Bala, depart in the morning at 7:20, call at Bala Park and Mortimer's Point, and meet the other ships at Port Carling. From there she would cruise to Rosseau, with several stops on the way, beginning the return trip at 3:00 p.m. The *Islander* in turn made two round trips daily from Bracebridge to Port Carling, connecting with the *Sagamo* at Beaumaris. The *Ahmic* provided a local service from Rostrevor to Morinus and Port Carling, leaving at 10:00 a.m. for Bala and Bala Park to meet the *Cherokee*, and returning to Rostrevor by 7:30 p.m. The little *Charlie M.* helped out with a similar service on Bala Bay, leaving Dudley at 7:00 a.m. for Whiteside and Beaumaris (where she joined the *Islander* and *Sagamo*), then proceeding to Walker's Point and Gravenhurst. At 4:00 p.m., she would leave Muskoka Wharf, along with the *Medora* and *Nipissing*, to begin her return trip. The *Oriole* was meanwhile based at Stanley House, leaving daily at 7:00 a.m. for Craigie Lea, Redwood and Port Sandfield, arriving at Port Carling by 9:35 in time to meet the *Medora*, *Cherokee*, *Islander*, and *Kenozha*. At 10:00, the busy little boat would leave for Lake Joseph station and a series of flag-stops 'en route'; departing again at 2:30 to return to Port Carling by 5:30, and then return to Stanley House three hours later. In contrast, the *Nipissing* was given a rather light schedule, along the east side of Lake Muskoka (perhaps to reduce the strain on her engines); plying daily at 8:45 from Point Kaye to Port Keewaydin and the resorts around Milford Bay, then to Beaumaris and Gravenhurst by way of St. Elmo, and returning by 6:30. Thus did the Navigation Company try to service the far-flung

S.S. "Islander", S.S. "Oriole" and S.S. "Ahmic" at Port Carling, 1910.
Courtesy, *Public Archives of Canada*, PA 132142

S.S. "Kenozha" at Port Carling.

ports of the Muskoka Lakes during its heyday.

Old timers still remember a close call the *Kenozha* had around 1907, shortly after the railways were built past Bala Bay. On this particular June morning, the steamer had been chartered for a big Sunday School picnic to be held at Bala. She left Rosseau with a goodly number of passengers, and collected more at Windermere. This left her extensively filled, but at Port Carling, still another throng was waiting to come aboard. Captain Hansen realized that his vessel would be overtaxed, but rather than disappoint so many people, he decided to take the risk. The crowded steamer was rolling appreciably as she left Port Carling, but she was able to complete the cruise to Bala without incident.

It was on the return trip that things became exciting. As the steamer was passing the swing bridge at Coulter's Narrows, next to Bala Park, a shout was raised that brought people rushing over to the port side. The ship at once heeled over and her upper works struck the concrete bridge abutment; but for that she would have capsized. The captain, frantic and furious, rushed down to the forward deck and ordered the passengers back to their seats; then he explained that the ship was overloaded and warned that a sudden shift of weight could be disastrous. The passengers got the message, but just to be sure Captain Hansen himself patrolled the decks until the steamer returned to Port Carling. What could have been a major calamity resulted only in some badly shaken nerves for the crew, and a sheared-off bumper and scupper pipe on the *Kenozha*.

On the evening of August 24, 1908, the *Nipissing* ran into trouble between St. Elmo and Beaumaris. The big side-wheeler had been experiencing difficulties with her machinery, which she had inherited from the first *Nipissing*. On this occasion the piston suddenly blew out with a resounding blast, shattering to pieces the thick steel shaft connected to one end of the walking-beam and tearing a hole through the hurricane deck. No one was injured, partly because there were few people aboard at the time, but the steamer was left immobilized. Plaintively she whistled for help, and presently the *Cherokee* arrived, picked up the passengers, and took the *Nipissing* in tow. The setback was a severe one for the Navigation Company, which needed every one of its ships.

A more spectacular incident took place at Beaumaris on August 11, 1908, when the *Sagamo* and the *Kenozha* met to exchange freight and passengers. It was not until the exchange was complete, however, that the normal routine turned to disaster. The *Kenozha* backed away from the wharf first and started to turn around, but by then the *Sagamo* was also backing out. Instead of waiting for the flagship to pass, the *Kenozha* kept on moving forward. With a loud crash her bow struck the port side of the *Sagamo* near the stern. The *Sagamo* suffered only a few broken windows and a dent in the sidewall, well above the waterline, but the upper part of the *Kenozha*'s forepeak was crushed, and the smaller ship sailed no more that season.

The accident was a disaster for Captain Hansen. He had not been at the wheel when it happened, but the Court of Inquiry pinned the blame on the mate of the *Kenozha*, who had been drunk at the time. The captain was also censured for not noticing the condition of the mate, and for not being on the bridge during the embarkation. Both men were promptly fired by W.F. Wasley, and shortly afterwards, the mortified Captain Hansen left Gravenhurst with his family for Northern Ontario, where gold had been discovered at Elk Lake and makeshift steamers were busy transporting eager prospectors up the Montreal River from Latchford. Here, the captain found new employment, and later moved further north to the Porcupine country, near Timmins, and ultimately died there. He never returned to Muskoka.

The *Sagamo* was not spared the occasional humiliation either. On August 6, 1910, when the ship was approaching Lake Joseph Station to meet the train, for some reason she came in too fast and struck the wharf, rocking the train and throwing some of the train passengers off balance. Still not stopped, the big ship collided with a couple of launches, crushing one and damaging the other. One of the boat-owners was hurt. Another claim on the insurance companies!

A less serious mishap took place about the year 1912, when the *Islander* was embarking from the wharf at Gregory. Captain Elder rang for "reverse", but the engineer, confused, gave him "forward", with the result that the steamer ran straight into a boat-house. The ship was only slightly damaged, but the boat-house was wrecked and the insurance company received yet another claim.

S.S. "Kenozha" and S.S. "Sagamo" at Clevelands House wharf, Minett, 1910.
Courtesy, *Public Archives of Canada* PA 129954
J. Micklethwaite Collection

Except for the occasional misadventure such as these, the steamers sailed under sunny skies and the Navigation Company knew nothing but prosperity, until 1912. In some ways, this year was a 'watershed'. Major Hugh C. MacLean, the publisher, who had been a company director since 1905, virtually took control by purchasing the holdings of four of the former directors, including James Playfair, who now retired as president in MacLean's favour. The Company's head office was moved to Toronto, and a new Board of Directors, consisting entirely of Toronto gentlemen, was elected. Two of its members, W. K. George and G. T. Somers, were also Directors of the Dominion Bank of Canada, from whom Major MacLean borrowed some of the money used to buy out the Playfairs. A number of the new board members had cottages in Muskoka, including the Major himself, who owned North Bohemia Island on Lake Rosseau. Many of the new directors, however, seldom attended meetings, which generally left MacLean a free hand. The Major's interests already included three publishing companies turning out newspapers and magazines and after 1909, he also served as a director of the Navy League of Canada. The Muskoka Navigation Company was rather a minor enterprise to him, and its day-to-day operations, except for the Royal Muskoka, were left almost entirely in the hands of W.F. Wasley. For the next 33 years, though, the Company was always assured of a steady stream of free advertising in the MacLean publications. In 1913, for the first time since 1901, the Company issued a dividend of five percent. It also assumed responsibility for the Royal Muskoka Hotel bonds, previously guaranteed by the Grand Trunk Railway.

In some ways the MacLean takeover came at an inauspicious moment. The season of 1912, like that of 1902, was wet and chilly, dampening tourism, and out west the crops failed, adding fuel to a depression in 1913. Despite this, and also despite an epidemic of forest fires in August

1913, an estimated 30,000 tourists returned to Muskoka; mostly by train, though more were coming in automobiles. The effects of the depression might have been very serious had it persisted.

During the winter of 1913-14, the directors of the Navigation Company were apparently feeling generous, and in January, they treated their captains and longtime employees to an "appreciation dinner" at the Engineers Club in Toronto. All the officers came except Captain Henry of the *Cherokee*, and were immortalized in a photograph, in uniform, along with Chief Engineer Harry Baillie and shipyard foreman Dan McRae. Besides the dinner and a welcoming address, the captains were shown the sights of Toronto in the winter, including multimillionaire Henry Pelatt's celebrated Casa Loma. In effect, they were celebrating 48 years of successful steamboating in Muskoka, in which Commodore Bailey, Master of the *Sagamo*, had participated almost from the very beginning. Of the others, Captain Joshua Kake of Gravenhurst, the most junior officer, had served 15 years; Captain William Henry Bradshaw of Bracebridge, 17 years; Captain A.P. Larson, 18; Captain Elder, 22; Captain Ralph Lee, 24; Captain C.E. Jackson, 29; Captain McAlpine, 33; and the absent Captain Henry, 40. The Company, during that time, had built or purchased sixteen steamers, of which nine were still in commission.

The season of 1914 began with all the steamers in action. It was a pleasant, warm summer that drew the usual visitors from the south, to join the locals for the usual regattas, dances, fireworks displays and moonlight cruises. Once again, as in 1913, the Royal Muskoka was honoured with an extended visit by Canada's new Prime Minister, Sir Robert Borden and his wife, who arrived on July 23rd. and proceeded up the lakes on Major MacLean's yacht. A week later, Colonel Sam Hughes of Lindsay, the energetic Minister of Militia and Defence, paid an official visit to Bracebridge and took a cruise downriver on the *Islander*. Except for Hughes and a few others like him, nobody paid much attention to a headline in the newspapers about the shooting of an Austrian archduke in a far away place called Sarajevo.

On the evening of July 30th, however, Premier Borden abruptly cut short his holiday at the Royal, caught the *Medora* to Barnesdale, and took the first train back to Ottawa to face again the world of realities. The clouds of war hovering over Europe had suddenly turned darker, and in the Balkans the storm had already broken. Within a few days it was official: all of the Great Powers of Europe were at war. Obviously there was no way for Canada to avoid the conflict, and a startled young country found its government calling for 25,000 volunteers to serve with the colours: meanwhile the price of flour and sugar skyrocketed. The response to the call was immediate and enthusiastic. Young men stepped forward to sacrifice themselves; proud and tearful wives and sweethearts crowded to a thousand railway stations to see them off; and millions more people in all walks of life cheerfully accepted a score of privations to help the war effort, or to relieve some of those left at home. Mercifully, no one then had any way of knowing that the eruption of August 5, 1914 was only the beginning of a dreadful holocaust that would drag on for nearly four and a half years. Thus, violently, began the 20th century. For better and for worse, the world would never be the same again.

The War promptly put an end to the depression, as factories were inundated with orders for munitions and military *matériel*, and farmers were urged to produce all the foodstuffs they could. However, the national emergency meant that carefree days at a comfortable summer resort or cruises on a sedate steamer were no longer in fashion, and furthermore, qualified engineers and good crew members became scarce. There is no question that the Navigation Company was forced to tighten the belt and curtail services until conditions more or less returned to normal. No dividends were declared until the War was over. On the positive side, however, the War discouraged overseas travel, forcing many people to spend their summers in Canada, rather than abroad.

Scarcely had the conflict broken out than the *Nipissing* completed her last trip. For several years now, her aging engines had been giving trouble. We have already noted how she broke a piston near Beaumaris in 1908. Early in August 1912, the vessel was again put out of service for a few weeks with a broken shaft. Another time she was cruising past Buck Island, south of Beaumaris, when the arm of the walking-beam jerked the head of the steam cylinder out. Steam gushed forth, and Captain Jackson could only drop anchor and whistle for help. Soon the passengers were transferred and the *Nipissing* was ignominiously towed back to Gravenhurst.

Officers of the Muskoka Navigation Company, 1913.
(Front Row, Left to Right): William H. Elder, Master of the "Islander"; Edward F. McAlpine, Master of the "Medora"; George Bailey, Commodore, Master of the "Sagamo"; Charles E. Jackson, Master of the "Nipissing"; Ralph W. Lee, Master of the "Kenozha".

(Back Row, Left to Right): Jon MacKenzie, Chief Engineer; Joshua Kake, Master of the "Oriole"; A. Peter Larson, Master of the "Ahmic"; Dan McRae, Chief Engineer; Harry Baillie, Chief Engineer; William H. Bradshaw, Master of the "Charlie M." (Absent from the above: John Henry, Master of the "Cherokee".)

Despite these setbacks, the graceful side-wheeler carried on until the summer of 1914, but finally the day of reckoning could no longer be deferred. She was backing out of Milford Bay one day, and the captain had just signalled "forward engines", when the walking-beam broke, immobilizing her machinery. The disabled ship began drifting towards the rocks. Hearing her continuous whistle calls, a youth named Francis Fowler came out to investigate in a little four horsepower gas boat. The passengers, aware that something was wrong, crowded over to the rail to watch with some amusement as the little boat began pushing the stern of the big ship away from the rocks. Then the motorboat took the steamer in tow and started heading for Beaumaris, at a speed of perhaps three miles per hour. Soon the *Islander* arrived to pick up the passengers, and apparently she also towed the *Nipissing* back to Gravenhurst. That proved to be the *Nipissing*'s last voyage. Spare parts for old machinery were difficult to obtain in wartime, and for the next ten years the old side-wheeler languished at the Navigation Company dockyards. Now and then she was used as a dormitory by some of the yard crews, and even by the Assistant Traffic Manager, with permission from Mr. Wasley.

Though far removed from the ravages of war, the Muskoka steamers experienced a number of dramatic incidents during this period. A lady from Mortimer's Point recalls an adventurous all-day excursion involving several of the boats on August 23, 1915. At that time the *Ahmic* and

S.S. "Nipissing" (Final Version) at Port Carling.
Courtesy, *Public Archives of Canada* PA 132122

S.S. "Nipissing", retired

Steamers at Beaumaris, around 1914
Gathered at the wharf are the Strs. "Charlie M." (left foreground), "Islander", "Kenozha" and "Nipissing".

the *Charlie M.* were providing a daily service on the west arm of Lake Muskoka, with the *Ahmic* sailing from Bala, and the *Charlie M.* from Whiteside. Usually they met near the Kettles, a well-known shoal off Mortimer's Point. On this particular morning, the *Charlie M.* collected about seven or eight excursionists from Acton Island and the Point, but on her way up to Beaumaris, she grounded on a rock near Rossclair and broke a steam pipe. Clouds of steam hissed out, and the little vessel began tooting for help. Her rescuer proved to be the *Islander*, on her way from Bracebridge to Beaumaris. She collected the passengers and towed the *Charlie M.* alongside to Beaumaris. Soon the *Cherokee* arrived, and the passengers boarded her to continue their cruise. Unluckily, a beautiful mahogany motor launch occupied by several elderly ladies in wicker chairs happened to manoeuvre astern of the big ship, unknown to the captain, and the *Cherokee* started to back up, right into the launch. Several people shouted in alarm and the captain stopped engines, but the steamer bumped into the launch, which capsized amid the eddies and sank, leaving the ladies sputtering and screaming for help. Fortunately, several stalwart fellows on the wharf immediately jumped into the water to rescue them and no one was drowned; later the launch was also raised. After these two incidents the party cruised all the way to Port Cockburn and had a marvellous time. However, their adventures were not yet over. Upon returning to Beaumaris, they found the *Charlie M.* on hand to take them home. Most were nervous about trusting her again, but everyone was assured that the little craft had been properly "fixed up". Off she went for the west arm, only to hit the same rock again! A bump, thump and scrape, and everyone's heart missed a beat, then the *Charlie M.* cleared the shoal and docked safely at Rossclair. It later turned out that a storm a few days earlier had shifted the buoy.

The enforced retirement of the *Nipissing*, meanwhile, had left the Company with only eight steamers in active service, and soon that number was reduced even further. In 1917, the railway dropped its overnight run to Muskoka Wharf, sending instead just two trains per day from Toronto. At the same time, the Navigation Company cut its routes from nine to seven and dropped the morning all-day run to Lake Joseph. The *Sagamo*, which had always assumed that route, conspicuously disappears from the schedules, and only the Lake Rosseau steamer (probably the *Medora*) continued to call at Muskoka Wharf. In 1918, the belt was tightened even

S.S. "Sagamo", laid up at Gravenhurst.

further: the steamers' routes were trimmed from seven to a mere five, and the *Cherokee*, though providing a morning service from Gravenhurst once again, was in fact doing so only three times a week, and plying on the alternate days from Bracebridge. Again there is no mention of the *Sagamo*. There seems to be little doubt that the lordly flagship never turned a wheel throughout the last two years of the War.

All this increased the workload of her sister ships. But worse was yet to come. In the spring of 1918 the steamer *Kenozha*, now the line's oldest ship, was entering her 35th season, and some of her tired old timbers were getting frail, despite periodic replanking. Her former master, Captain John Henry, who was now on the *Cherokee*, used to come and look her over now and then. He did not like what he saw. "The poor old girl's getting pretty dozy," remarked the captain sadly, and it was clear that the *Kenozha*'s days were numbered. Perhaps she was reprieved by the War, because the Company needed her, and in wartime she could not be replaced. Fate, however, spared her an ignominious end in the scrap yards. In the early morning hours of August 15, 1918, she met the same fate as the original *Nipissing* 32 years earlier, and in the same general area too. She caught fire at the wharf at Stanley House, on northern Lake Joseph, where she was berthed for the night, and her crew of fourteen barely had time to abandon ship before she became a crackling inferno. Captain Lee and his purser, who were asleep in the bridge cabins, had to jump over the side, leaving behind their clothes, money and personal effects. The blazing ship was cut loose from the dock and drifted slowly across the bay. Finally she grounded, burned to the waterline, and sank. The stranded passengers were picked up by the *Cherokee*, and later the machinery was salvaged, but the skeleton of the old *Kenozha* is said to be still visible in the shallow water at the north side of Stanley Bay.

The *Kenozha* was the second ship of the fleet lost by fire, but as events turned out she was not the last. The War ended in November 1918, and the following year the *Sagamo* came out of retirement. Soon, however, the Company suffered another loss. On the evening of July 6, 1919, Captain William Bradshaw brought his charge, the *Charlie M.*, back to the Gravenhurst docks, and then took the 10:00 p.m. train home to Bracebridge for the weekend. Later that same night someone phoned to tell him that his vessel had just burned near her boathouse. Captain Bradshaw bumped his way back down to Gravenhurst the next morning in his brother's Model T Ford to see for himself, but it was all-too-true. Somehow the little *Charlie M.* had taken fire and was now a sunken, useless hulk. The remains have since disappeared beneath landfill at the Gravenhurst waterfront.

S.S. "Kenozha" on Bala Bay.

Str. "Charlie M." at the Gravenhurst Dockyards.
The retired Str. "Nipissing" can be glimpsed at the right.

Steamers were not the only victims of the fire scourge during those ill-favoured years. Several of Muskoka's grandest hotels were also destroyed. On the evening of March 13, 1913, the old Bala Falls Hotel, which had been in business since 1886, burned to the ground. Two and a half years later, in October of 1915, the lovely Summit House at Port Cockburn, now the oldest resort on the lakes, took fire one night after all the guests had departed for the season, creating a fearful holocaust that speedily turned the great mansion into a heap of glowing cinders. The hapless proprietor, Alexander Fraser, barely had time to send a last pitiful telegraph message before taking to his heels. Only the abundance of recent rain and the lack of any wind that night prevented a general forest fire that would have destroyed everything for miles. Faithful patrons returned the following summer to tent on the point where the Summit House had stood, but inevitably they soon drifted away to other resorts like the Royal. One year later, at 2:30 in the morning of October 16, 1916, a like fate befell the Prospect House at Port Sandfield, which after a lifetime of 34 years was completely destroyed within a matter of hours. In 1917, the Maplehurst Hotel near Rosseau also burned. None of these resorts were rebuilt, though Maplehurst carried on for many years in the form of cabins. Bala and Port Sandfield both survived nonetheless, as other hotels expanded to replace the ones destroyed, but for Port Cockburn, the loss of the Summit House was a fatal blow. It had ceased to be part of a through transport route once the C.P.R. and the Canadian Northern bypassed it for Barnesdale, and once the hotel was gone, there was no longer any reason for the lake steamers to call, except to drop off the mail, and soon there was very little of that! Early in 1918 the post office was closed, and except for a few cottages, Port Cockburn quickly lapsed into a deserted bay at the head of the lake. Today, there is little to remind one that this spot was once one of the liveliest on the lakes. The Stanley House meanwhile took its place as the most northerly calling place on Lake Joseph.

S.S. "Sagamo" and S.S. "Cherokee" at Port Cockburn.
Visits to the Summit House by two steamers simultaneously were very unusual!
Courtesy, *Public Archives of Canada*, PA 129952
J. Micklethwaite Collection

S.S."Sagamo", passing Prospect House, Port Sandfield, 1910.
Courtesy, *Public Archives of Canada* PA 32250

Despite these casualties, and the brief depression that followed the conclusion of the War, the Muskoka communities groped their way back to a form of normalcy. With the advent of the 1920s, this seemed to be achieved. Prosperity returned, industry was humming, the resorts were full, and the steamers were again sailing with crowded decks. But times had changed. The "Roaring Twenties" were not the same as the Edwardian era. In some ways conditions were no longer favourable to passenger ships. More adaptations were necessary, as steamboating entered its seventh decade in Muskoka.

Were there any steamboats on any of the lesser Muskoka Lakes? There were, but they were small, few and obscure. A steamer was apparently launched on Three Mile Lake, east of Windermere, in 1886. Its duties must have included towing logs to the mill at Dee Bank Village, collecting and distributing provisions for farmers around Ufford and Raymond, and no doubt, conducting fishing parties as well, but the outcome of the venture is unknown. A decade later (1896-97) we hear of a steam launch running pleasure trips on Skeleton Lake, which was then seldom visited, and in about 1903 the little steamer *Fairy Belle*, run by Captain Charles Fullerton of Skeleton Bay, was moved to the lake to tow for a local sawmill. An 'alligator' is mentioned on Pine Lake, near Gravenhurst, in 1893, and another on Kahshe Lake, south of Gravenhurst at the turn of the century, towing for a mill near the exit of the Kahshe River.

Kahshe Lake also saw a couple of pleasure steamers. The first was a launch called the *Flying Belle*, which was imported on a wagon from Gravenhurst around 1906 and used as an adjunct to a small resort called "Duncan's Tourist House". The guests would usually detrain at Kilworthy Station and proceed in horse taxis to meet the steamer, which was also used to haul scows of freight or take people on dance cruises in the open air, on the scow! As visitors began erecting their own cottages on Kahshe Lake, the *Flying Belle* found additional employment scowing in lumber and furnishings for them. The little steamer served on Kahshe Lake until the War years, but disappeared with the advent of private motor launches; she may have been taken to other waters. One other large steam launch, the *Rob Roy*, which had already spent eleven years on Sparrow Lake, was also taken to Kahshe Lake around 1911 and put to work taking tourists and supplies from Klueys Bay to various points on the lake.

Steam Launch "Flying Belle", on Kahshe Lake.

Post Office and Store, Kilworthy, Ont.

A G.T.R. train passing through Kilworthy, Ontario.

General view of Huntsville, Ontario, 1905.
The three steamers are the "Joe" (left), "Empress Victoria" and "Gem". The prominent building to the left is the Kent Hotel.
Courtesy, *Mrs. Barbara Mills*, Georgetown

CHAPTER 2
The Heyday of the
Huntsville Navigation Company
(1905-1928)

Following the death of its founder, Captain Marsh, in 1904, the Huntsville, Lake of Bays and Lake Simcoe Navigation Company Ltd., like its south Muskoka counterpart, entered a short period of reorganization. In 1905, Dr. J.H. Webb of Waterloo, Ontario, was elected its interim president, while W.H. Patton, a Toronto businessman, remained Vice-president. Two other Toronto men were on the Board of Directors, along with the Manager, William Duperow, who continued as secretary and treasurer. The Company then had 55 shareholders who had subscribed a total of $58,800 in share capital, with easily the largest amount, $21,850, held by the Marsh Estate. Plans continued for the construction of new scows and steamers, particularly for the Lake of Bays Division. Outwardly, everything was business as usual.

Behind the scenes, however, a traumatic upheaval was in the making. Charles Orlando Shaw, Manager of the Anglo-Canadian Leather Company tanneries at Bracebridge and Huntsville, was stealthily buying up shares in the Navigation Company, including those owned by the Marsh Estate. His motive seems to have been a long smouldering resentment at the allegedly unfair defeat of his yacht, the *Sarona*, by the *Joe* in August 1904. It is also likely that Shaw saw the Navigation Company as a worthwhile investment and an interesting new side venture for his talents. But the implacable industrialist was never a man to swallow an insult, nor could he ever be diverted from any course on which his mind was set. The fact that William Duperow had not only relished his victory, but had even issued prizes to commemorate it, seems to have inspired in Shaw a relentless desire for revenge.

And revenge he got. One morning Duperow, while working at his office at the Huntsville wharf, was surprised to see the short, stocky, red-faced figure of C.O. Shaw striding in, demanding to see the books of the Navigation Company. When Duperow politely asked by what authority he was making such a demand, Shaw threw down his trump card, a sheaf of documents confirming that he, Charles Orlando Shaw, now owned $27,400 of the Company's stock; about 47 percent. No doubt Shaw gloated over Duperow's sudden loss of composure, as the manager obediently produced the records he asked for. Contrary to some people's recollections, Shaw did not dismiss Duperow right on the spot: the manager in fact remained at his post at least until 1906. But things were never the same again.

Shaw soon made his authority felt. He started laying down the law to his manager. Within months he also called a shareholders' meeting, which probably few attended, since most were from Toronto and Hamilton. First on the agenda was the election of a new Board of Directors. All of the old members, except Duperow, were removed, and C.O. Shaw was elected President, along with a new slate of six directors. H. Foster Chaffee, a Toronto businessman, became the new Vice-president, while John McKee of Huntsville, one of Shaw's minions, became the new Secretary and Treasurer; replacing Duperow, who was demoted to General Manager. Meanwhile Shaw continued to buy up the holdings of some of the minor shareholders.

It is difficult to present an objective picture of Charles Orlando Shaw. There is no doubt that he was an extremely aggressive and successful businessman, although of a type seldom held in high esteem today. A construction engineer by training, he came from a family that had been running tanneries in the United States and Canada for at least three generations. C.O. Shaw himself was born in Dexter, Maine, in 1858, and lived for a time in Boston, until the 1890s, when the continuing search for tanbark drew him out to Cheboygan, Michigan, where his firm, Shaw, Cassils and Company of Montreal, opened one of its plants. Meanwhile his cousin, William Sutherland Shaw, was busy founding and managing tanneries in Bracebridge and Huntsville.

Charles Orlando Shaw.
Huntsville industrialist and President of the Huntsville and Lake of Bays Navigation Company, 1906-1942.
Courtesy, *Huntsville Pioneer Village*

S.S. "Joe" at the fateful regatta at Grunwald, (August 1904).
Courtesy, *Mrs. Barbara Mills*, Georgetown

C.O. Shaw, however, felt he could do better, and in 1898 he came to Huntsville to make good his boast. While Sutherland Shaw left to open a new tannery at Boyne City, Michigan, the Huntsville tannery, under his cousin's direction, expanded to become the largest producer of sole leather in the entire British Empire, turning out (by 1906) about 313,000 sides of leather annually. The Company, renamed the Anglo-Canadian Leather Company in 1905, became one of the largest in Canada.

All this was achieved, in part, by the furious energy and exacting demands of C.O. Shaw. He was the sort of man who was always busy himself and could not stand seeing any of his employees idle. It is said that he once ordered one of the tannery hands dismissed, over the protests of the foreman, simply because the man happened to be wearing a wristwatch, which in Shaw's eyes meant he was a clock watcher. No man alive, it seems, could breathe more devastating venom into the two deadly words, spoken in a deep, soft voice: "You're fired." Within just a few weeks of his arrival in Huntsville, the tannery employees went on strike, unable to endure the work loads demanded by the new manager, or, for that matter, his snappish temper; but, with no union to back them up, nor any funds in reserve, the men were soon forced to capitulate and go back to work. In 1904, deciding that the locals around Huntsville expected too much in wages, Shaw brought over about 40 families from Milan, Italy: many of them were musical, and from their ranks were to come some of the musicians of the celebrated Anglo-Canadian Concert Band, founded in 1914.

By this time, Shaw was recognized as one of Huntsville's foremost businessmen, and for a time he served as councillor and mayor. Yet for all his wealth and opportunities, Shaw did nothing for community betterment, unless it also happened to be beneficial to himself. He led a very frugal life, belonged to no clubs, and attended few social functions, except the occasional movie. Nor has he left any memorial around Huntsville, unless we count Bigwin Inn on the Lake of Bays. Even his once famous concert band, for many years the pride and delight of Huntsville, was, in truth, simply another enlargement of his own ego, in that Shaw himself, being an expert cornetist, liked to perform in the band. One might add that, having developed the concert band to a high level of excellence and attracted a member of John Philip Sousa's Band to conduct it, C. O. Shaw abruptly disbanded the ensemble in 1928 — perhaps in a moment of pique, or because it was costing him too much in money or energy — to the intense disappointment of music lovers everywhere, and especially the people of Huntsville.

This, then, is the general image we have of C. O. Shaw: a dynamic, ruthless egoist who seemed to care only for his work and his music, both of which he did extremely well. To his employees, Shaw was a menacing tyrant and they dreaded him, although Shaw himself may have felt that terror was essential to keep his men in line. He was, in short, a man cast in the same mold as the late 19th century "robber barons" of American Big Business; men such as Cornelius Vanderbilt, who coined the phrase, "the public be damned", or John D. Rockefeller I, whose guiding motto was to "pay a profit to nobody." Charles Orlando Shaw was proud to be a businessman of that ilk, and apparently he never modified his views one iota.

It comes as a relief to find that this little ogre of a man had a few human traits. He was a good family man, and most of them idolized him. Deep down, he had a sense of humour, and could smile at a blunt-spoken maintenance man at Bigwin Inn who dared to answer him back. Sometimes he could be quite charming — providing that no one disagreed with him! He was known to take a personal interest in his employees, sometimes beyond the dictates of business efficiency, and he was even guilty of the occasional act of decency. One evening around 1911, hearing that a girl had sustained a ruptured appendix at a cottage on the Lake of Bays, he asked the crew of the *Empress Victoria* if they would make a special trip to the Portage, along with a team of doctors and nurses: they responded with alacrity and the girl was saved. Privately, C. O. Shaw was actually kindhearted, but he evidently felt that any visible sign of benevolence would be taken for weakness, and therefore kept his kindnesses a secret. He sometimes provided housing for faithful employees, but he always demanded complete subservience from them. He was sometimes known to come to Bigwin Inn at season's end and play cards with his staff, but woe betide any bellboy caught lounging with a cigarette! Shaw could also order the Wardell store at Huntsville to send blankets free of charge to an injured tannery hand who was shivering in his

Anglo-Canadian Leather Company Tannery, Huntsville.
The tugs "Hildred" (left) and "Phoenix" can be seen in the river, plus several scows.

William John Moore, Manager of the Huntsville Navigation
Company, 1907-1953.

garret in dead of winter, but he thought nothing of marching straight up to the counters and demanding immediate service, no matter how many others might be waiting in line. An extraordinary man was C. O. Shaw, though hardly a loveable one.

His takeover of the Huntsville Navigation Company in 1905 came as bad news to some of its employees, and many of them soon resigned. Captain Alex Casselman, who had commanded the *Joe* during her race with the *Sarona*, soon left, as did Captain Fred Marsh of the *Mary Louise* (Captain Fred Marsh later co-founded the Perrin & Marsh Steamboat Line on Lake Temagami). The genial Captain John Fraser of the *Empress*, the Line's senior officer, held on for a few more seasons but then packed his bags for the west. William Duperow soon did the same. It is not absolutely certain that Shaw made the manager's life miserable, but there can be no doubt that the new president could not tolerate men of strong personality and independent judgment. For all his charm and good humour, Duperow had both. Inevitably he dared to disagree with Shaw, and

68

inevitably the two parted company. In 1907 Duperow left for the west, where he went to work for the C.P.R. and did very well; becoming Administrative Manager and Western Passenger Agent at Winnipeg.

Duperow's departure meant that a new manager was needed, and Shaw lost little time in finding one. His choice was William John Moore, a tall, red-haired man from Gravenhurst who had previously been Manager of the Rathbun Company sawmill on Muskoka Bay. In accepting Shaw's invitation and moving to Huntsville, Moore was taking on a lifetime job. He remained General Manager and Secretary-Treasurer of the Huntsville Navigation Company for the next 40 years. He also handled Shaw's office work in the wintertime, and his private work too. For years the tall, spare figure of Mr. Moore, coming to and from his rather drab little office at the town wharf, usually carrying an umbrella, rain or shine, was a familiar sight at Huntsville. To his subordinates, Moore was a strict, though reasonable boss. To the public, he appeared an indefatigable worker, totally devoted to his company's interests. His friends, however, knew that behind a rather gruff facade lurked a warm, gentle and fascinating personality. Gradually W.J. Moore became a respected, then popular, citizen of Huntsville, and eventually he was elected to the town council, which was something of an achievement for a Catholic living in a staunchly Protestant community.

There was certainly plenty of work to be done. The Huntsville Navigation Company was then riding the wave of local and national prosperity, and until the outbreak of war in 1914, it knew nothing but success. By 1906, the Line employed about 50 to 60 men, with wages and operating expenses totalling $23,000. It was also towing all of the tanbark and sawlogs for the local mills, to say nothing of the Royal Mail. In the passenger department, Duperow, and Moore after him, had repeated engagements attending press and sportsmens' club meetings in the central United States, at which they handed out thousands of leaflets outlining the charms of the North Muskoka Lakes, only five hours from Toronto. Visitors could board an evening train at Pittsburgh or Buffalo and have breakfast at Huntsville the following morning before boarding the steamers for the resorts of their choice. All this paid off handsomely, as an estimated 3,500 tourists travelled on the Huntsville steamers in 1905 alone.

The fleet, meanwhile, continued to grow. Inherited from Captain Marsh were the *Empress Victoria, Joe, Phoenix* and *Hildred* on the Huntsville lakes, plus the *Mary Louise, Maple Leaf* and *Lady of the Lake* on the Lake of Bays. Linking them was the newly-built Portage Railway. It is said that C.O. Shaw, to his annoyance, discovered a debt of $25,000 still owed by the Company, probably stemming from construction of the railway, and consequently the entire fleet was mortgaged to help pay it off, and to finance expansion. In 1906, the Line was engaged to tow a record 50,000 feet of sawlogs and 15,000 cords of wood and tanbark to the mills of Huntsville, and consequently it doubled its fleet of scows between 1903 and 1906.
between 1903 and 1906.

The steady growth of the tourist business required the addition of several new passenger ships. The first to arrive was the *Florence Main*, which we have met earlier on Lake Muskoka as Captain Mortimer's unsuccessful challenge to the Muskoka Navigation Company. C.O. Shaw bought the 80 foot vessel late in 1904, even before his takeover of the Huntsville Navigation Company, and had her shipped from Bracebridge on two railway flatcars. The vessel reached Huntsville on April 2, 1905, and was immediately recaulked and repainted for service. The *Florence Main* spent the next two seasons on the Huntsville lakes, apparently towing tanbark, but she was not to remain in this role for long. As Shaw's priorities fluctuated, he soon found other uses for the boat.

In 1906, meanwhile, Shaw decided to import another steamer, his third, to the Huntsville lakes. This craft was the *Dortha*, a beautiful yacht of 34.67 tons. Built at Hamilton in 1894 as the *Lizzie* and renamed in 1895, the *Dortha* had been the property of Senator George T. Fulford of Brockville. Fulford, however, died in the fall of 1905, and the following February his heirs sold the boat to Shaw, who brought her to Huntsville by rail as soon as the ice left the lakes. Powered by a 25 hp. upright engine, the *Dortha* was 77.4 feet in length by 19 feet in beam, and was easily the most elegant craft ever seen at Huntsville. She featured a clipper bow and a fantail stern, with varnished "gingerbread" cabins embellished inside with red plush cushions and walnut panelling, while the floor of her dining room was inlaid with "V" patterns in which every panel was made of

S.S. "Empress Victoria", leaving Huntsville town wharf.
Courtesy, *Mrs. Barbara Mills*, Georgetown

Steam Tug "Phoenix" and crew.
Courtesy, *Mr. Owen Swann*, Huntsville

a different type of wood. She even carried a small piano. Shaw launched his latest acquisition at the Huntsville station wharf at the first possible moment in 1906. He may have intended the *Dortha* for his own private use, but very soon she was running passengers regularly to Port Sydney; replacing the *Joe*, which Shaw decided to transfer to the Lake of Bays. A few attempts were made to use the *Dortha* as a towboat, but these were dropped, owing to her tendency to roll. In January of 1907, the new vessel formally became part of the Navigation Company fleet.

Now a confirmed passenger steamer, the *Dortha* was not permitted to retain her yacht-like appearance for long. In the fall of 1908, Shaw decided to have her remodelled extensively in drydock to make her look more like her sister ships. This was accomplished by building a whole new hull around the vessel, leaving the old ribs and cabins intact. At the same time, she was given a new steeple compound engine. Except for her name, no one would have recognized the new, straight-stemmed double-decked ship that emerged in 1909 as the *Dortha*. Her outward character was totally changed, and only the pilot house remained unaltered. Perhaps in view of that, on August 31, 1909, the vessel's name was changed by Order-in-Council to the *Ramona*.

Re-registered at 83.26 tons, the *Ramona*, though much plainer and slower than the *Dortha*, was still a handsome ship, and was licensed for 240 passengers. She continued to ply between Huntsville and Port Sydney, usually with a crew of four, and docking overnight at the Belleview Hotel. Friday was always "meat day" as the little steamer was stocked up early in the morning

S.S. "Florence Main" (Second Version).
The vessel has now been converted into a double-decker, with an enclosed bow and a new hurricane deck. More cabins will be added later.
Courtesy, *Mrs. Jean Lindsay*, Clarkson

S.S. "Joe", at The Locks.

The "Dortha" in Locks of Muskoka River
at Huntsville, Ont.

Steam Yacht "Dortha" at The Locks.
Courtesy, *Mr. George Johnson*, Port Sydney

S.S. "Ramona", at The Locks.

River scene at Baysville, Ontario.
The small steamer near the bridge appears to be the passenger tug "Niska", in her original version.
Courtesy, *Mr. Charles Mickle Cane*, Toronto

before making her rounds, stopping anywhere that a white flag was raised; she was a freighter as well as a passenger ship, and together with the *Gem* shared the Mary Lake route.

A fine new passenger steamer for the Lake of Bays service had been on the Company drawing boards as early as 1904, but this project had been shelved until the Portage Railway was completed. Under Shaw, the interrupted scheme went ahead, partly because both the *Mary Louise* and the *Lady of the Lake* were growing old and unequal to the demands on them. The whole problem of the Lake of Bays division became even more acute when the *Maple Leaf* burned at Baysville in July of 1906, but by the following autumn, the hull of the new steamer was ready to hit the waves.

It was a cool, breezy day when the new flagship of the Huntsville Navigation Company made her début. A small party gathered at South Portage for the event, including C.O. Shaw, W.J. Moore and J.R. Reece, a prominent local official who had been given the honour of christening the new ship. Reece, who had lost a leg many years earlier during his service with the British Army, nearly fell off the stand, but otherwise the brief ceremony proceeded as planned, the bottle was smashed, and the steamer *Algonquin* slid stern first into the lake amid the cheers and applause of the party. The hull was immediately towed across to the railway dock to have the boiler installed. At long last, the Lake of Bays was getting a fine new passenger steamer.

Yet the steamer *Algonquin* never turned a wheel on the Lake of Bays. Shortly after her launching, C.O. Shaw suddenly decided that the new ship, being the Company's largest (she was 120 feet in length by 23.8 feet in beam and ultimately registered 200.4 tons) should ply on the Huntsville lakes instead, where the crowds were likely to be larger. The Line already had six steamers on the lower lakes and only two on the upper lakes. No matter! The *Joe* and the *Florence Main* would be transferred to the Lake of Bays in place of the *Algonquin*. Some of his aides must have shuddered at the implications, but once his mind was made up there was no dissuading Shaw. Unluckily, the engine and boiler of the flagship were already in place, having been hauled overland from Huntsville, but work on the superstructure was suspended until the following year.

In the spring, the wheels were set in motion for the multiple transfer. All three of the steamers involved were much too large to be carried on the tiny railway, and the road across the Portage was very narrow. The *Joe* was the first to go, using timbers, cables, horses, rollers and six pulleys to winch her across. Supervising the job was a brother of Captain Robson, Jim Robson of Birkendale, who is said to have been a genius at improvisation. He once moved a barn loaded with hay a distance of 300 feet along a twisting road near Port Sydney, and another time floated a broken water pipe under the river at Huntsville to the surface in a matter of hours, to the amazed disbelief of the Town Council. Obviously Robson was just the man to engineer the moving of the *Joe* and the *Florence Main*. Both needed several weeks to complete the one mile trek, but by July the two of them had safely reached the Lake of Bays. The *Joe* now began plying to Dwight, Point Ideal, Glenmount and Baysville, while the aging *Mary Louise* continued to run to Dorset. The *Florence Main* was still used primarily as a workboat, but C.O. Shaw was already making big plans for her.

The *Algonquin* was laboriously winched across the Portage in the spring of 1907, after the transit of the *Joe*. The task, which was assigned to Warren Moore, one of the tannery men (no relation to the Manager), took several weeks, since the steamer was already completed as far as the second deck, and the boiler alone added fifteen tons to her weight. Despite everything, the big ship was slowly inched across the divide. All went well until she was approaching the wharf at North Portage, where she was to be launched, bow first. Then, unhappily, some of the rollers dropped from beneath her hull, perhaps into a depression in the road, and within moments the unsupported oak keel snapped under the strain — just what the men had been dreading. It was decided to launch her anyway, and the new vessel was then towed to Huntsville. A broken keel is usually fatal to any ship, but the *Algonquin*'s was massively reinforced with timbers, after which the superstructure cabins and hurricane deck were built. By the summer of 1907 she was plying daily to the Portage.

Despite her injury, the *Algonquin* was a fine ship, even though her bow bobbed perceptibly up and down when she was in motion, and for safety she was never run at full speed. Her overall length, including the fantail, was about 128 feet, and her handsome lounge cabin was further

S.S. "Algonquin", Flagship of the Huntsville Navigation Company. Courtesy, *Ontario Archives*, Acc. 9939, Reel 14, #11

S.S. "Algonquin" (left) and S.S. "Empress Victoria" at Huntsville. Photograph taken from the railway bridge.

S.S. "Algonquin" at the Canal.
The cordwood alongside will be used as fuel.

enhanced by an overhead clerestory, in which the tiny windows were paned with coloured glass. Unlike the *Empress*, the *Algonquin* did not have a pull-down stack, and consequently the old bridge over the Canal between Fairy and Peninsula Lakes had to be raised to accommodate her. Owing to her size, the new flagship required a crew of seven or eight, and partly for this reason she usually operated only from late June until Labour Day, leaving the *Empress* and *Ramona* to look after the shoulder seasons. Newspapers, coffee and light refreshments were available on board but no full-course meals: C.O. Shaw would not hear of the idea.

Usually commanded by Captain William Sangster of Huntsville, a dapper, dour little man who became a favourite with Shaw, the *Algonquin* at once began cruising twice a day to the Portage; always connecting with the trains from Toronto at the railway wharf, both early in the morning and at about 3:40 in the afternoon. She carried freight as well as passengers, and it was not uncommon for her to load up half a boxcar's worth of commodities every trip. On the morning runs, she would stop at the Huntsville town wharf to pick up anything left by the *Ramona* or the *Empress*. While out on the lakes, she would stop at any docks big enough to receive her to drop off freight and passengers or pick them up on a flag signal. Sometimes she would also meet the *Ramona* in mid-lake to transfer cargoes; the deep-throated roar of the flagship's whistle bringing a shrill reply from the *Ramona*. Sometimes the steamers would also stop and let people off onto private boats coming alongside or pick them up 'en route'; as for example one Saturday night when a group of raftsmen, finding themselves stranded at the Portage, took off in a small boat, hoping to intercept the *Algonquin* in a nearby channel. The steamer, however, took the opposite course through a very narrow passage, but happily Captain Sangster spotted the small boat, backed towards the frantically waving men, and took them to town. (There were seldom any passengers on the return trip on Saturdays anyway.) The Canal was a problem for the big ship, which could barely squeeze through it, and every so often she

S.S. "Empress Victoria", at Grassmere.

S.S. "Mary Louise", on the Lake of Bays.
The vessel has obviously seen better days!

would run aground amid the water lilies. As a rule she could work free by herself, but occasionally the *Phoenix* or *Ramona* would be summoned to the rescue.

As the *Algonquin* came into her own, her predecessor, the *Empress Victoria*, now usually called simply the *Empress*, slowly subsided into a standby ship, seldom sailing in the summers anymore, except for special events, though she continued to ply in the off-seasons. Her former part-time route to Port Sydney was now handled by the *Ramona*. In time, a tow post was installed on the *Empress*, which began spending more and more time as a towboat, perhaps replacing the little *Hildred*, which fades from the record after 1910. Gradually these exertions wore out the once proud lady. She lasted until the season of 1913, but the following year, she was pronounced unfit for further service and dismantled. It is said that her corroded boiler broke while it was being removed, leaving the bottom of it still in place. Once everything of value had been stripped away, the little ship, now twenty years old, was towed into Lake Vernon, to a point about 200 feet from the mouth of the Big East River, and there snubbed to a submerged pole, soaked with kerosene, and set on fire. The crew of a passing tug was just in time to see her lurch suddenly to one side, then to the other, and then disappear into the depths forever. The following May the registry office was informed that the steamer *Empress Victoria* was no more.

Her old running mate on the Lake of Bays, the *Mary Louise*, had already met a similar fate. This little propeller, which by 1907 had seen 23 years of active service, was looking quite scuffed and battered towards the end, and would probably have been retired in that year had not the *Algonquin*, her intended successor, been transferred to Huntsville. As it happened, the *Mary Louise* was reprieved until the fall and then beached at South Portage. The machinery was removed, and one evening the old ship was purposely set on fire. Later the hulk was towed across the bay and scuttled below the bluffs. It is said that her propeller shaft was still turning during this short final trip, as if unwilling to concede that this really *was* the end. Not far away, near the boat-houses of South Portage, lay the remains of the *Lady of the Lake*, herself dismantled a few years earlier.

Their successors were the *Joe* and the *Florence Main*, newly arrived from the lower lakes in 1907. Two steamers were not enough for the burgeoning business of the Lake of Bays. C.O. Shaw already had a third one under construction at South Portage, though why he did not leave the *Algonquin* there and build his new ship at Huntsville is a mystery, perhaps to be explained simply as another example of Shavian caprice.

The new ship was the *Iroquois*, a splendid, steel-framed vessel started at South Portage in 1906. She was very similar to the *Algonquin*; slightly smaller (118.5 feet by 23 feet and registered at 198.05 tons) but deeper in draft, probably because the Lake of Bays, with its lengthy expanses of open water, is rougher and stormier than the lower lakes. Construction dragged on for about a year, with most of the parts being built in advance by the woodworking plant and machine shop of the tannery. The launching took place on July 21, 1907, just four days after the induction of the steamer *Cherokee* at Gravenhurst. Within a few weeks the *Iroquois* had completed her trials and was plying regularly to Dorset.

Commanded initially by Captain Joseph St. Amond of South Portage (usually known as "Captain Santimore"), the *Iroquois* proved a very steady ship, never swerving from her compass bearings. She was licensed for 150 passengers, but in practice sometimes took twice that. One of her most distinctive features, in addition to her deep, heavy whistle, was a powerful 500-watt searchlight mounted on the pilot house. Like the *Algonquin*, the *Iroquois* was seldom run at full speed because she showed a tendency to vibrate at more than "three-quarters ahead".

The construction crews who had worked on the *Iroquois* were present at the launching, and C.O. Shaw, who was in a good humour, invited them to come along for a cruise to Norway Point, where a new hotel, the Wa-Wa, was under construction: his yacht, the *Sarona*, would take them back to Huntsville. Both the *Iroquois* and the *Florence Main* were crammed to capacity when the little railway finished bringing over all the crowds from Huntsville. The two steamers then backed away and separated as they began their rounds. It was getting late by the time the *Iroquois* left Norway Point, having dropped off almost all her passengers except the workmen. Then, on the return trip, a series of whistle blasts directed the ship over to Fox Point, where the *Florence Main* was languishing with a broken propeller shaft. The *Iroquois'* crew went aboard, helped draw the shaft, and towed the *Florence Main* across to the Portage. Even though it was close to midnight, there was no rest for the crews; they had found a derelict scow drifting in the bay, which

Scene at South Portage, around 1910.
At the wharf are the Strs. "Mohawk Belle" and "Joe". Note the scowloads of tanbark, destined for the Huntsville tannery.
Courtesy, *Mrs. Marie Tryon*, Scarborough

S.S. "Iroquois" at South Portage.
To the left are the two locomotives of the Portage Railway.

had to be retrieved and they still had to go to work in the disabled *Florence Main*.

The construction men, meanwhile, wanted to get home. They walked across the Portage in thick fog, wondering if the *Sarona* would still be waiting for them. She was, but the fog was like pea soup, and the *Sarona* had to creep across Peninsula Lake. Finally the wheelsman, judging the canal to be very close, stopped engines. Everyone peered into the mist, looking for some sort of landmark. At last a marker buoy was spotted, near the channel entrance. From here the yacht found the canal and groped her way through.

There still remained Fairy Lake of course, and the steamer started to cross that too. But then the wind arose, making navigation even more difficult. The helmsman tried to steer by the direction of the waves as they splashed against the hull, which in theory was a good idea, but he forgot that shorelines are capable of deflecting the angles of waves. As a result, the *Sarona* wandered off course, and almost piled up on the rocks off Haverland Farm. The rocks were spotted in time, and the yacht, recovering her bearings, changed course and steamed into Huntsville around 6:00 a.m.

Shortly after the *Iroquois* entered service, the building crews were put to work on the *Florence Main*. She was a well-balanced boat with a powerful condensing compound engine, but as a passenger ship she left something to be desired. As built by the Mortimers she was quite narrow and tippy, so much so that the water was sometimes known to wash the gangways as the vessel turned. Besides, she was only a single-decker, which greatly limited her carrying capacity. C.O. Shaw now ordered a massive rebuilding of the *Florence Main* to make her hull three feet wider (achieved by building a new hull around the original), and to give her a full-length second deck. The ship that emerged from the ways in 1908 was quite a beauty, re-registered at 83.21 tons and certified for 175 passengers. Shortly afterwards her upper works were also rebuilt and Shaw also resolved to give her a new name. In 1909, he began calling her the *Mohawk*, but then discovered that there was already a vessel registered under that name. The change of name had to wait, but in 1911, Shaw started calling her the *Mohawk Belle*, and this name became official in 1913.

Commanded by the affable Captain Robert Parsons of Burks Falls, who had lately been on the *Ramona*, the *Florence Main* (*Mohawk Belle*) now assumed the run to the south and central portions of the Lake of Bays; leaving Baysville early in the mornings and calling at Port Cunnington, Point Ideal and Dwight, before meeting the Portage train around 9:30 a.m. Then she would make a return trip to Baysville, arriving by noon and repeating the whole process in the afternoon. The *Iroquois*, based at Dorset, served such places as Birkendale, Ronville, Edgewood and Norway Point twice daily, joining her sister ship at the Portage. The *Joe* now became primarily a workboat, scowing lumber, gravel and tanbark around the lake, although sometimes she continued to take passengers. On the Huntsville lakes, the fleet now consisted of the *Algonquin*, *Ramona*, *Phoenix*, and (until 1913) the *Empress*. All of the boats were now painted with red bottoms, white hulls, green guardrails, orange sidewalls above the windowsill lines, red deck rims and mouldings, varnished upper cabins, and black stacks, by order of C.O. Shaw.

Those years were the boom years for the Huntsville Navigation Company, as they were for its South Muskoka counterpart. The country generally was prosperous, business was brisk, and there was still no sign of decline in lumbering or resort building. By 1906, Deerhurst was taking about 100 guests, Ronville 200 and Grunwald 150, while B.H. Cunnington was expanding his lodge at Port Cunnington to take 50 guests. Dorset, despite a disastrous fire in 1907, still had two hotels. In 1908, Thomas White and his family founded the Britannia Hotel (and Kingsway Post Office) on the west side of the Lake of Bays; this resort still survives. That same year the Wa-Wa Hotel also took shape at Norway Point. This resort, a two-storey double-winged building capable of housing 100 guests, was founded by the Canadian Railway News Company of Toronto, which owned a number of hotels and provided most of the catering services on the Canadian railroads. Needless to say, the Wa-Wa was built with the advice and blessings of C.O. Shaw.

As the sole means of transport to practically all these resorts every summer, the passenger steamers were usually packed. In spring they were used for towing and in autumn they transported hunters for the hunting season. Almost the only negative sign during this entire period was the loss of the mail contract to Baysville around 1910: apparently it was possible to

Steam Yacht "Sarona".
Courtesy, *Mrs. Barbara Mills*, Georgetown

deliver the mail faster by road from Bracebridge than roundabout by boat from Huntsville. It has also been said that C.O. Shaw developed a grudge against Baysville for some reason, which may help to explain why the Navigation Company more or less dropped its calls there before the War.

Despite this setback, the Company prospered, its receipts rising every year. The *Mohawk Belle*, however, grew leaky as water permeated between her two hulls, and in November 1911, she suddenly started taking water one day and had to be run ashore near Baysville: her freight and patrons were later rescued by the *Joe*. Finally C. O. Shaw decided to have her completely rebuilt and enlarged. She was lengthened at the bow to 94 feet and given a whole new hull, built around a steel frame. The semi-circular smoking lounge was retained, and cabins were provided for the captain and purser. Now registered at 146.74 tons, the *Mohawk Belle* was ceremoniously relaunched by Mrs. Shaw in 1913, but the crew were none too pleased with the changes made. They now found the ship so light at the bow that docking became difficult whenever a head wind was blowing, and the sheer of the forward decks was now so steep that the deckhands had trouble rolling cargoes into place. Also, the vessel proved temperamental, top heavy, and given to rolling. If passengers hugged one side in rainy weather, the steamer listed. Nevertheless, the *Mohawk Belle* was to carry passengers for about another twenty years.

A few additional steam yachts and launches from this period need a brief acknowledgement. One was the *Florrie T.*, a small 28.5 foot launch built in 1906 by William Tipper of Etwell, near Hoodstown, who named the boat after his daughter. Powered by a slide-valve engine and a vertical, steel-cased pipe boiler, the *Florrie* was used for picnics and special cruises, sometimes as far as Port Sydney and the Portage, and occasionally to take people to Huntsville to do their

S.S. "Florence Main" (Third Version).
The vessel is now completely enclosed between decks, and has a new pilothouse and new upper cabins. Captain Robert Parsons stands, second from the right.
Courtesy, *Mr. Owen Swann*, Huntsville

S.S. "Joe" at Baysville Narrows.

S.S. "Mohawk Belle", docked at Baysville,
The steamer, in her original version, has just been rechristened from the "Florence Main".
Courtesy, *Mrs. Marie Tryon, Scarborough*

Hotel Britannia (Kingsway P.O.), Lake of Bays.
Courtesy, *Mrs. Marie Tryon*, Scarborough

Wa-Wa Hotel, at Norway Point, Lake of Bays.

Port Cunnington Lodge, Lake of Bays.
Courtesy, *Mr. Brian Westhouse*, Parry Sound

S.S. "Mohawk Belle" (Second Version).
Courtesy, *Miss Ruth Tinkiss*, Bracebridge

shopping. On one occasion, she took a record crowd of 32 passengers to Ravenscliffe for a picnic, but most of the participants, it should be noted, were children. Sometimes, she also towed the family scow into town with loads of cordwood, tanbark, lumber or cement, and once at Martin's Narrows on Vernon Lake she came to the aid of a Navigation Company scow whose crew were vainly trying to propel it with poles against a head wind. The *Florrie T.* ran until 1918, but by then her pine planking was starting to rot at the waterline, and after a year of idleness, she was dismantled, the machinery sold, and the hull left to fall to pieces near the Tipper boat-house.

The little steamer *Dolphin*, was patterned after the *Florrie T.*, built just a few years earlier. Powered by a rocking valve engine, the *Dolphin* was owned by Sydney Goldthorp, a neighbour of the Tippers. Goldthorp operated the *Dolphin* on regular Saturday shopping trips to Huntsville, charging 25 cents per passenger. A somewhat tippy little craft, the *Dolphin* once struck a log while returning to Etwell, began taking water, and had to be beached in shallow water. A passing minister picked up the stranded occupants in his motorboat and took them home. He also alerted the Tippers, who came in the *Florrie T.* and took the *Dolphin* in tow. The *Dolphin* lasted until the 1920s, but finally, when she became leaky and unseaworthy Mr. Goldthorp sold the machinery and let the hull go loose. It drifted down the lake, but later the wind blew it back to the place where it was built. In effect, she came home to die.

Another contemporary steamer was the *Opeongo*, a 36 foot launch built at the Canal in 1908 by William H.D. Morgan, a skilled carpenter who had once been hired to build cabins for the rangers of Algonquin Park, in and around Opeongo Lake. Driven by a balky side-crank engine and a vertical, fire-tube boiler, the *Opeongo* was used primarily as a supply boat, peddling milk and produce from the owner's gardens to the tourists and cottagers around Peninsula Lake. She was very slow, and, shortly before the First World War, was converted into a gas boat. Morgan ran the craft until about 1920, when she was sold to a Huntsville resident who continued to use her to distribute vegetables. Many years later, she was re-engined and used for pleasure cruises. The hull now lies on the bottom of the river above the Locks, but long before that the name *Opeongo* had been forgotten.

Steam Launch "Dolphin", on Lake Vernon.
Courtesy, *Mr. Wilfred Tipper*, Etwell

Ex-Steam Launch "Opeongo", at The Locks.
Courtesy, *Mr. Frank Cottrill*, The Locks

Steam Launch "Ahteamec", on Mary Lake.
Courtesy, *Mr. George Johnson*, Port Sydney

One more custom-built steam launch was the *Ahteamec* ("whitefish"), built at Toronto in 1912 by Professor William Simpson, former owner of the little *Pinta*. The *Ahteamec* was 39.5 feet in length (40 foot vessels being more stringently regulated!), had a steel frame, and was fitted with a double-crank, triple expansion engine and a unique "porcupine" water tube, pipe boiler designed by the owner himself. Simpson, who had built a new cottage on Vernon Lake, regularly used to meet his family at the Huntsville station wharf with the launch, which scarcely made a sound as she puttered along.

Simpson died around 1928, and for the next few years the boat was practically abandoned in its boat-house. Then, around 1932, it was purchased, sight unseen, by Allan and Wilfred Clarke of Port Sydney, and a sorry sight it proved to be, half sunk in the ice. The Clarkes raised and replanked the boat and eventually managed to take her to Port Sydney under her own power. For a few years they used the *Ahteamec* to salvage logs on Mary Lake, and flirted with the idea of a regular passenger service, there no longer being any boats on that route. But the reams of red tape were impenetrable, and moreover, the boat, which had no keelson, developed a bulge beneath the engine and grew leaky. Some of the mechanical components, including the propeller, vacuum pressure gauge and water pump, either broke or wore out, and could not be replaced. Finally the Clarkes gave up, beached the craft, and later (1938) cut it up for scrap and burned the hull. The machinery ended up in a steam enthusiast's collection.

One yacht that deserves a brief mention was the *Minota* (19.41 tons), a splendid steel-framed draft some 65.5 feet in length. Built in Toronto in 1891, the *Minota* had a single deck, a 5 hp. high-pressure engine, a clipper bow and a fantail stern. She was painted white, with a red bottom and a black and red stack, while her name appeared in raised gold letters at the bow. Owned by Dr. Beattie Nesbitt, a Toronto speculator with strong ties to Muskoka, the *Minota* spent most of her life on Lake Simcoe, until 1911, when the esteemed Dr. Nesbitt was suddenly making headlines across the country amid fraud charges and the collapse of the Farmer's Bank. The good doctor fled to the United States and hid in Chicago until the authorities finally caught up with him. Meanwhile his assets, including the yacht, were seized and confiscated. The *Minota* was sold in November to the Huntsville Navigation Company and taken to South Portage, but, strange to say she was never launched and never used. Instead, she just sat at the Portage for years and gradually fell apart: her steel frame was still visible as late as the 1940s. It might also be noted that C.O. Shaw's big yacht, the *Sarona*, made fewer and fewer trips as the years went by, until finally in 1919, Captain Sangster and two assistants were ordered to get rid of her. They did this by removing the power plant at the Portage, then towing the hull alongside the *Phoenix* to the mouth of the Big East River. The unkempt old boat was then set on fire, but her massive oak timbers didn't want to burn. Finally she was scuttled, beside the *Empress*.

There were also a few new tugs and workboats built in North Muskoka after 1905, but some of them are so poorly documented that even their names are uncertain. A few were imports from other waters while several were converted pleasure boats. Some were owned by the various lumber and woodworking companies, others were run by freelance boatmen.

Though most of the mills at Huntsville were content to let the Navigation Company do their towing for them, there were a few exceptions. One of these was the powerful Muskoka Wood Manufacturing Company, which had a large steam sawmill in downtown Huntsville and several more in the surrounding districts. The firm was known to cut up to 6,000,000 feet of lumber every year and until 1907, these consignments were usually towed in by the *Phoenix*, but then the company chose to import a tug of their own from Georgian Bay. This craft was the *Mabel M.*, a small, 39 foot steam vessel with a black hull and gray cabins, registered at 4.51 tons and built originally at Port Elgin in 1901 to carry fish. The *Mabel M.*, commanded by Captain May (past Master of the *Phoenix*), served the Muskoka Wood Company until June of 1914, when she took fire at her wharf at Huntsville and burned to the waterline. Her machinery was salvaged, and the owners brought in a second tug, the *Glad Tidings* (6.76 tons) to replace her. Powered by a 3.8 hp. engine, the *Glad Tidings* was built in Orillia in 1902, and had been used mostly for towing on the Severn River. She lasted on the Huntsville scene until 1924, normally under the command of Captain May.

Steam Yacht "Sarona", near Huntsville.
Courtesy, *Mrs. Barbara Mills*, Georgetown

Mr. Frank Hutcheson of Huntsville, whose father was Vice-President of the Muskoka Wood Manufacturing Company, recalled an unlucky incident that once befell the boat while she was under his command. One season, Frank obtained permission to run the steamer; after all, he had served in the Royal Navy and he knew the lakes well. A few weeks passed uneventfully, but one day he and his friend Claude Wardell, owner of the Wardell store in Huntsville, decided to borrow the tug to take two girls for a picnic on the upper Muskoka River. They passed through the locks safely, but Wardell asked to take over the wheel and Hutcheson agreed. Unhappily, in his exuberance Wardell chose to cut a corner downstream, with the result that the gudgeon (a steel skeg on the bottom of the boat) grounded on something and sheared off the rudder pin. Shortly afterwards, as the tug swerved to come ashore at Remington's Rapids about halfway to Mary Lake, the rudder fell off. Now out of control, the 42 foot steamer grounded in the river, heaved up at the stern, holed herself and began filling with water. The only thing to do now was beach the boat, walk to the nearest telephone, and call for help. Bad tidings from the *Glad Tidings*! The party was presently picked up and the tug towed back to Huntsville for repairs, but young Hutcheson's days of command came to an abrupt end.

The *Glad Tidings* was destroyed by fire in February of 1924, and the Company did not replace her. The management was annoyed by the boatmen's habit of spreading the logs out thinly, so as to prolong the season and reduce their own exertions as much as possible. Consequently, the firm provided the river drivers with small boats called "pointers", each equipped with a gas motor and especially designed for coping with logs, thereby cutting out the need for tugs. In any case, the days of the log drives were fading out anyway.

Another firm that ran a tug for several years around Mary Lake was the Parker Lumber Company, which was founded about 1889 by an English gentleman named William Parker. He also gave his name to the Hamlet of Parkersville, near Utterson. In time, the Company had sawmills humming at Parkersville, Utterson, Martin's Siding and Mary Lake. In 1907, two of Mr. Parker's sons bought a 30 foot steam launch called the *Mayflower*, which they used for towing logs from the Locks. Now and then, the boat was sent from the mill to Port Sydney for provisions, and occasionally, to treat the river men to a cruise. The *Mayflower* was dismantled around 1922 when the Parkers' timber limits gave out, and it disappeared with the ice the following spring.

Another operator was Alfred Olan of south Fairy Lake, who built a steam sawmill at Breezy Point around 1901. Shortly afterwards Olan acquired the old steam launch *Swift* from J.E. Fisher of Huntsville, and used her as a towboat for about a decade. By 1914, the *Swift* began rotting so badly that she could not be repaired. At the time, Olan's son Ben was just completing a staunch new 34 foot craft, more or less for fun and Alfred Olan promptly acquired the vessel. It gave excellent service for over a decade, towing logs and scow-loads of sawdust, which was burned for fuel, and taking the Olans and their neighbours to Huntsville every Saturday. The tug, known as the *Water Lily*, had an oak frame and tamarac planking, and inherited the engine from the *Mabel M.* About 1925, the *Water Lily* went to the Muskoka Lakes, where she became a dredge tender. In 1937, she was rebuilt and renamed the *Scrapper*.

Very similar were the activities of the Cottrill family, who for many years combined farming with sawmilling at the Locks. Benjamin Cottrill, head of the family, had extensive experience in lumbering before settling near Mary Lake. For a time he managed Sydney-Smith's mill at Port Sydney; then in 1903 he took over a mill at the Locks, buying logs and timber limits everywhere and selling dressed lumber all around the lakes. Such operations called for a towboat, and eventually Mr. Cottrill purchased Frank Kent's yacht, the *Seabird*. Like many pleasure boats past their prime, the *Seabird* finished her days towing timber booms and scowing lumber, sometimes direct to the customers' own docks. Finally in 1915, too waterlogged for further service, the *Seabird* was abandoned about a mile below the Locks.

Her successor was built in the lock chamber and launched in 1916. The new tug was an odd-looking but sturdy craft, some 37.5 feet in length and registered at 11.56 tons. She had a pipe boiler and a high pressure engine, apparently obtained from the *Seabird*, but these proved insufficient and within a year, she was refitted with a two-cylinder compound engine and a larger boiler, giving her speeds of up to 12 miles per hour. She had a short, hinged stack and could pass underneath the swing bridge at Huntsville, unless the waters were high. She was called the *Jennie C.*, after one of Mr. Cottrill's daughters, and was usually commanded by his son Taylor. Around the same time, the family greatly enlarged the sawmill, and were soon delivering lumbering to Port Sydney, Huntsville and Dwight.

Despite a fire one night near the Locks, the *Jennie C.* continued to ply for the Cottrills until 1928, often taking some of the neighbours to church on Sundays. Finally, she grew rotten and had to be scrapped. The family then obtained another tug, gave her the engine from the *Jennie*, and carried on into the 1930s.

On the Lake of Bays another little fleet of tugs was busy puttering about during this period, though most of them require little commentary. One was the *Bobs*, a small launch owned by Sandy and Alec McLennan of Dorset and used for various odd jobs. Another was the *Equal Rights* (6.27 tons), a 42.3 foot craft built at Birkendale in 1909 to replace her burned-out predecessor, whose engine she inherited. Unlike the original, which had been built as a yacht, the second *Equal Rights* was strictly a workboat. She towed logs to the Birkendale sawmill for about a decade, and was then sold and taken to Huntsville. There she was used for a few more years before she was dismantled. Her boiler went into another tug in 1921.

Another handsome launch was the *Minelle* (2.94 tons), a 36 foot craft built at Owen Sound for the Crump brothers of Ronville Lodge in 1899. In 1906 they sold her to Arthur Bailey, a machinist from Fox Point, who used her for towing and scowing during the 1910s, until one stormy spring night when the boat pulled loose from her dock, taking a few loose stringers with her, and disappeared into the dark, never to be seen again. An alligator tug was sent to look for it but no trace was ever found. Still another nameless tug was owned by Alec MacKinnon of Baysville, and used for shipping everything, including passengers, until about 1910 when it sank near the present Baysville dam; the craft in question may have been the *Bobs*.

Better known is the steamer *Lillian M.*, a large pleasure boat owned by a Baysville carpenter, Arthur Henderson, who named the craft after his daughter. Furnished with a compound engine and a pipe boiler, the *Lillian* was first used as a pleasure boat. Later she was sold and became a supply boat for the Langmaid store at Baysville during the 1910s and '20s. It was not uncommon for her to leave town with all her seats stacked with groceries, not to return for over sixteen hours. Around 1930, the boat went to Alfred Chevalier of Birkendale, who rebuilt the hull and used her

Steam Tug "Water Lily", near The Locks.

Cottrill Saw and Gristmill at The Locks.
Courtesy, *Mr. George Johnson*, Port Sydney

Steam Tug "Jennie C."
The little craft is attending boat-house construction on Fairy Lake.
Courtesy, *Mr. Frank Cottrill*, The Locks

Steam Launch "Lillian M.", Lake of Bays.
Courtesy, *Mr. George Burk*, Dorset

to tow for his sawmill near Sea Breeze. During the 1940s the *Lillian M.*, still steam-powered, was again sold and returned to Baysville. The new owner hoped to use her as a tug on Hollow Lake, but she was accidentally crushed by a bulldozer while she was being relaunched at Baysville. The wreck was taken overland to the Locks and scrapped.

Earlier we noted that the powerful Mickle-Dyment Company put a tug called the *Herbert M.* on Kawagama (Hollow) Lake in 1889. The original *Herbert M.* was dismantled in 1908 and replaced by the second *Herbert M.*, a larger vessel some 51 feet in length and registered at 26.95 tons. She was a trim, handsome boat, and apparently she hauled huge booms of sawlogs and scows full of provisions across the stormy waters of Hollow Lake for nearly twenty years, until her owners had exhausted their limits in the area. She was stroked off the registry in 1927. The Shier Lumber Company of Bracebridge also had a smaller tug, the *Margaret S.*, on the lake at the same time.

From Hollow Lake the logs had to be fed down the sometimes turbulent Hollow River to Johnny-Cake Bay, near Dorset, on the Lake of Bays. There, a tug and an alligator would take over.

The tug, as of 1913, was the *Niska*, and she had quite a remarkable career. She was the direct successor to the steamer *Nishka*, a yacht built by the Stroud family of Milford Bay in 1897 and subsequently sold to the Mickles. After one season (1912) as a tug on Sparrow Lake, the *Nishka*

Strs. "Iroquois" and "Niska" (Original Version) at South Portage.
Courtesy, *Mr. Alvin Saulter*, Gravenhurst

Steam Alligator "John Bull" at Dorset.
Courtesy, *Miss Ruth Tinkiss*, Bracebridge

Steam Tug "Niska" (Second Version) under reconstruction.
Courtesy, *Mrs. Allan Fraser*, Bracebridge

was lengthened amidships from 36 to 50 feet and shipped by rail to Huntsville by Captain Grieves Robson, formerly Master of the *Equal Rights*. The rebuilt *Nishka*, however, leaked so badly that she had to be overhauled immediately upon arrival at South Portage. Even so, she still leaked, and Captain Robson never trusted her. As a result, in 1913 he had the vessel pulled to pieces at Birkendale and rebuilt, with two engines, a new Scotch boiler, and a steel frame. The *Niska*, as she was now called, was 50 feet in length by 11 feet in beam and registered 22.64 tons. She had bunks aboard, and could average ten miles per hour. Although a tug, she was licensed for twenty passengers. Altogether she would serve for 44 years, and before her demise, she would be the only steam tug left anywhere in Muskoka.

The *Niska* was Captain Robson's boat until 1923, and he used her for anything that would pay: towing blocks of logs in the spring (even at night), scowing freight, and taking passengers on special trips. For some time, she was the only steamer that plied to Baysville, after the Huntsville Navigation Company more or less refused to send the big ships there. She was a workboat, often towing for the Mickle and Shier Companies in partnership with the *John Bull*.

The *John Bull* was an enormous alligator, owned by the Mickle Company and built at Dorset around 1908, with hooded paddle wheels, a 500 lb. anchor, and over a mile of cable. She had a cookery and bunkhouse aboard, and her wailing wildcat whistle, rising slowly in pitch whenever the cord was pulled, made a terrifying noise. Her stack, and even her pilothouse, were collapsible, to allow her to pass beneath the bridge at Dorset. Like most alligators, she was monotonously slow, but she could handle three blocks of logs at a time, whereas the little *Niska* could take only one. Nevertheless, for many years the two of them teamed up for towing. The tug usually hauled the logs across Johnny-Cake Bay to Dorset, but at the Dorset Narrows, the blocks would have to be dismantled and pulled through. Afterwards the *Niska* had the job of reassembling the tows for the alligator to winch across the lake. Each boom consisted of twenty sticks, and each tow had both a common boom and a storm boom in case of rough weather. While the *John Bull* puffed and wheezed her way to Baysville, the *Niska* gathered up any wayward logs, then headed for Baysville to shepherd the logs through the Baysville Narrows and on into town, while the alligator chugged back to Dorset. Once the logs were in the river drivers' hands, the tug would hurry after the alligator to boom the next consignments, and also make sure that a channel was kept clear for the *Iroquois*. Winds could be a major problem on the Lake of Bays, sometimes delaying the drives for as much as a week. This in turn left the river drivers with nothing to do but drink and brawl; since they were paid by the month, they could not be laid off.

In 1923, after a career of 46 years on the lakes, Captain Robson retired and moved south to Barrie. His tug was sold to the Mickles, who used it for another four years. Then, having exhausted their limits, they resold her to a Huntsville lumber dealer, who shortly went bankrupt. In 1929, the *Niska* went to the Cottrill brothers at the Locks, who were creditors of the former owner. They settled the unpaid inspection dues, came to Baysville, broke the government seals placed on the tug, pumped her out and fired her up to go to the Portage. There she was loaded onto a cradle, dragged over the spring snows by a bulldozer, relaunched on Peninsula Lake, and steamed to the Locks. Here she was rebuilt, and became the successor to the ailing *Jennie C.*, whose engine she received, and whose duties she assumed. The *Niska* was now almost the only tug left on the North Muskoka Lakes. We will continue with her adventures in another chapter.

Now we must turn our attention back to the Huntsville Navigation Company and the tourist industry. One of the unfulfilled ambitions of Captain Marsh had been to build his own summer resort on the North Muskoka Lakes, much as the Muskoka Navigation Company had built the Royal Muskoka. At first C.O. Shaw seemed content to let others build resort hotels in the region and besides, his tanneries had lost a lot of money during the brief business shock of 1907, though this was soon recuperated. In 1908, the Wa-Wa Hotel was started at Norway Point with the blessings of Shaw, who acted as a consultant in planning it. When asked to name his reward, Shaw requested only that a suite be reserved for him at all times; this was done, and the tannery tycoon periodically took advantage of it.

Within a year, however, the arrangement soured. Some say that Shaw was once asked to 'pay' for his room. Others say that he arrived unexpectedly at the hotel to find it filled to capacity and his own suite occupied by someone else. Whatever the reason, 'C.O.' was offended, left the Wa-Wa and never returned. Then and there, he resolved to build his own resort. He already had a site in mind for it on Bigwin Island, on the Lake of Bays.

Bigwin Island, the only really large one on the lake, is two and a half miles long and about a half a mile across, with an area of 670 acres. Named for the Ojibwa Chief Joseph Big Wind—who died in 1940 at the ripe old age of 1,223 moons—(nearly 102 years)—the island had been a favourite Indian campsite for at least a century, and probably longer. In the 1860s, a factor for the Hudson's Bay Company, Thomas Goffatt of Orillia, decided it would make an excellent site for a small trading post, which explains why the Lake of Bays was long known as "Trading Lake". Once the 'White Man' began arriving in numbers, the Indians were, as usual, crowded out, and after 1900 the shy, retiring Ojibwas silently withdrew to their reserve at Rama, on Lake Couchiching. C.O. Shaw, who had developed a fondness for camping on Bigwin Island, bought it outright around 1910 for a reputed $2,000 (amid some controversy as to the legality of the deal), although as a gesture of generosity, or atonement, he promised that Chief Big Wind should be buried with his ancestors on the island.

Though an architect was hired to work out the details, it was Shaw himself who planned the new hotel, which had the twofold advantages of providing additional work for his steamers and a useful tax write off for his tanneries. Predictably, Shaw planned things very well, The hotel, he decided, should directly face the offending Wa-Wa across the lake, and vastly excell it. The Bigwin resort would have 280 rooms and be able to handle 700 guests. It would have a dodecagon dining room and dance pavilion directly overlooking the water, plus a great central building behind, featuring an enormous lounge and two dormitory wings adjoining; all magnificently proportioned and furnished. Furthermore, it would all be built of concrete and masonry: none of your flimsy wooden firetraps for C.O. Shaw! Work was started in 1912, and soon most of the local workboats (notably the *Joe*) were busy scowing tons of gravel over to the island. It is said that when the winter first set in, Shaw came over and ordered all work to stop, because, he insisted, concrete mixed in freezing temperatures would crumble. The foreman nodded, then presented Shaw with a sledgehammer, showed him some freshly set concrete, and invited him to demonstrate his point. Shaw obliged, and took several good cracks at it, but failed to make a dent in the masonry. For once in his life, Charles Orlando Shaw changed his mind, conceded that 'maybe it would be all right', and allowed the work to continue. Unknown to him, the workmen had been mixing salt with the concrete.

Construction proceeded steadily until 1914, but then the War broke out. Labour became scarce and the work had to be suspended. Nonetheless, a great deal had been done, and during the War, tourists often came across from Norway Point to marvel at the massive unfinished structures. When finally the War ended and men began returning home, the work was rushed to completion in barely a year—to the amazement of observers and the amusement of C.O. Shaw. By mid-June of 1920, the hotel was in business.

Aerial view of Bigwin Inn, Lake of Bays.

There was nothing quite like Bigwin Inn. It stands on the southwest side of the island, facing Glenmount and Norway Point. The central building featured a rotunda, library, tuck shop, newsstand, medical office, telegraph office, post office, beauty parlour, table tennis courts and a children's playroom, not to mention a huge lounge opening onto the porches. Adjacent were the dormitories—all fireproof, of course—and a tea house for snacks. Not far away, and linked to it by crimson-tiled, covered walks, was the combined dining room-dance pavilion and boat-house, suggesting an impregnable mass of masonry rising straight up out of the water. Around these buildings were spacious lawns and terraces, offset with groves of oak, maple and beech, as well as four stone bungalows, each with 'all the comforts of home'. Water was supplied from a crystal clear artesian well near the hotel. There was plenty to keep the guests amused: a swimming pier, diving tower, croquet lawn, sailboats, canoes, rowboats, three bowling greens, four clay tennis courts, and an eighteen hole golf course. The meals were superb, and usually there was a chamber orchestra to entertain at lunch and dinner. Frequently the concert band would be on hand to play at an evening dance.

It is rather surprising to find that Bigwin Inn was, in a number of ways, built and operated by local amateurs, rather than imported professionals. The nine magnificent fireplaces in the central building were each executed from local rock by a Huntsville stonemason who sketched his plans on shingles, which he casually threw away once he had finished with them. The first Manager of the hotel, James G. Reid, was head drummer in the Concert Band, but Shaw felt he had potential and sent him off to take a course in management. Reid continued to run Bigwin Inn for eleven years. The first bookkeeper was a local man, and the first four bellboys were amateurs too; C. O. Shaw preferred college students, or at least Boy Scouts for the job. Not surprisingly, things might occasionally go wrong. When the first guests arrived in June of 1920 on the *Iroquois*, the bellboys were so intent on lining up straight and looking their best that they forgot to collect the visitors' trunks, which ended up in Dorset.

Bigwin Inn was North Muskoka's answer to the Royal Muskoka, though in most respects it was a cut above it. The new hotel was a very elegant, dignified place, extensively patronized by millionaires who wanted class and quiet, and that was what Shaw, by preference and policy, gave them. He insisted on formal dress for dinner every evening, and usually ordered the band to play

Dining room and dance pavilion, Bigwin Inn.
Courtesy, *Mr. Brad Robinson*, Dorset

light classical airs. Cigarettes were grudgingly tolerated, but not open liquor: guests who wanted to drink had to be very discreet about it. The days were usually devoted to golfing, canoeing and croquet. Evenings were characterized by bridge, billiards, chitchat and ballroom dancing, where the ladies, bedecked with jewels and long gowns, were in their glory, showing off their own charms and their husbands' wealth. Four times daily, the steamers called to collect or leave off passengers and provisions. Bigwin Inn was a great success in its heyday, but it would prove a different matter in later years, when public taste began to change.

At least once during the 1920s, Bigwin's communications with the outside world were severed, literally by a fluke! At that time the alligator *John Bull*, now under Captain Wesley Hill, was still engaged at winching Mickle's and Shier's logs across the lake to Baysville. One day the big tug dropped anchor in front of Bigwin Island and began letting the cable run, as usual. But "Nipper" Hill realized that the anchor was dragging, and remembering the hotel's underwater telephone cable, he decided to stop and check things out. The anchor was raised, and sure enough, the cable came up with it, entangled in the flukes. Naturally, the men put it back, then resumed their work. Shortly afterwards, however, a motorboat from the hotel came alongside, bearing Captain Elder and a very irate C.O. Shaw.

"Who's in charge of this boat?" snapped Shaw.

"I am," replied Nipper, who added jokingly, "Want a fight?" (That was not the right thing to say to Shaw, who was in a fighting mood!) The blistering hotel owner informed Hill that his anchor had ripped the hotel's telephone cable loose, disrupting all the phones. "Sorry," replied Hill, sobered.

"Sorry?" cried Shaw. "What good's it going to do me if you're sorry? I've got businessmen at my hotel who can't make important calls. I'm going to report you for this." Then the motorboat sped away. As usual, Shaw carried out his threat, but the jury hearing the case refused to convict Captain Hill.

Meanwhile, how were the passenger ships faring? Very well, it seems, until the War, which 'put the damper on excursion cruises'. It also put a lot of men into uniform, and consequently crew members became scarce. It is said that the *Iroquois* had to be tied up for most of the duration, to await the return of happier times. The resorts, too, felt the pinch and some of them closed their doors, permanently. Grunwald, on Mary Lake, was an immediate victim of the War, because of its Germanic name and appearance, and on the night of November 11, 1918, it mysteriously burned to the ground. The disappearance of Grunwald hastened the decline of the Port Sydney branch of the steamer service. The previous fall had seen the closing of the Belleview Hotel at Port

Sydney, where the *Ramona* had hitherto docked for the night, and apparently no other place would put up the steamer's crew overnight. It is likely that the *Ramona* made no more regular trips to Port Sydney after 1917, and certainly by 1920 neither Baysville nor Port Sydney figured any longer as ports of call.

Similarly, time was running out for Albert Sydney-Smith's steamer, the *Gem*. The quaint little propeller was still seaworthy, having been rebuilt a second time in 1912, but business fell off badly during the War: the cheese factory closed, and by now, many of the villagers had their own motorboats. In the winter of 1918, Captain Lyle Casselman, who had been commanding the *Gem* for most of her days, was killed in the bush by a falling tree. The Mary Lake steamer service probably died with him, and the *Gem* was placed in drydock for a few years. Sydney-Smith then purchased a 30 foot motor launch called the *Lillian*, which continued to take passengers to Huntsville twice a week, but even this service lapsed when her owner died in 1925. The *Gem*, meanwhile, was sold and spent her last years as a tug.

The war years were also the last for the steamer *Joe*, now a freighter and passenger ship on the Lake of Bays. The late Mr. Alvin Saulter of Gravenhurst, who worked as an engineer for the Huntsville Navigation Company and the Portage Railway for many years, recalled an anxious moment on the vessel during the season of 1916. It happened early one Saturday evening, starting around 6 p.m. when the *Joe* was despatched to Dwight with the mail. The only ones aboard were the Engineer, Bill Murray of South Portage, and Saulter himself, who had been acting as fireman. On this occasion, Murray took the wheel and left Saulter, then a youth of nineteen, at the engine controls. Both the *Joe* and the *Mohawk Belle* were at the Portage at the time; they backed out simultaneously, raced each other across the bay, then separated. It took the *Joe* about 45 minutes to reach Dwight, during which time Saulter noted that the engine was working under some strain. On the return trip the machine began pounding. Saulter, apprehensive, went to the pilothouse to report it but Murray simply shrugged and said, "Don't worry about it, it'll be okay." Saulter went back below, but the pounding only grew worse. Again he reported it but the engineer remained unperturbed. As Saulter returned to the engine room a third time, it happened! The connecting shaft from the flywheel to the rocker arm on the air pump snapped off as the bolts broke, and instantly the end swung around and put a hole through the bottom planking of the boat. Saulter shut off the engine, brought word to Murray, and added, "I told you something was going to happen!"

Murray went below, to find about an inch of water in the hold. The *Joe* was only a little more than halfway back to the Portage. The engineer decided to disconnect the shaft and run back on high pressure. By the time this was done, the bilges had over a foot of water in them, just about overflowing the men's boots. The syphon was turned on and the *Joe* managed to reach Portage Bay in about ten minutes, at reduced speed. Still, the water was gaining. "Do you think we can make it across the bay?" asked Murray nervously. "I think we can," replied Saulter. "Besides, if the *Joe*'s going to sink, better it be out of sight." That was cold comfort, but the *Joe* did make it to South Portage, where the matter was reported to Assistant Manager Bill Elder. All they could do at that point was keep the siphon going all night, while Murray and Saulter were ordered to keep an eye on it. Saulter took the second watch, but he was so dead-tired that he couldn't stay awake. As a precaution, he tried sitting on the engine room railing, but soon dozed off and started to fall. Instantly awake, he instinctively flung out his arms to grab something, and caught a hot steam pipe! Saulter spent the rest of the night nursing a badly burned hand. The next day the *Joe* was put on the marine railway at the Portage, where the repair crews went to work on her.

Unfortunately, the *Joe* had little more time left. She ran until the end of the season of 1918, but by then she was getting leaky, and the following spring, with the *Iroquois* again back in service, the *Joe* was dismantled and sunk at South Portage, in a bay north of the railway terminus, and the screech of her whistle became a thing of the past. She had served seventeen years on the North Muskoka Lakes.

This left the Navigation Company with only five steamers, of which three—the *Algonquin*, *Ramona* and *Phoenix*—were on the Huntsville lakes. Following the armistice and demobilization, the country was starting to return, more or less, to normal, and soon the resorts were reviving. By 1920, Bigwin Inn had been rushed to completion—though not, it seems, without imposing a severe financial strain on the boat line: for all his drive and determination, C. O. Shaw was a poor

Str. "Gem" (Third Version) in The Locks.
Courtesy, *Mr. George Johnson*, Port Sydney

financier, and in 1920 he had to admit his son-in-law, Charles W. Conway, a bank manager by training, to the Company Board, presumably to straighten things out. Conway, a financial expert, accomplished this in short order. The steamers, meanwhile, were again sailing with crowded decks: automobiles and motorboats had yet to make a serious impression on the boat service.

New refinements were also added. A marine drydock was built at the rear of Bigwin Island, where the *Mohawk Belle* henceforth spent the winters (the *Iroquois* wintered at the Portage), and a private telephone line opened from Huntsville to North Portage. In November of 1919, the line went dead after a fresh fall of about two feet of snow. Four men were sent to the Canal on the *Ramona* to investigate. They found almost the entire line down, poles and all, amid the snowy forests south of Peninsula Lake. Deciding there was little they could do, they left their shovels in the bush, hurried overland to the Portage, and were just in time to catch the *Ramona* back to Huntsville. Later, as the snows melted in the spring, a crew of six or seven men was able to rebuild the line in less than a week.

Just three years after Bigwin Inn formally opened its doors there occurred, across the lake, the worst resort disaster in Muskoka's history: the Wa-Wa Hotel fire. The Wa-Wa, now fifteen years old, had 198 guests checked in on the fatal night of August 20, 1923. All was quiet and normal until about ten minutes before midnight, and most of the guests were in bed. Minutes later, however, a pair of young people spotted a glow around the baggage room, where the north wing adjoined the rotunda and dining room, and raised the alarm. Moments later, a cloud of smoke billowed out, and in no time at all, the centre of the building was engulfed in flames which spread rapidly to the two wings. There were no fire gongs to rouse the guests, and the firewall partitions had little effect. All was confusion and pandemonium as people in their nightclothes groped for a way out. Fortunately, the upper storey rooms had escape ropes, but a few people were trapped in the hotel's two lofty towers and had to jump to their deaths. The hotel staff did their duty manfully, fighting the fire with everything at hand and helping people get out, but eight perished and many more were hurt. Hoses were turned on, but they proved to be in poor shape;

The Wa-Wa Hotel, Lake of Bays (burned August 20, 1923).

and then the engine house for the pumps burned too. In 45 minutes, it was all over.

As the holocaust spread, people came flocking to the scene by boat from Bigwin Inn, Glenmount, Grandview and the nearby cottages. Everyone rushed to provide food, blankets and clothing; winning high praise from the sufferers, most of whom had lost all their belongings in the inferno. Bigwin Inn became a temporary hospital, as guests gave up their rooms to make way for the injured.

Meanwhile, news of the calamity had been telephoned to Huntsville. Early in the morning, Captain Elder was roused and ordered to take the *Ramona* to Peninsula Lake immediately to speed the evacuation. At the Portage, Lou Thompson, now Superintendent of the little railway, hurried across the divide alone on a locomotive in record time (two and a half minutes), roused the crew of the *Iroquois*, and fired up the steamer's boiler using kerosene to do it! Just as the dawn was breaking, the *Iroquois* arrived at the scene of the fire. It was a heart-rending sight. Nothing was left of the hotel except the stone entrance steps and a vast heap of glowing hot cinders. Crowds of anguished people were milling around, some of them suffering from burns or fractures. Some had already been ferried away to Bigwin Inn or Glemount. The steamer gathered as many of the sufferers as she could, ran them to the Portage, and then, joined by the *Mohawk Belle*, returned for more. Later the *Mohawk Belle* and the *Algonquin* had the melancholy task of bringing back the bodies of the dead, in caskets, to Huntsville. In the meantime, a special train was despatched from Toronto to take the people home.

While the resort industry reeled from the impact of the Wa-Wa disaster, and the authorities tried to find someone to blame for it, C.O. Shaw, who no doubt felt smugly vindicated in building Bigwin out of concrete, lost little time in drawing an added advantage from the Wa-Wa's demise. Automobiles were becoming commoner as roads were gradually improved, and some of the guests coming to Bigwin Inn were arriving by car rather than by train. These people were reluctant to leave their cars at Huntsville: most preferred to motor direct to the hotel. This meant that a parking place on the Lake of Bays was becoming an urgent priority. Seizing his chance, Shaw lost little time in buying the site of the Wa-Wa and building a garage for his guests' cars. In time, riding stables, an amenity not available at Bigwin, were also established at the Norway Point landing.

The new parking lot meant that a new boat was needed, to shuttle guests to and from the Island. The boat arrived in the spring of 1925. She was the *Ella Mary*, a big 66 foot steam yacht of 24.64 tons with a triple expansion Polson engine, previously used around Belle Island in northern Lake Muskoka. Shortly after her transfer to the Lake of Bays her name was officially changed to the *Bigwin*. Usually commanded by elderly captains nearing retirement, the *Bigwin* began her endless ten minute trip back and forth between the hotel and Norway Point, charging a fare of 25 cents. Occasionally, she varied her routine with visits to Glenmount for Sunday church services or the rare pleasure cruise on the Lake of Bays. In time, she was converted into an oil burner, and much later (1956) she was dieselized. Technically, she belonged to the Huntsville Navigation Company only until March 1928, when Shaw transferred her legal ownership to a separate entity known as the Bigwin Boat Livery Ltd. of Bigwin Island.

Steam Ferry "Bigwin", at Norway Point.
Courtesy, *Miss Ruth Tinkiss*, Bracebridge

The Navigation Company fleet in 1925 still consisted of only five steamers. In the spring of that year, just as the *Bigwin* arrived, the *Phoenix*, last of the Company tugs, was broken up at the Fairy Lake locks. After 24 years of towing scows and bucking logs, the old tug had finally outlived her usefulness. She was not replaced, since the towing business was manifestly slackening off. Her boiler was transferred to the *Ramona*—which proved a mistake, since the *Romana* was a much larger vessel than the *Phoenix* had been.

Indeed, very few new workboats were put into service on the Huntsville lakes after 1920. One exception was the *Weneeda* (1.57 tons), a 35.7 foot screw tug with a square stern, built in 1921 by James Austen Scriver, an energetic Huntsville mechanic and woodsman with long experience both in the bush and on the boats. The tug, which inherited the boiler from *Equal Rights*, was usually commanded by Scriver's son Joshua, and used to tow logs from the Big East River to Huntsville for the lumber companies. The *Weneeda* had a short life, primarily because the Scrivers refused to spend any more money on her than was absolutely necessary, and before the decade was out, she was scuttled somewhere near Huntsville. The scrapping of the *Phoenix* presented another opportunity for towing, and J.A. Scriver now won a contract to bring in bark for the tannery. He was also shrewd enough to load the bark on skids and stone-boats, which eliminated the need for unloading and stacking it, and as a result, the operation paid. In 1926, he bought the burned-out hulk of the steam yacht *Llano* from Captain Archer at Bracebridge, rebuilt it, and put her to work towing. The *Llano* lasted into the 1930s, by which time the Depression was in full swing and trucks were taking over deliveries of logs and bark. For a couple of summers Mr. Scriver used the *Llano* as a houseboat at Huntsville; then he sold her and moved to Oshawa. The *Llano* was apparently taken back to the Muskoka Lakes, where she finished up as a stone-hauling hulk at Port Carling.

The only other freelance boatman to take up steamboating around Huntsville during the 1920s was Norman ("Gibby") Keith, who worked for a time as engineer under the Scrivers. It was Keith who acquired the old steamer *Gem* from Albert Sydney-Smith around 1921 and stripped her down into a single-decked tug, which he used for all sorts of jobs: towing logs, scowing shingles to Huntsville for the Cottrills, and even salvaging logs on Mary Lake. Like Scriver, Keith took little care of his boats, and soon the *Gem* was looking very grimy indeed. In 1924, he sold the boat to Captain May, who carried on with her for about seven more seasons. Finally, after a career spanning a third of a century, the aging *Gem* was dismantled and abandoned on the north shore of Lake Vernon, not far from Huntsville. Her late owner, Squire Sydney-Smith, who had been the presiding genius at Port Sydney since the 1870s, predeceased her on October 2, 1925, at the age of 83.

"Gibby" Keith remained in the towing business just a little longer, and in 1924 built a small, 31.5 foot tug called the *Marion F.* (6.68 tons) to replace the *Gem*. She too was used to tow booms for some of the mills at Huntsville. Though Keith sometimes ran the vessel single-handed, the venture did not pay: towing was in decline, and there were simply too many tugs on the lakes. In 1926, Keith gave up, sold the *Marion F.* to a Magnetawan lumberman, and moved to Toronto. Thus by about 1931, almost all the Huntsville steam tugs were gone.

Though towing was dying out, there was little sign of a slowdown by the passenger ships during the twenties. Every day, on the *Algonquin*, began at 6:00 a.m. at the station wharf, as the stoker arrived to fire up the boiler, and the deckhands began the morning cleanup. At 7:15, she cast off her lines and headed over to the town wharf. Here, most of the local passengers would go aboard, the crew would load up all the provisions and freight, and the purser, in consultation with Mr. Moore, would sort out his tickets, count out a cash "float", check the manifests, and take the morning mail. At 8:00 a.m. the ship's deep-throated whistle erupted, both to signal "departure time", and to alert the bridgemaster to clear and swing the highway bridge. (Occasionally the thing was known to jam and refuse to turn.) When all was ready, the lines were cast off, except for one at the stern, which the captain used as a "spring line" to swing the bow out to the correct angle. When this was done, the spring line was let go, and the *Algonquin* glided over to the bridge channel, passing through with several feet of clearance on either side. From here it was downstream past several hairpin turns in the river, sounding a warning whistle at each one. Another dock stood at the Huntsville Municipal Camp Grounds near the "mountain". Here, any locals who had missed the boat at the town wharf could try flagging her down. Otherwise, she would head straight across the lovely blue expanse of Fairy Lake, which many passengers likened to the lochs of Scotland. The purser, meanwhile, would be going about selling tickets to the passengers and issuing transfers. After passing Scot's Bonnet Island and then the Twin Sisters and One Tree Island, the *Algonquin* would call at Haverland Farm (later Camp Swallowdale), then proceed to Grandview Farm (run for so many years by Miss Rose Cookson, whose home-cooked meals were proverbial), and perhaps to Fairyport, on the other side of the lake. Then, she would cut her speed and enter the Canal, trying to steer clear of deadheads, reeds and waterlilies, to say

S.S. "Algonquin", at Huntsville station wharf.
Courtesy, *Public Archives of Canada* PA 71078

S.S. "Algonquin" and Yacht "Sarona" at the Canal.
Courtesy, *Ontario Archives*, Acc. 9939, Reel 13, #24

S.S. "Algonquin", approaching Deerhurst, Peninsula Lake.

S.S. "Algonquin" at North Portage.

nothing of the occasional fisherman in his punt. At the Canal Post Office, the mailbag would be thrown ashore to the postmistress, then the steamer would continue past the overhead road bridge and out into Peninsula Lake, whose waters, unlike those of Fairy and Vernon Lakes, were crystal clear. Usually she would pass her smaller sister, the *Ramona*, at a shallow bay near this point. Then, it was on to Deerhurst on its grassy, rolling hilltop to unload passengers, provisions and the morning mail. Next stop was Pow Wow Point Lodge, followed usually by Grassmere, where Tally Ho and Limberlost Lodge stood, then on to Put In Bay and Springside, and finally, a broad sweep over to North Portage to meet the little railway train. By now it would be mid-morning. The steamer would finish unloading at the Portage, then wait for the tiny train to clack and whistle its way across the divide. This usually took about fifteen minutes each way, barely giving the conductor enough time to collect his fares. After connecting with the boats on the Lake of Bays end, the train would make its return, going forwards now, with the locomotive wheels squealing on the curves around Osborne's Lake and the North Portage terminus. (As a rule, two trains were formed at that time, one freight and one passenger, and the only places they could pass each other were at the two terminals.) If, as sometimes happened, a fire started along the tracks from engine sparks or a carelessly discarded cigarette, the train crews would stop and douse it with water from the locomotive or the lake. Once the train had returned, the *Algonquin* would begin her return trip, with usually fewer stops, and be back at Huntsville, hopefully, by noon.

After lunch, and after wooding up again, the steamer always headed back to the station wharf to meet the afternoon train. By the time it arrived, and all the passengers, baggage and waybills were accounted for, it would be mid-afternoon. The ship would then return to the town dock, collect the afternoon mail (and any additional passengers), and repeat her run to the Portage. The flagship ordinarily called only at the important stops: lesser points would be serviced by the *Ramona*, which ran at alternate times, mostly to carry freight and laundry for the resorts. Even after her return in the evening, the *Algonquin* might not be finished, since there might be a charter by one of the local service clubs for a Moonlight Cruise, often featuring a hired pianist and a dance on the afterdeck, or at one of the resort pavilions. She would invariably return after dark, though the captain always tried to get back through the Canal before the daylight faded. At such times, the young folks were known to loosen or unscrew the lightbulbs to shroud the decks in darkness as they gathered for some intimate evening socializing. Occasionally, a beam from the searchlight might make a sweep of the forward deck, startling the indignant couples and bringing a chuckle or two from the bridge. We might add that the *Ramona* was commanded variously by such men as Captain J. T. Burke of Huntsville (who died in 1922), William Langford of Huntsville, William T. Jones of Gravenhurst, Arthur Thompson of Walker's Point, or Captain Elder; the *Algonquin* almost exclusively by Captain Sangster.

On the Lake of Bays, meanwhile, the *Iroquois*, usually under Captain Joe St. Amond or Albert Leeder, would blow her departure whistle at Dorset at 8:00 a.m. and set off across Trading Bay amid the morning mist to Bayview Farm, the Maples, and Birkendale. From here, she would cross to Glenmount, then proceed to Bigwin, and then head west for the stately Britannia Hotel. From there, it was north to the Portage by mid-morning. Her partner, the *Mohawk Belle*, was now based at Bigwin. Commanded by Captain William P. Tinkiss or Robert Parsons, she would set off around the back of Bigwin Island to the local ports of call, such as Ronville Lodge, Port Cunnington, Fox Point, Dwight, Point Ideal and Bonavista, before joining the *Iroquois* at South Portage. After connecting with the little railway, the two steamers would back out from South Portage wharf, the *Iroquois* first, because she was faster, then separate and go their respective ways. In the afternoons, the procedures would be repeated. Through the twenties and thirties the fare from Huntsville to the Portage was 85¢, to Dwight or Bigwin $1.60, and to Dorset $1.75, one way.

S.S. "Iroquois" and S.S. "Mohawk Belle" meeting the train at South Portage.

Waterfront scene at Dorset, Ontario.
The Str. "Iroquois" is in port. Behind it stands the Alvira Hotel.
Courtesy, *Mr. Brad Robinson*, Dorset

S.S. "Mohawk Belle", docking at Glenmount.

On the lower lakes, the *Algonquin* had a few interesting times. Besides the occasional grounding or the odd trip through fog or thunderstorms, she once had trouble at the bridge near the Locks when she was entering winter quarters, in 1925. Usually there was a clearance of a few inches between the bridge and the ship's stack, but this time the water happened to be high, and as the steamer passed beneath the bridge the stack jammed right under it. Despite the current the vessel could not move. Efforts were made to pry it loose, but in vain. The solution to the problem was to remove some of the stop logs in the dam below and lower the water level. The *Algonquin* was able to break free the following day.

By this time, the Company flagship was leaking badly, and an inspection in the Locks in December in 1926 confirmed that her hull was in poor shape. It was figured that she might survive one more season, and consequently the ship, now twenty years old, was given makeshift repairs while plans were prepared for a new one. The old *Algonquin* staggered back into service in 1927, but soon a serious leak opened up along her broken keel, and the pumps had to be run day and night to keep the old lady afloat. Steadily it grew worse, until it seemed doubtful whether she could hold up until the fall. She just barely managed it.

Meanwhile, a crew of fourteen men, including Captain St. Amond, Bill Murray, Captain Elder and his son, J.A. Scriver, and many of the hands from the Portage Railway, were rapidly building and assembling the hull of the new ship. Directing the work and poring over the plans was Captain Sangster, now incurably ill with tuberculosis and not destined to live long enough to assume his new command; C.O. Shaw would actually shed tears when he died. Mindful of the weakness of the earlier ship, Shaw ordered a full steel frame from the new one, which was constructed at the tannery foundry. A sixteen inch "I" beam was obtained for the keel, plus some three inch angle-irons for the ribs. Once these were rivetted in place along with the steel deck plating, a gang from Collingwood arrived to finish the hull, using white oak planking two and a half inches thick and imported from Virginia for the purpose. By early June, the hull was ready for launching.

The big event took place on June 7, 1927, on the south side of the Vernon River near the railway bridge. The site had been prepared using horse-drawn hand scrapers to level the banks behind the new ship. A large crowd, part of it on the railway tracks, gathered to watch as Miss Helen Conway, a daughter of C. W. Conway, shouted in a loud, clear voice, "I name you *Algonquin* the Second!", before smashing the bottle over her bow. Then the retaining blocks were knocked loose, and the new ship slid flawlessly into the water. Close by, the *Ramona* blew her shrill whistle three times in salute.

The new *Algonquin* was designed as an exact duplicate of the original, meaning that she was 117.4 feet long at the waterline and 23.5 feet in beam. When completed, she drew over six feet of water and registered 170.61 tons. About three months after the launching, the old ship, her season and career over, was brought alongside the hull of the new. The engine, boiler and equipment of the old *Algonquin* then went into the new boat, under the supervision of Engineer John Smith of Huntsville, who was to serve on both. The superstructure cabins were likewise transferred. Then, as the new ship neared completion, the hulk of the old was towed into Lake Vernon, shortly before the freeze-up, loaded with stone and scrap iron, and set on fire in the usual manner. She burned to the waterline and finally sank, joining the *Sarona* and the *Empress Victoria* in what can best be termed the graveyard of the Huntsville steamboats.

A very different scene took place the following June 25th, when the new *Algonquin*, gleaming and resplendent in her fresh coat of paint, cast off her lines amid a cheering crowd at the Huntsville wharf and set off proudly on her first trip to the Portage, under the command of Captain Parsons. The new ship was a splendid asset, looking almost exactly like her predecessor except that her hull windows lacked the handsome top arches of the original. Also, her stem at the bow, instead of standing almost vertical like the other steamers, inclined slightly forward, which perhaps spoiled her appearance a little. Nevertheless, she was to give excellent service for the next 25 years.

The second *Algonquin* was the last new passenger ship on the North Muskoka Lakes. Though no one could have known it then, the grim years of the Depression were soon to unfold, and along with that, other conditions were soon to change, with a sort of relentless inevitability, and all to the detriment of the Huntsville steamboats. Already the routes had started to shrink, and towing was almost a thing of the past. The inexorable decline of the North Muskoka steamers would soon be painfully obvious.

S.S. "Algonquin", caught under the bridge at The Locks, 1925.
Courtesy, *Mr. Frank Cottrill*, The Locks

Captain William N. Sangster, Master of the "Algonquin".
Courtesy, *Mrs. Frank Stephenson*, Huntsville

S.S. "Algonquin" at North Portage.
The little train can be seen at the left.
Courtesy, *Mrs. Marie Tryon*, Scarborough

S.S. "Algonquin", Grand Old Lady of the Huntsville Lakes.

S.S. "Algonquin", (II) new Flagship of the Huntsville Fleet.
The vessel appears above passing the swing bridge at Huntsville.

Burks Falls harbour, around 1905.
In this scene are the S.S. "Wanita" (left) and S.S. "Wenonah", both still wearing the colours of the Muskoka and Georgian Bay Navigation Company.

Robert James Watson, industrialist and politician.

CHAPTER 3
The Magnetawan Steamboats
(1906-1935)

We left the Magnetawan steamer services just at a point of reorganization which they, like their counterparts around Huntsville and South Muskoka, were obliged to undergo immediately after 1905. Until that time, two enterprises had dominated the boating scene on this route; the Muskoka Navigation Company and the Magnetawan Navigation Company, the latter operated by the energetic Walton family. As we have seen, however, the Muskoka Navigation Company decided to seek its fortunes solely on the Muskoka Lakes after 1905, while the Waltons chose to abandon the Magnetawan for the Pickerel River system in northern Parry Sound in 1912. The way was open for newcomers to try their hand.

The man who first stepped in was Robert James Watson, an entrepreneur who took up several careers during his very busy life. During the late 1880s, we find him running a flour business in Bracebridge. For a time he was also a steamboat Captain, and in 1888 was commanding the tug *Rosseau* for the Muskoka Leather Company tannery (Beardmore's), of which he later became Manager. Afterwards, around 1894, he was invited to manage a new tannery at Burks Falls for the Magnetawan River Tannery Company. Later still, he became very active in politics, and actually stood for election himself in 1910. In short, R.J. Watson was an energetic and popular individual, though perhaps too restless to remain at any enterprise indefinitely.

It was on November 11, 1905 that Watson, hearing that the Muskoka Navigation Company was pulling out of the Magnetawan region, decided to do what C.O. Shaw was then doing at Huntsville: he bought up all of the Line's assets on this run, including its two steamers, the *Wenonah* and the *Wanita*, which between them carried almost all of the passengers and much of the freight between Burks Falls and Ahmic Harbour. For a year, he carried on with them as usual. However, by the year 1906, the *Wenonah* was twenty years old and probably past her prime, and Mr. Watson decided to have her converted into a towboat to scow tanbark to Burks Falls, while building a large new replacement steamer for the passenger business. Probably for this reason, he mortgaged all his vessels in 1907 for a total of $15,550.50, at rates modern borrowers would envy (7%), but apparently his enterprises were thriving, since he was able to discharge the entire debt in less than sixteen months.

The *Wenonah* was drydocked in 1906 and the paddlewheels and one engine were removed, along with the sidewalls and both the upper decks. What was left afterwards was a large, single-decked screw tug, which was immediately put to work, endlessly hauling scowloads of tanbark, split and peeled by the farmers. Three men, a captain, engineer and deckhand/fireman, were needed to crew her, sometimes working from 4:00 a.m. until 6:00 p.m. every day.

The *Wenonah* was not fated to serve as a towboat very long. One afternoon during the summer of 1908, the old steamer, commanded by Captain Stephen Croswell of Ahmic Harbour, left the wharf at Midlothian for Magnetawan with an empty scow in tow. She did not get far before sparks from the fireboxes apparently ignited the cordwood being used for fuel, and soon flames were spreading around her stack. Unable to check the blaze, the crew took to the scow, and were soon picked up by local people who had seen what was happening. The engine, still functioning, took the burning vessel over to the foot of Echo Rock on the south side of Lake Cecebe. Here she finally filled and sank. The engine and boiler were later retrieved, but the bottom of the hull, containing the remains of the steel firebox, can still be seen to this day. The loss was a serious one, and apparently the tannery henceforth hired some of the local tugs to tow for it.

S.S. "Wenonah" (Second Version) as a Tug (1907).

STEAMER ARMOUR, BURK'S FALLS, ONT.

S.S. "Armour", Flagship of the Magnetawan Steamboat Line.

Steamers at Burks Falls wharf.
In this fine shot, the S.S. "Armour", (left), S.S. "Wanita" and S.S. "Wenonah" (as a tug)
are docked for the winter, around 1907.

A new passenger steamer was built during the winter at Burks Falls and completed in 1906, and a very handsome vessel she proved to be! Larger than any other ship on the river, though slightly shorter than the *Wenonah*, she was 87.5 feet in keel, about 93 feet overall, had a beam of 17.5 feet, and registered 115.29 tons. She had a steel frame and a new fore and aft compound engine delivering 16.6 net horsepower, plus a powerful searchlight atop the pilot house. Her spacious dining room at the stern was large enough for six tables, not counting the captain's. Her construction caused a thrill of anticipation around the community, and Mr. Watson announced a contest to decide what her name should be. Someone suggested that she be called the *Armour*, after the township encompassing Burks Falls, and this became official on the day the bottle of champagne was broken over her bow and she slid into the Magnetawan for the first time. The Village of Burks falls declared the day a holiday, and all the tannery men were out to watch the festivities. After the usual preliminaries, the *Armour* sounded her hoarse whistle for the first time to herald her inaugural trip.

Though the *Armour* was a very fine ship, she initially had trouble on the river, largely because she sat high out of the water and proved top-heavy. On her maiden cruise to Lake Cecebe, she grounded on a sandbar at the entrance to the lake and rolled partway over—which must have made a fine impression on her frightened passengers! Presently her running mate the *Wanita*, under Captain Will Kennedy, arrived to pick up the people, and the *Glenada*, owned by the Waltons, showed up to help roll the big ship loose. She was then pumped out and towed back to Burks Falls. On the recommendation of her Master, Captain Mortimer, four tons of concrete ballast were poured into her hold. This made the *Armour* a little more stable, though she was still known to have occasional trouble passing the sandbars in low water, and the Magnetawan swing bridge when the waters were high.

S.S. "Armour", passing Millar's Swing Bridge, Magnetawan River.

The new steamer had her work cut out for her. Every day she would leave Burks Falls about 8:00 a.m., after the arrival of the train from Toronto, taking passengers and excursionists on the upper deck and consignments of groceries and hardware on the lower, and head downstream, stopping at various landings on the river. Usually she met and passed the *Wanita* near Millar's swing bridge, close to Lake Cecebe, where there was just enough room for the two of them to pass. Whistle salutes would be exchanged, and sometimes the two steamers came alongside in mid-river to exchange passengers. From here it was on to Lake Cecebe, where the *Armour* would call at Midlothian wharf, and sometimes Rockwynn Lodge or Cecebe, plus Kil Kare, Camp Comfort, Clifton Island and other places on a flag signal. By the time she reached Magnetawan and locked through, it was usually about noon. On Ahmic Lake, she had dozens of potential stops, mostly at cottages but also at settlements such as Port Anson, resorts such as Forest Nook and Cedar Croft, and camps such as Camp Kentuck and Camp Chikopi. If there weren't too many calls in a day, she would arrive at Ahmic Harbour about 2:00 p.m. Soon she was on her way back, returning to Lake Cecebe around 4:00 p.m. and Burks Falls by 6:00, in time to meet the evening train at the wharf. The *Wanita* meanwhile plied the opposite course, meeting the southbound noon train at the Falls. Naturally, the boats also carried the mail, plus trainloads of campers at the beginning of July and August, and hunters in the late fall: on those days reduced rates were charged. Sometimes beef cattle would be herded to the local landings too. There was nothing the boat crews liked less than carrying livestock, on account of the mess they made, and whenever possible animals were loaded last, in the hope that there wouldn't be any room left for them. More often than not, the cattle ended up being driven to town overland. (In those days the roads were little better than cattle trails anyway!)

Predictably, the *Armour* and her sister ships became an institution on the Magnetawan. People for miles around made a point of taking at least one cruise on the steamer every season. Picnic cruises were often held at Geddes Landing on Lake Cecebe, where there was a fine bathing beach, and the owner thoughtfully provided tables. The steamer would drop the people off there and pick them up again on the return trip about three hours later. Dominion Day and the twelfth of July were usually celebrated at Burks Falls, and to handle the rush, the *Armour* would have to

View of Ahmic Harbour, Ontario.
The S.S. "Armour" is at the wharf.

Cedarcroft Resort, Ahmic Lake.

S.S. "Wanita", stopping for passengers.

S.S. "Wanita", meeting a train at Burks Falls.

Albert Alexander Agar,
President of the Magnetawan Steamboat Line.

116

make a special late trip to Ahmic Harbour, spend the night there, and help the *Wanita* run the crowds back in the morning. Both ships would return late that day. Meals were served on board: the fare was good but expensive, with breakfast costing 75¢ and dinner $1.00. Moonlight cruises were especially popular, with dancing on the brightly-lit decks of the *Armour*. If there wasn't a band available, someone could always be found with an accordion. One old-timer vividly recalls such a cruise to Rockwynn and back, shortly after the *Armour* was launched, during which a vocalist enthralled the company with a new song called 'Let Me Call You Sweetheart'. Hymns were sung on the return trip, interspersed with the occasional hoarse whistle blast as the *Armour* slowly rounded each bend, piercing the velvety darkness of the river banks with the beam of her searchlight until the lights of Burks Falls came into view.

R.J. Watson did not remain in the boat business very long. No doubt he found his hands already full trying to manage the tannery. Furthermore, his political career was on the upswing. In 1910, he became the first Liberal to win the Federal seat of Parry Sound, a rare achievement for an ex-steamboat Captain, although he lost his seat shortly afterwards during the Reciprocity Election of 1911. In view of all these concerns, on November 12, 1908, he sold the *Armour* and the *Wanita* to a Burks Falls gentleman named Albert Alexander Agar, who had married Watson's daughter Maude. Watson retired from steamboating and later, after his forays into politics were over, he moved out west to Vancouver. Eventually he died in 1935.

Agar, the new owner, became one of the leading businessmen of Burks Falls. He was brought up on a farm near Kleinburg, north of Toronto, and about the age of nineteen decided to pack up and head north. Arriving at Burks Falls in 1894 with a team of horses, a spirit of adventure, and $200 in his pocket, he put up at the Burk House Hotel and found work teaming on the local roads. Soon he was transporting provisions for the contractors building the Ottawa, Arnprior and Parry Sound Railway for J.R. Booth. Eventually Agar became bookkeeper at R.J. Watson's tannery, and in 1906 began keeping the records for Watson's steamers as well. Having become interested in the boats, and having married one of Watson's daughters, it was natural for this ambitious young man to buy the boat business from his father-in-law when the opportunity arose. Henceforth he would dominate the steamboat scene on the Magnetawan almost until its days ran out.

A.A. Agar soon proved to be a very adept businessman, and at one time served as Reeve of Burks Falls. Personally he was an amiable, pleasant, well-dressed man, though it is said that he never missed an opportunity to make a dollar. As a result he prospered, and later bought a hardware store in Burks Falls. Some of the old timers claim that his business methods were sometimes a bit devious, but he made up for this by contributing loyally to his church, sending provisions to needy people during the winters, and sometimes letting people take cruises at cut rates. For better or for worse, he was one of the 'big men' on the Magnetawan.

Agar moved rapidly to consolidate what Watson and his predecessors had built. In 1909, he named his enterprise the Magnetawan River and Lakes Steamboat Line, and early in 1910, he purchased the tug *Theresa*—the same *Theresa* first used at Rosseau Falls—from her previous owner, George W. Ross of Port Anson, in order to get back into the towing business. It was a timely purchase, since the Waltons had just recently been obliged to dismantle two of their own tugs that were growing old. This meant that towboats were momentarily scarce on the Magnetawan. Agar then declared war on the Waltons and did his best to undercut them in the towing business. One time he also tried ordering Captain Will Walton not to dock the *Glenada* at Burks Falls, with the result that Walton relieved him of a few teeth in the melée that followed. By 1911 however, the Waltons threw in the sponge, sold the *Glenada* to Agar, and afterwards left the district to try steamboating on the Pickerel River in northern Parry Sound. At the same time Agar acquired a third tug from the Knight Brothers Company of Burks Falls.

Agar's Line now dominated both the transport and the towing businesses between Burks Falls and Ahmic Harbour, with few competitors, and, not surprisingly, the freight rates went up, much to the anger of the people. A few efforts were made to break the near-monopoly of the Magnetawan Steamboat Line, but with little success.

Agar's fleet, however, did not always enjoy smooth sailing. One November day in 1910, about 40 hunters from the Lake of Many Islands, having trekked down the Nipissing Road to Magnetawan with two deer each, boarded the *Armour* to return to Burks Falls. The men were singing, and perhaps a trifle intoxicated. At any rate, as the steamer was casting off her lines and starting to turn around, the hunters all crowded over to the rail to wave goodbye to their host, Fred Schmeler, owner of the hunt camp. The vessel heeled over alarmingly, sending dishes flying in the dining room, and the deckhands hastily threw the lines back around the dock posts until Captain Mortimer had the situation under control. Another time, on July 12, 1911, while the ship was cruising to Burks Falls on Lake Cecebe, a fire broke out on the *Armour's* hurricane deck near the stack, but the blaze was speedily put out, with few of the passengers realizing that anything was wrong. The same thing happened again at Marsden's Landing on the river, west of the swing bridge, and again one day at Burks Falls, but each time the fires were immediately put out and damage was slight. One of these incidents, however, may account for the rebuilt officers' cabin the *Armour* received late in life.

Such incidents were minor compared to the disaster that befell the *Wanita* in 1911. The little ship had been laid up for the winter at Burks Falls in December, when fire broke out, and soon the vessel was largely gutted. Apparently Agar figured that she was burned beyond redemption, since he sold the engine from the wreck. Yet he obviously had second thoughts, because about a year later he had the *Wanita* rebuilt, this time as a single-decked tug, and put her back in service in 1913. The *Wanita* towed for him until the end of 1920, when she was sold to the Knight Brothers.

The fire, meanwhile, left the *Armour* without a running mate. To rectify that, Mr. Agar decided to adapt the steamer *Glenada* as a passenger ship. The *Glenada* was a solid, sturdy vessel, but she had been built primarily as a workboat, with only a single deck. Agar now had her remodelled into a double-decked steamer, and as such, she proved much more satisfactory than the *Wanita* had been: she was both larger and more stable. Like the *Wanita*, she had a longer season than the *Armour*. Being cheaper to run, the *Glenada* would open the season in May, as soon as the ice broke up, and would continue until the freeze-up, whereas the *Armour* operated only during the summer months and during the hunting season. Again unlike the *Armour*, the *Glenada* remained a part-time towboat. Both ships were used to carry cattle.

S.S. "Glenada" (Second Version) at Burks Falls (1916).
Courtesy, *Mr. John Baker*, Toronto

Captain Joe Mortimer and crew (S.S. "Armour").

S.S. "Armour" approaching the lock at Magnetawan.

Another constant menace to the boats was, of course, logs. Log drives on the Magnetawan, bound mostly for the sawmills at Byng Inlet on Georgian Bay or upriver to the Knight Company sawmill and wood specialty plant, continued as long as steamboating did; in fact, the two died out almost simultaneously. As a result, deadheads were a constant menace. At least once, the *Armour* got a log caught inside her propeller at Magnetawan. To alleviate the problem, every second year the Steamboat Line had to engage a scow with two men and a pair of horses aboard to remove the logs. The scow would be towed to each obstruction reported by the boatmen, and the log secured by a line from a boom and hauled up by the horses until the boom could be swung and the log deposited on board. The process would be repeated until the scow was full, at which point it was taken to shore and emptied. Presumably the salvaged logs now belonged to the Steamboat Line.

In spite of, or because of, Agar's near control of the boat business on the Magnetawan, a few independent operators tried to avoid paying his rates by building or acquiring steamers of their own. One of these was Frank McDuff, a settler from Grand Valley who bought a sawmill on Lake Cecebe early in the century and sold some of his lumber at Burks Falls. About 1909, McDuff imported a 30 foot steam launch called the *Susie Kennedy* (which was then five years old), and used her to tow booms from the Distress River and other points to his mill, plus scowloads of lumber into town. Agar, annoyed by the competition, once tried to order the *Susie* not to dock at Burks Falls, but the captain refused to be intimidated. The *Susie Kennedy* plied until 1912, when the mill was closed; afterwards her engine and boiler were sold and the hull left to rot away.

Another pair of businessmen who tried to circumvent Agar's freight rates were the Troyer brothers of Magnetawan. J. Wilfred Troyer, a merchant and owner of a general store in the village, was incensed by the fact that imported commodities at Magnetawan cost nearly double what they did in Burks Falls. In 1919 he suggested to his brother, Henderson Troyer, who had just returned from the War, the idea of running a supply boat to bring in provisions for the stores of Magnetawan. As a result, Henderson bought the steam yacht *Pukwana* (once the *Willoudee*) from Lake Joseph, and began using her to carry groceries, hardware, farm machinery and the like from Burks Falls. He also conducted pleasure cruises, now and then, to Ahmic Harbour in the evenings for dances. Taking passengers from Burks Falls was more difficult, since the *Pukwana*, which was only about 54 feet long, was not big enough to carry all the trunks they usually brought with them. In fact, the vessel was not really large enough to be a freighter either, and when heavily loaded she proved almost unmanageable, being only 8.9 feet in beam. In the summer of 1920, the Troyers tried putting false sides on the *Pukwana*, but she had scarcely been relaunched, when she mysteriously caught fire one night as she lay at her dock. A crowd gathered and pushed the burning boat out into the river, but not before the blaze spread to the Troyers' new freight shed. Both the boat and the shed were destroyed but some of the flour and feed in the building were saved. Arson was suspected, though nothing could be proved. It is said that the remains of the *Pukwana*, including her anchor, were discovered above the locks at Magnetawan in 1965, when Lake Cecebe was temporarily lowered.

It is doubtful that the Troyer brothers made much money with the *Pukwana*, but nonetheless they were not quite ready to quit. They purchased another small steam launch called the *Martha*, which had already been in serviced locally for many years, first towing logs for a sawmill at Port Carmen on Lake Cecebe, then hauling cartage from Burks Falls to Magnetawan, and later still (1912) taking fresh milk, meat, vegetables and bait from the farm of Isaac Bell of Port Anson to the resorts and cottages of Ahmic Lake. Naturally, the *Martha* was also used to run picnics or take people to dances at Ahmic Harbour, and would sometimes whistle at the *Armour* if she met the big ship on her rounds. In 1920, as his sons were moving away, and private butcherings were now forbidden by law, Mr. Bell sold the *Martha* to the Troyers, who at once converted her into a motor launch and continued freighting for another year or two. It is said that the vessel's new Captain, John Stewart of Magnetawan, upon reaching Burks Falls one day, happened to meet Mr. Agar, who pleasantly assured him that he (Agar) meant Stewart no ill will, but still hoped that his boat would sink with all hands. Stewart remembered that comment later in the day, when he ran out of gas on Lake Cecebe and found that the anchor had been stolen! The *Martha* did not sink, but the Troyers gave up the boat service shortly afterwards, though the launch was still in Wilfred Troyer's possession as late as 1946.

Steam Yacht "Pukwana".
Photo taken during the vessel's days on the Muskoka Lakes.
Courtesy, *Public Archives of Canada* PA 132152

Steam Launch "Martha".

Besides these short-lived ventures, a handful of independent steamers, mostly tugs, were also used on the Magnetawan during this period. The little steamer *Linden* (2.75 tons) was built by Henry Walton in 1902, but within just four years was sold to Captain Levi Fraser and shipped south to Gravenhurst. In 1903, a little 36 foot steam launch called the *Amanda* (3.76 tons) was built at Ahmic Harbour for William Stewart of Croft Township, who acted as caretaker for some of the local cottagers. The *Amanda* lasted until 1910, when she burned on Ahmic Lake. Her little high-pressure engine was transferred to another steamer on Whitestone Lake, near Dunchurch.

A much larger steamer, the *Theresa* was shipped by rail from Bracebridge to Burks Falls in April of 1904 to tow for a firm called the Magnetawan Hardwood Company, which ran a sawmill at Ahmic Harbour. Within a year, however, the 26 ton tug was resold to the Knight Brothers Company Ltd., which was then the leading industrial concern and almost the economic backbone of Burks Falls. The Knights, of course, used the *Theresa* for towing logs, along with a houseboat called the *Ark*, which served as a floating diner and boardinghouse for the log drivers. Around 1905, she was on hand to rescue the Walton steamer *Emulator* when that vessel ran ashore at

Goose Lake. Late in 1908, however, the Knights sold the *Theresa* to George Ross of Port Anson, who, as noted, resold her to Agar in 1910. Commanded by Captain Tom Kennedy of the *Wanita*, the *Theresa* gave Agar his first real opportunity to enter the towing business. Soon, he secured lucrative contracts from both the tannery and the Knight Company, such that in 1913, he also converted the *Wanita* into a tug. The *Theresa* served until 1919, when she grew rotten and had to be broken up in drydock at Burks Falls. The hull was abandoned downriver near the "Devil's Elbow", in an artificial channel called the "Cut": today the spot is silting up and filling with reeds.

The Knight Company meanwhile required a new tug to replace the *Theresa*, and in September of 1908, purchased another vessel from the Muskoka Lakes. This was the *Gravenhurst*, the craft built by Captain Peter Campbell in 1902. She was shipped in by rail and put to work towing and scowing, until 1911, when she, too, was sold to Agar, who now owned three tugs. The sturdy little *Gravenhurst* continued to tow until 1918, when she took fire on the river, apparently a few miles from Burks Falls, and burned to the waterline.

The loss of the *Gravenhurst* and the scrapping of the *Theresa* meant, of course, that at least one replacement tug was needed, and in 1919 a vessel was built at Burks Falls by order of Mr. Agar. The newcomer was the *Mike* (33.60 tons), a 52.85 foot screw tug apparently named for Mike Pritchard, a marine engineer who had sailed for many years with Captain Croswell, and would continue to serve on the *Mike* herself. A sturdy, steel-framed vessel with a fore and aft compound engine and a sharp pitched whistle, the *Mike* served the Agar Line for only two years before she was sold to the Knight Company. Compared to the *Wanita* she was rather slow, and could do only about 12 m.p.h., but she was so good at turning in tight corners that Captain Croswell claimed that she could "turn on a half dollar".

The *Mike* had the usual adventures during her term on the Magnetawan. One time she went aground on the rock in Noel's Bay, on the south side of Ahmic Lake, failed to break free, and whistled for help. Finally the *Glenada* arrived and pulled her loose. Another time, around 1920, the tug got caught on a sandbar near Knoepfli Falls, the outlet for Ahmic Lake. An alligator called the *Shoepack* (spelling uncertain) spotted her and tried to drag her off; failing, she ran over to Camp Chikopi, snubbed her cable to a tree, and easily winched the *Mike* out of the mud.

The *Shoepack* survives in a few photos today, and in the memories of some old-timers, but seemingly not in any official registries. She was owned by the Croft Lumber Company of Huntsville, and possibly came from that region, but her year of construction is unknown. She was a crude little craft, about 35 feet long, with a dark red hull and a hinged stack for passing under bridges, and her four-bladed paddle wheels were driven by a chain pulley that had the annoying tendency to work loose. One time she even dropped a paddle wheel overboard. She was capable of towing four scows at a time, using her engines directly instead of winching, but she could not be steered or turned in a crosswind: to do that, one of the crew had to shift the towline from side to side at the stern.

The *Shoepack* arrived at Burks Falls on a flatcar sometime before 1910, and was put to work winching booms to the Croft Company mill on Ahmic Lake, assisted by a gas-powered tender called the *Pagan*. She also scowed hay and oats to the lumber camps around Neighick, Crawford and Burnt Lakes, dragging herself overland or through muskeg patches that would have paralyzed a conventional tug.

Older men still recall eventful times on the *Shoepack*. One dark, windy night in 1920 the tug got lost on Ahmic Lake with a boom in tow. The *Pagan* was sent ahead with a light to find the dock at Rocky Reef. After much groping around she finally reached Chikopi, from which point the crew realized that Rocky Reef must be to the left. The alligator followed the light, and the wind carried the tow neatly around the reef.

Another time the tug chugged into McArthur's Bay on Ahmic Lake to pick up another consignment of logs. While these were being rolled into the water, the boat scraped against a fallen tree, gouging her side. The tow was taken to the mill without incident, but then the alligator was sent to Ahmic Harbour to collect a ton of oats. She did not get far on the return trip before the engineer complained about all the water in the hold. A search revealed a hole in the port side near the stern, just below the waterline. The siphon was turned on, but the ungainly little craft wallowed deeper and deeper in the water as she crawled back to the mill. At last she made it, but the crew lost no time in heaving the feed bags out onto the bank. The *Shoepack* was then winched

Steam Tug "Theresa", with logging crew, Lake Cecebe.
To the left is the "Ark", a houseboat used to accommodate the log drivers.

Steam Tug "Gravenhurst" on the Magnetawan River.

Steam Tug "Mike".

Steam Alligator "Shoepack", near Ahmic Harbour.

ashore and patched. She operated until 1925, when she was finally put on skids near the Croft mill and left to rot away.

A few private steamers call for brief acknowledgement. One small tug, perhaps a converted launch, was used for about ten years by Bill MacLachlan of Magnetawan to sweep logs in to his sawmill at nearby Jenkins Creek. In 1921 the owner died and the craft was beached. In 1926, John Henry Blackmore, owner of a sawmill at Port Anson, imported the tug *Marion F.* from Huntsville. Older residents still recall how comical she looked as she struggled along with an enormous scow in tow. One time in 1927, Mr. Blackmore heaved the anchor overboard near Port Anson, but got his ankles caught in the line and he went over too! He disappeared from sight, unable to free himself, but luckily the Engineer heard the splash and pulled the anchor up, saving Blackmore's life. By the 1930s Blackmore had scuttled his tug, and began hauling his lumber to town by truck. There was also a steamer called the *Pocahontas* on Ahmic Lake, but almost nothing is known about the vessel, save its name. Finally, Daniel Rice, who founded the Forest Nook summer hotel on Ahmic Lake early in the century, is known to have used a steam launch named the *Forest Nook* to ferry in his guests. It was ultimately beached, and later burned, at the site of Camp Kentuck.

We have little information as to how the passenger ships of the Steamboat Line weathered the War, and it can only be surmised that the effects were much the same on the Magnetawan as elsewhere: diminished travel to the camps, cottages and resorts, but probably no reduction in freighting. The War may also have done the boats a bit of a favour by retarding road improvements. By the beginning of the 1920s, things seemed to be returning to normal, but even in the north country, times were changing.

One very obvious novelty was the appearance of the motorcar, and shortly afterwards the transport truck. An automobile was seen in Burks Falls as early as 1912, and in fact triggered the carriage accident that claimed the life of Walter Knight, but anyone motoring in the Magnetawan area was taking quite a risk. By 1918, an automobile succeeded in rattling its way from Burks Falls to Magnetawan Village, and by 1921 three taxis, along with seven horse-teams, were stationed at Burks Falls. Gradually the roads were gravelled, especially on the hills, and sometimes even widened to two lanes! By 1925 one could motor from Burks Falls to Magnetawan, a distance of about 25 miles, in one and a half hours, with no more than a single flat tire. The steamers, though more comfortable, could not match such speeds, nor did they possess the exciting novelty of the motorcars, which were getting faster all the time. Trucks began to appear too, and storekeepers soon found that they preferred their merchandise delivered direct to their doorsteps, rather than merely to the nearest wharf.

Very early one morning in 1925, the *Armour*, much delayed, steamed into Burks Falls about 4:00 a.m. She had to leave again at 7:00, and hence the postmaster had to collect the mail and rouse the proprietor of one of the local stores, dropping off all the orders for groceries. Not having a truck available to move everything down to the wharf, the men borrowed one. The rig had a 4-90 shift, with both the clutch and the brake on the same pedal; the driver, unused to this, couldn't stop the vehicle as it coasted down to the dock, and the two front wheels of the truck went off the edge of the wharf. The river happened to be fairly low, and the ship's crew saved the day by reversing the *Armour* until she was opposite the truck. Then everyone, standing on the deck, gave a mighty heave and managed to hoist the vehicle back onto the wharf.

Another change, also unwelcome to the boats, began during the 1920s, as the Canadian National Railways cut out more and more of its usual calls to the wharf at Burks Falls, contenting itself instead with stops at the main line station only. This forced travellers to take taxis to the wharf. The taximen, of course, offered to drive their customers all the way to Magnetawan or Ahmic Harbour.

All of these developments spelled trouble for the Magnetawan Steamboat Line, but predictably, Albert Agar was not about to surrender without a fight. For a time, he tried providing his own taxi service between the station and the wharf. He also had his assistant, Morris Lounsbury, whom he had lured north from London to run his hardware store, board trains at Katrine station, four miles south of Burks Falls and canvass for passengers to continue their travels by steamer. The taximen of course resented this, and fights broke out at Burks Falls station as boatmen and cabbies alike tried to grab people's luggage. On one occasion, Lounsbury

Burks Falls wharf.
Meeting the train is the S.S. "Wanita".

started a rumour that Bill Raaflaub, proprietor of the principal taxi service at Burks Falls, was no longer running cabs, and Raaflaub retaliated by giving Lounsbury a black eye at the station. Agar himself sometimes got caught up in those rows. The situation became so bad that the C.N.R. finally sent in its own police to keep order. In an effort to settle the problem the taximen were ordered to remain in their cabs on railway property, while the boatmen were prohibited from canvassing on trains.

Occasionally, too, Agar had problems over the wages he paid. In 1921, after some sharp words on the subject, the skipper of the *Glenada*, Captain Edward Pink of Burks Falls, walked right off his ship, along with the engineer. The mail contract made it imperative to keep the *Glenada* running, so Agar hastily pressed Captain Tom Kennedy into service. Kennedy, who worked primarily on the tugs, was unused to double-decked passenger ships, and promptly ran into trouble. On his first day out, while approaching the dock at Rocky Reef, he waited too late to signal 'reverse' (or the new engineer failed to respond fast enough), with the result that the steamer collided with the wharf, shoving it sideways a good three feet, and knocking all the people on it off balance. The next day Captain Pink was back at the wheel, having obtained the raise he asked for!

Despite every expedient tried, including the cancellation of the meal service as an economy measure, the Magnetawan steamers were now fighting an uphill battle. As they lost their freighting monopoly to the trucks, they also became less essential for moving logs and lumber, since trucks proved capable of handling these too. In any case, the last log drives went through Burks Falls about 1928. In 1922, the tannery shut down, depriving the boats of a valued customer. Private motorboats were also becoming commoner. Soon all of the camps and lodges had their own launches and a few were being used commercially for cruises. As receipts fell, the passenger ships had to rely more and more on excursion cruises, but the season was short and the profits insufficient to sustain them. By and large, the only remaining hope was the all-important mail contract.

One summer's day in 1926, Dr. Thomas Culluns of Baltimore, Maryland, who had been cottaging at Ahmic Lake for decades and who regarded the steamer cruise as half his holiday, was met by Mr. Agar upon arrival at Burks Falls. The two were old friends, and as the doctor prepared to board the *Armour*, Agar wanly wished him a pleasant trip, adding that it would

S.S. "Glenada", running mate for the "Armour".

S.S. "Armour", docked at Midlothian wharf, Lake Cecebe.

probably be his last. Culluns, shocked, asked why. Agar explained that Wilfred Troyer was then getting up a petition for a morning mail service, by truck, to be handled by Stan Wurm of Magnetawan, and without the mail contract, the steamers could not keep running. Indignant, the doctor made a special point of getting off at Magnetawan for a talk with Troyer, whose store derived a lot of business from the Ahmic Lake Cottagers' Association. Culluns was a prime mover in the organization, and apparently he promised that Troyer's store would 'never get another nickel's worth of business from the doctor or his friends, unless . . . . ' The very next day the two of them drove straight to North Bay by car and had the petition quashed. The steamers continued to ply for a few more years, but they had only gained a brief reprieve. Nothing could prevent the endless proliferation of speedboats, automobiles and trucks, and nothing could stem the spreading network of macadamized roads. Time was running out for the steamers of the Magnetawan.

In 1928, a plan was unveiled to rebuild the road from Burks Falls to Mangetawan, eliminating the worst curves. This would reduce the time of a motor trip between the two places to about half an hour. That, apparently, was the last straw. On Labour Day evening, 1928, the *Armour* steamed back to Burks Falls as usual. Later on, towards midnight, the townspeople were aroused by fire alarm bells. Flames could be seen from the harbour. It was the *Armour*, ablaze almost from stern to stern. The fire brigade hurried to the scene and a large crowd gathered, but nothing could save the steamer. As the mooring lines burned, the doomed vessel began to drift away, threatening the Knight Company woodpiles across the river, but Captain Croswell braved the searing heat to resecure her. Soon it was all over — although the wreck was soon raised and converted into a fishing-tug on the Great Lakes. Perhaps the fire was not an accident. Perhaps the graceful *Armour* had simply given up and committed suicide, now that she was no longer needed. It mattered little. What did matter to the despondent citizens was that something very special had gone out of their lives forever.

This was not quite the end of the steamer service. The *Glenada*, shorn of almost any hope of breaking even, struggled on for a few more seasons and continued to carry the mail on Ahmic Lake, but soon the Depression started and after 1931 she was benched at Burks Falls. Several years later, around 1935, she, too, took fire in drydock, and became a total loss. Her owner, Albert Agar, retired from the boat business and carried on with his hardware store. Later, he bought a small grocery store, more or less as a hobby, until his eventual complete retirement from business. During the late '50s, he developed heart problems, and in 1959, aged 84, he died.

The only other steamers still in service on the Magnetawan in 1931 were the *Wanita* and the *Mike*, both owned by the Knight Company. This fine old firm, which had been the mainstay of Burks Falls for nearly half a century, folded in the fall of that year, another victim of the Depression, and that spelled 'finis' to log towing. Both of its tugs were sold in 1932. The *Mike*, still in good condition, thanks to a major refit in drydock some years earlier, was taken to Meaford on Georgian Bay, there to be converted into a fishing boat: she lasted into the 1940s. The aging *Wanita* was less fortunate. She languished at Burks Falls until July of 1934, when Captain Croswell received orders to fire her up and take her back to Ahmic Harbour. On July 19th the unkempt old tug made that final trip, with a small group on board, although she was now so leaky that the pumps had to be kept running continuously to keep her afloat. As she passed her old familiar ports of call, everyone stared at her as if they couldn't believe their eyes. No steamboat had been seen on the river for several years. The surprise was greatest at Ahmic Harbour, when the *Wanita*'s shrill whistle echoed around the bay in the late afternoon. She had, however, merely come home to die. That same night, at about two o'clock in the morning, she took fire, and also set the old wharf shed ablaze. A passing motorist raised the alarm, and the old tug was pushed away from the dock, to burn and sink in the bay. She had served on the river since 1896. Her remains are still visible today.

On that melancholy note, steamboating came to a close in the valley of the Magnetawan, after more than half a century. Today, although few resorts remain in the region, the Magnetawan lakes are as popular with anglers and cottagers as ever. Speedboats, sailboats and canoes now fill the scene every summer, and the locks at Magnetawan Village remain very much in service. But of the old passenger steamers which did so much to open up the region, nothing remains save a few photographs and relics in local museums, plus a bronze plaque recently unveiled at the harbour of Burks Falls, honouring their memory.

S.S. "Armour", returning to Burks Falls.

Str. "Mike", one of the last Magnetawan Steamboats.

McKellar Village, 1871

Str. "W.B. Armstrong" on Lake Manitouwabing. A successor to the "Ada", this craft is shown near McKellar in 1892.
Courtesy, *Parry Sound Library*

CHAPTER 4
Steamboating in the Almaguin Highlands
(1881-1924)

Besides the central Magnetawan, many of the other small lakes and rivers of the Almaguin Highlands, briefly, had steamers of their own. All of these were either alligators, lumber tugs, or small pleasure boats. None were very impressive and few of any particular interest. We document them only in the interest of completeness.

STEAMBOATS AT KEARNEY: (1900-1924)

Nestled among the hills of eastern Almaguin, only miles from the border of Algonquin Park, lies the pleasant little town of Kearney, on the upper reaches of the Magnetawan. Named after its first settler, who arrived from Emsdale about 1879, Kearney was originally a small lumber town. Later (in 1895) it became a station on the Ottawa, Arnprior and Parry Sound Railway. Today the community relies largely on tourism, trapping, cottaging and outfitting sportsmen headed for the Park. The permanent population has never exceeded 600, and it is said that Kearney owes its incorporation to its two hotels, which pressed for it in 1908 when the local township voted to ban the sale of liquor.

The little community is reflected in the waters of the Magnetawan, portions of which have been dignified by the name of lakes. From the dam at Kearney, one can navigate from East Lake (now Hazzard Lake) upstream to Hungry Bay, past the highway bridge, up the channel to Loon Lake (now Perry Lake), and sometimes, depending on the depths, up to Beaver Lake (now Bethune Lake), for a total distance of about two miles.

Three small steamers are known to have used this waterway. The first was a passenger boat called the *Queen Anne*, imported on a railway flatcar around 1900 by a man named Misener, who intended to cater to tourists. The *Queen Anne* was about 50 feet in length, pointed at both ends, and had a tall stack and a wooden canopy. She could take about 25 passengers at speeds of approximately five miles per hour. Business proved very slack, except on Sundays, and it is not surprising that the owner gave up after just a few years, sold the vessel elsewhere, and left the area.

A second steamer, an alligator with hooded paddle wheels, was imported to Kearney in 1913 by the Canada Pine Lumber Company, which had just opened a sawmill in the village. This nameless, weatherbeaten tug was used for about five years to warp logs downstream from Beaver Lake, until the mill was closed. The craft was then moved to other waters.

The third and last steamer at Kearney was a nameless steam punt, built in 1913 by Charles Allair, a local blacksmith. The Allair steamer was square at both ends, about 25 feet long, with sloping sides, a tiny pilothouse and canopy, and a single cylinder engine, giving her speeds of about seven miles per hour. She was used for over a decade to run picnics and excursions, and occasionally to salvage drifting logs, until one day in 1924 when the boiler fire, having been chucked overboard at Kearney, somehow refloated under the stern, still smouldering, and set the whole craft on fire. Mr. Allair salvaged the machinery, and later built a motorboat to replace the steamer.

STEAMBOATS AT DUNCHURCH: (1900-1924)

The pretty little village of Dunchurch stands five miles west of Ahmic Harbour, by the shores of Whitestone Lake, which is so irregular in shape that the shoreline almost pinches the lake in two at the site. To this charming spot came Mr. and Mrs. George Kelcey, by way of the Great North Road from Parry Sound in 1872, and here they decided to open a hotel, develop businesses, and encourage settlers. Given the honour of so doing, Mrs. Kelcey named the budding village after her native town in England. In time, stores, churches and sawmills were built, and Dunchurch soon enjoyed the benefits of a tri-weekly stage service to Parry Sound. In 1886 a stage also began connecting with the steamer *Ada* at Ahmic Harbour.

A feeder to the Magnetawan, Whitestone Lake extends only about five miles north from Dunchurch and another three south of it. Consequently, the only steamers on the lake were a few tugs. The first of these was the *Black Bear*, a 35 foot craft built for a lumberman named Albert McCallum, who ran a 200 acre farm up the lake to service his lumber camps. The *Black Bear's* duties were to take provisions to the camps and tow logs to her owner's mill. After a number of years, the *Black Bear*, improperly caulked, sank one winter in Whitestone Lake. She was then sold to Thomas Dobbs of Dunchurch, who refitted the vessel to tow for his own sawmill (1908-09), and also, to conduct the occasional Sunday picnic cruise. The steamer seems to have had much the same effect as the automobile now has on teenage girls. So many were attracted for outings that the boat was soon dubbed the "Lady Catcher". Around 1910, the tug reverted to McCallum, who perhaps used her for a time on Ahmic Lake before transferring her westward to Shawanaga Lake. Here she towed for the Rosseau Lumber Company and the Beagan and Simpson Company, both of which were exporting by way of Boakview station on the Canadian Northern Railway. Later still, the *Black Bear* went to Georgian Bay, and ultimately to Kidd's Landing on the Pickerel River. Her hull was left to rot there at Smokey Creek about 1932.

Thomas Dobbs needed a tug to replace the *Black Bear*, and in 1911 he built the *Dreadnought*, a 35 foot craft with a tiny pilothouse which received the engine from the burned-out *Amanda* on Ahmic Lake. Operated by his sons, the *Dreadnought* towed for all the local mills for four years, and, like the *Black Bear*, she was in great demand for excursions. Then early one morning in May of 1915, the *Dreadnought* went up in flames at her dock at Dunchurch, and by the time the alarm was raised she was beyond saving. After that, the Dobbs family relied on gas boats to tow for them.

A few minor steam tugs were also used on Whitestone Lake. One was a tiny twenty foot towboat, brought in from Ahmic Harbour to tow on Eagle and Whitestone Lakes after the *Dreadnought* burned. This little craft went to Shawanaga Lake around 1917. Another little steam launch called the *Mystic*, said to have been built at Magnetawan, was won in a raffle by Robert Robertson, a relative of the Dobbs family, who used her on Whitestone Lake for towing and recreation early in this century. And finally, there was another nameless steam punt, imported from Shawanaga Lake around 1917 by John T. McLennan, who owned a sawmill on the Whitestone River, about three miles from Dunchurch. This boat burned at Dunchurch within a few years and was replaced by a second, similar tug which was sold with the mill in 1924. This craft was probably the last steam vessel to serve in the region of Dunchurch.

STEAMBOATS AT McKELLAR: (1881-1916)

The village of McKellar, about ten miles southwest of Dunchurch on the highway to Parry Sound, is also at the centre of a cluster of lakes, themselves part of the watershed of the Seguin River. The Armstrong brothers, Samuel and James, practically founded McKellar around 1867 as a by-product of their logging operations, and later imported the little steamer *Ada* to Lake Manitouwabing in 1881. The *Ada* was transferred to Ahmic Lake in 1886, but the Armstrong family obtained another steam tug, which they called the *W.B. Armstrong*, to take over towing on Trout Lake, Minerva Lake and Lake Manitouwabing. The Armstrong mills burned before the end of the century, and by then the owners had either died or moved away.

A revival was started in 1899, when John Thompson, son of one of the local hotel proprietors, built a new sawmill at McKellar, capable of cutting 18,000 feet of lumber daily. His son Herbert soon took over the mill, modernized it, and built a steamer to bring in the logs. Named for Herbert's half-sister Irene, the tug was about 30 feet in length, with a compound engine and a vertical boiler, and could move at a very respectable eighteen miles per hour. Often she went to collect tows of up to 50,000 logs each from such places as Hurdville and Broadbent. Most of the actual towing was done at night, when there was less chance of contrary winds. Herbert Thompson himself frequently commanded the *Irene*.

Inevitably, the *Irene* was a part-time pleasure boat, and on weekends or holidays she would leave McKellar with a boat load of picnickers bound for Robson's Lake, Birch Island, Cameron's

DISTRICT OF PARRY SOUND
Main Steamboat Waterways

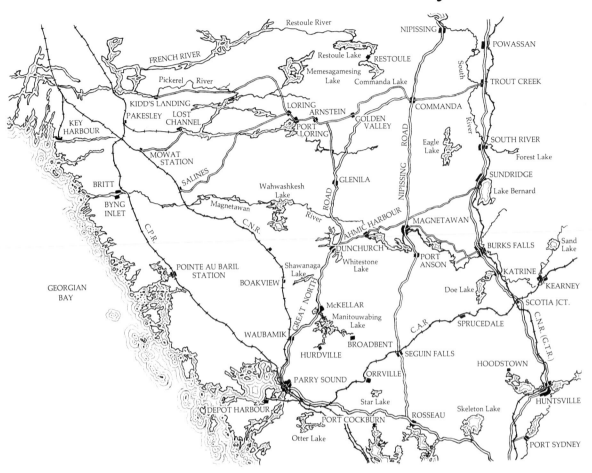

Steam Tug "Irene", on Lake Manitouwabing.

Point at the mouth of the Seguin River, or the island where Chief Manitouwaba himself lies buried. Groundings were frequent, and consequently the steamer always took a punt in tow. The *Irene* was, of course, a wood-burner: at one time her owner tried firing her up with coal but the engineer, unaccustomed to this fuel, used too much and burned out the boiler grates only a few miles from dock. The grates were replaced as quickly as possible, since the tug was indispensable.

The *Irene* worked until about 1916, when Herb Thompson sold both the mill and the boat and built another mill on Lorimer Lake. The new owners of the McKellar mill preferred using motorboats to do their towing, and left the aging *Irene* to rot away on skids. She was the last steamboat to run on Lake Manitouwabing.

It is possible that every single lake in the Parry Sound District had a steamer on it at one time or another. The task of trying to track them all down becomes nearly hopeless. As early as 1886, a steam launch is mentioned on tiny Star Lake, south of Edgington (Orrville), where it was used as an adjunct to a small hotel called the Star Lake House. In 1888 we hear of another small steamer—perhaps the same one?—on Otter Lake, southeast of Parry Sound; also used for recreation cruises: this craft, called the *Otter*, could carry up to 20 people, and was apparently owned by a settler named James S. Miller, who took a few summer guests at his "ranch".

More steamboats are known on lakes farther north, but almost all were tugs. The Huntsville 'Forester' mentions an alligator at work on Restoule Lake, near Lake Nipissing, in 1895, apparently for the Hardy Lumber Company of Trout Creek: this craft was swamped and wrecked in June of that year while being winched upstream at Five Mile Rapids on the French River, drowning the engineer. The Company replaced her with two new 37 foot alligators, the *Hardy* and the *Victoria*, which both arrived from Simcoe, Ontario, in 1896. The Holland and Graves Lumber Company of Buffalo, N.Y., (later Graves and Bigwood) also bought alligators from Simcoe, including the *Holland & Graves* (1901) and the *Wahwashkesh* (1903); the latter probably for use on Big Deer (now Wahwashkesh) Lake near Ardbeg. Old-timers still remember the craft at work, as late as the 1920s, hauling logs destined for Graves and Bigwood's enormous sawmill at Byng Inlet on Georgian Bay. The alligator, which had a cable two miles long, was eventually dismantled and replaced by pointers. There were also three tugs on Lake Bernard.

Steam Alligator "Hardy" and raft, Parry Sound District.
Courtesy, *Ontario Archives*, S 2318

STEAMBOATS AT SUNDRIDGE: (1895-1912)

The attractive little village of Sundridge is spread out along the northwest side of Lake Bernard, about ten miles north of Burks Falls. Now a popular tourist town of 800 people, the community was first settled around 1875 when a Scottish wagon maker named James Dunbar arrived at Stoney Lake, as it was then called, by way of Gravenhurst, Rosseau and Magnetawan. He was soon joined by his son and brother and other families who trickled in looking for land. Though there was no waterpower available at the lake, James Dunbar erected a sawmill around 1881, laboriously hauling the machinery overland and across frozen lakes. He also made a survey for a village, to be called "Dunbarton", but since that name was already in use near Toronto, someone suggested the alternative of "Sunny Ridge". This name was applied for, but when a post office was opened, the villagers were surprised to find that the name had been condensed into "Sundridge" and so it remained. The community grew rapidly after the railway came through in 1886, and in 1889 Sundridge became an incorporated village.

James Dunbar went on to build several sawmills around Stoney Lake (later renamed Lake Bernard to avoid confusion with Stoney Lake in the Kawarthas). He also built a flat-bottomed side-wheel steamboat, about 70 feet in length, to tow logs on the lake: the 'Forester' makes note of it in 1895. The tug was confined strictly to Lake Bernard, which, unlike most others in the district, is an oval shaped sheet of water about six miles by three, with no islands. The people of Sundridge liked to charter the craft for cruises and picnics to such places as Flanagan's Landing (a farm south of town), Flat Rock (about two miles down lake) and Anderson's Landing at the south end. Navigation was generally safe at distances of 200 yards from shore, and the Dunbar tug, laden with up to 70 passengers, usually made a day of it, poking along slowly in a complete circuit of Lake Bernard. (For those who wanted more elaborate and varied cruises, the answer was a quick trip by train to Burks Falls for an outing on the *Armour*).

The Dunbar tug lasted until about 1910, but one day she managed to go aground on a submerged piling near town while on her way to collect a boom. Unable to free it, the family abandoned ship in a rowboat towed astern. The tug remained caught, became holed, and was finally towed ashore and left to rot away. The wreck was visible at the Sundridge waterfront for years.

Before we leave Lake Bernard we must mention two more nameless alligators; one used by the James Brennan sawmill downlake from Sundridge from 1894 to 1905, and the other by the

Dunbar Tug, Lake Bernard (Sundridge).
Courtesy, *Mr. Merrill Dunbar*, Sundridge

South River Chemical Company, which manufactured charcoal at South River. The alligator, used on Forest Lake near South River, spent one season (1912) towing cordwood on Lake Bernard before it was beached about a mile east of Sundridge. Henceforth sailing craft and motorboats dominated the scene on Lake Bernard.

CHAPTER 5
Steamboating on the Pickerel River
(1895-1935)

The only other waterway of any consequence for navigation in the Parry Sound District, aside from Lake Nipissing, is the Pickerel River system, which drains a considerable territory directly south of the French River on its way to Key Harbour on Georgian Bay. The portion that interests us is the section extending west from Port Loring to Lost Channel, a distance of roughly 25 miles. The upper portion, near Port Loring, is known as Wilson Lake. Farther west, along the sixteen mile stretch to The Elbow, it widens out again to become Toad Lake. At The Elbow, one channel extends northwest into Dollars Lake and the outlet of the river. The other channel, though deceptively inviting, is a dead-end. During the 1890s a newly arrived drive foreman, known as "Black Jack" Kennedy, one of those "know it all" types, once conducted a timber drive into this channel, ignoring advice to the contrary, only to find himself stranded with his logs in a swampy bay. The bay consequently became known as the "Lost Channel".

The Pickerel River region has always been rather remote. For centuries, it was known only to Indians and fur traders, until the 1870s, when a two-pronged assault was launched: by lumbermen pushing inland from Georgian Bay, and by settlers arriving from the south. Around 1875, a road of sorts, known as the Pickerel Hills Road, was blazed by one of the lumber companies from Glenila, seven miles north of Dunchurch, up to the modern site of Loring, a distance of 42 miles. Several settlers, despairing of the sandy soil at Glenila, moved up this road, but for many years they were terribly isolated, and had to carry in all their provisions from Dunchurch, on their backs. Gradually things improved. A post office was opened at Loring, which took its name from the wife of the local Member of Parliament. A store and a school followed in 1885, then another store and a blacksmith shop in 1886. At the same time, the Northern Railway was extended north through Trout Creek and Callander, and soon another tote road was opened from Trout Creek to Commanda, on the Nipissing Road, and then east to Arnstein and Loring. This made it possible to team supplies in from Trout Creek Station to Loring, a distance of 42 miles, instead of hauling everything in from Parry Sound, 65 miles away. By about 1900, the Village of Loring could boast two sawmills, a few shops, one hotel, and a population of about 110.

The new roads also increased the flexibility of the lumber companies. By the 1880s, at least five firms, some American, were operating dozens of camps in the region, cutting logs and feeding them into the rivers to get them to the mills on Georgian Bay. Dams were built to raise the levels of Wilson Lake and Dollars Lake.

Horse-powered capstans mounted on cribs were still the standard means of moving the log booms across these lakes, although, before the turn of the century, the Turner Lumber Company imported an alligator called the *Traveller* from Georgian Bay to Wilson Lake to speed up the process. The *Traveller* could, of course, portage herself past the local dams. For several years, she was the only steamboat on the waterway.

The routes were shaken up again in 1906; this time by the Canadian Northern Railway and the C.P.R., which were simultaneously extended from the Sudbury basin to Muskoka and southern Ontario by way of the Town of Parry Sound. Suddenly, the logs bound for Georgian Bay could be collected by rail, wherever the tracks bridged the rivers, or wherever stations might be erected. Thus Mowat Station, Salines (now Drocourt), Ardbeg, Boakview and Waubamik, to name only a few, all became important collection and distribution points. Salines is only 26 miles

PICKEREL RIVER SYSTEM
Main Steamboat Routes

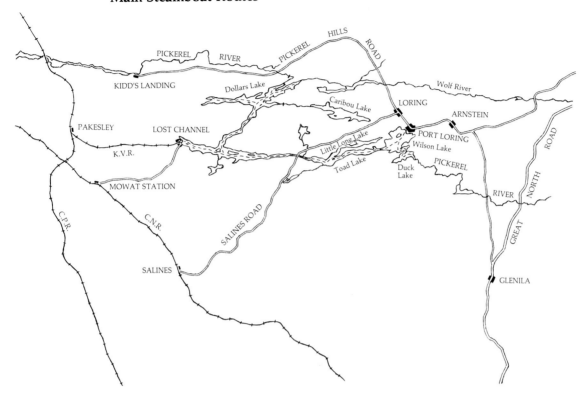

from Loring, and in 1908, a new road was built to connect them, but this did not work well, since the station at Salines was only a flag stop. As a rule, the road was used mostly in winter.

This, briefly, was the general picture of transport around the Pickerel River region before the coming of the Waltons.

Captain Arthur Walton and his family moved to Magnetawan in 1890 and soon had a couple of steamboats freighting and towing everywhere from Burks Falls to Ahmic Harbour. In 1911, however, the Waltons, apparently unable to compete with A. A. Agar, gave up and sold their last steamer to him. At a mere 68 years of age, Arthur Walton was in no mood for retirement and since steamboating was always in his blood, he and his sons began prospecting for some new region that could use a boat service. In 1912, they visited Loring, met the local lumber barons (who needed tugs), and decided that the prospects of the area were good. They purchased a few houses and a small sawmill near Wilson Lake, just south of Loring, then sold their homes and surplus possessions at Magnetawan and prepared to move. Just after freeze-up they trekked up the Nipissing Road, hauling all their goods by sleigh, including a new steam engine and boiler ordered from the Waterous Company of Brantford. There, by the desolate, lonely shores of Wilson Lake, they set to work, cutting wood, buying timber and chopping ice for summertime use. A few months later, their wives and children joined them. Docks and sheds were also built, and work was started on a new steamboat, at what was now being called "Walton's Landing" on Wilson Lake. (The boiler was used to steam the planks.)

The steamer, launched in 1913, was a rather ungainly big craft, built of solid white oak, and registered at 51.67 tons. The locals dubbed her 'the Ark', and wondered when the Flood was coming. She was 69 feet in length by 14.7 in beam, but she drew only 3.9 feet of water, and had an especially shallow draft at the bow, to simplify landing where docks were not available. The big steeple compound engine and Polson boiler, good for 8.1 hp, gave the vessel a speed of about ten miles per hour. Though hardly a beauty, the new ship was very practical, and could carry over 100 passengers and a lot of freight. She was named the *Kawigamog* ("where the waters turn back"), the original Ojibwa name for Lost Channel.

The *Kawigamog*, though still lacking a deck or superstructure, was deemed ready for launching on June 4th. A large crowd, including people from Loring, Arnstein and Golden Valley, all gathered to witness the event, while the schools declared the day a holiday. The vessel's brass valves shone and the boiler gleamed in the sun. A grey blanket covered the bow, until Captain Walton pulled it away to reveal the name beneath. His wife Becky then broke the bottle, and with Edgar Walton at the wheel, the big craft slid down the greased skid-ways into the water. Within a short time his brother Will, down in the engine room, had steam up. Two mischievous youngsters were found "stowing away" on board during the launching, and were afterwards put to work applying pitch to the upper parts of the hull.

At first the *Kawigamog* could operate only as far as the Wilson Lake dam. Within a year, however, Captain Walton managed to persuade the Ontario government to take over and rebuild the lumbermen's dam at the outlet of Dollars Lake, raising the levels so that Wilson and Dollars Lakes would henceforth be maintained at the same level, and the Wilson Lake dam could be removed. This cleared the route direct to Lost Channel. Instead of having to team goods in from Trout Creek or Salines Station, forwarders could now collect their provisions at Mowat Station and haul them over a twelve mile tote road to Lost Channel. Here the *Kawigamog* took over. This was far superior to any previous arrangement, but the road to Lost Channel, which the Waltons helped to build, was so rough that merchandise often got broken in transit.

The effects of the new service soon became evident. At Lost Channel, the Waltons built a storehouse and a wharf; at the other end they erected a sawmill and petitioned for a post office at Walton's Landing, which was renamed Port Loring at Arthur Walton's suggestion. Soon, Port Loring had a new hotel, a store, a church and a school, and began to assume the appearance of a village; today it has about 300 inhabitants. All this was bitterly resented by the residents of Loring proper, who did not relish the rise of a rival community right next door, and for many years, people from Port Loring might be subjected to insults and catcalls at the neighbouring village, and vice-versa. Eventually the merging of their two respective Presbyterian churches into one helped to heal the breach.

The steamer usually ran six days a week, leaving Port Loring for Lost Channel and back, under the command of Captain Walton, or one of his sons. She could make the trip one way in just two hours, but as the number of stops increased the average trip took three hours. Sometimes she moved surplus cargoes such as flour, feed and lumber in scows. With the advent of winter, a three-point plow was attached to her bow: with that she could buck her way through ice three inches thick, and clear a passage for the local tugs. Sometimes people walked out on the ice in winter to meet the steamer and collect the mail. Also the *Kawigamog* served as a part-time towboat, though, as the years went by, the various lumber companies began importing their own tugs, reducing the role of the big steamer.

One of the *Kawigamog*'s first assignments was to tow a block of 8,000 pine logs from the outlet of Caribou Lake to George Bruce's mill at Bruce's Bay, near Lost Channel. Payment was to be by the hour. It took about six hours to move the logs. On the way, however, Patrick McKelvie, the drive foreman, demanded that the tow be delivered direct to the mill. Captain Edgar Walton suggested leaving the logs at the entrance to the bay, and letting the tail wind carry them the rest of the way: this would shorten the towing time and save Mr. Bruce some money, but McKelvie wouldn't hear of it. The Waltons shrugged, and did as he ordered. Once she arrived, however, the steamer was cornered in the bay with 8,000 logs behind her. Edgar noted this, but McKelvie didn't care. The Walton brothers demanded a meeting with the mill boss, and there they pointed out that, according to law, a vessel was considered relieved of her charge only when the tow was released and the vessel clear. That meant that the steamer's crew were entitled to continuing payment as long as their ship was unable to get out of the bay. The mill boss sharply ordered his foreman to get out there and clear a path for the boat. It took McKelvie and twelve of his men, armed with pike poles, a good four hours to open a way through the logs, and all the while the boat crew relaxed, had a leisurely lunch, and thought of all the money they were making: enough, it turned out, to pay for a new condenser from Peterborough, that the steamer needed.

In addition to all the usual navigating hazards, the *Kawigamog* had to contend with the bridge on the Salines road, which was too low to let her pass. For that reason, she had a hinged stack, and every time she approached the bridge Captain Edgar would shout the order, "Stack down!" as she glided under it. Then it was "Stack up!" and full speed ahead.

S.S. "Kawigamog", under construction at Port Loring.

S.S. "Kawigamog", on the Pickerel River.

One day in 1920, the *Kawigamog* had an unfortunate encounter with the Salines bridge. The order to lower the stack was given, as usual, but young Aubrey Walton, then aged thirteen, was distracted somehow and failed to attend to it. There followed a scraping, rending, squealing crash and an awful jolt, as the steel piping bent and twisted on impact with the span. Down below, the hands thought the steamer had gone aground. Then the engine room began filling with smoke. Curses erupted as the men groped their way out to confront a terrified, tearful Aubrey Walton. The top of the stack was wrecked, and it had to be jury-rigged for the remainder of the trip. Sometime later the bridge was raised, but meanwhile young "Daub" spent the summer working in the galley to help pay off the cost of a new stack.

Was the *Kawigamog* very successful, operating in such a little-known, sparsely settled region? Business must have been slow at first, with most of the proceeds coming from freighting. The outbreak of war in 1914 must have reduced the flow of passengers. But gradually matters improved. Local people began chartering the vessel for Sunday picnics or evening dances at Lost Channel. Hunters hired the ship to take them to their camps in the fall: at such times a cook would be engaged and meals served. What the service really needed, however, was better promotion for tourists, a few resort hotels, and easier access overland to Lost Channel. Surprisingly enough, all three ingredients were soon supplied.

The first such development was a hunting lodge, opened on the south side of the Pickerel River in 1917 by Clarence C. Courtney of Pittsburgh and his wife, who had toured the area on the *Kawigamog*. The resort, known as Kawigamog Lodge, catered primarily to hunters and anglers. The steamer, of course, brought in most of the building supplies for the lodge, and afterwards its daily allotment of milk and groceries, not to mention guests. The Courtneys made excellent hosts and soon added six cabins as annexes to their lodge. The meals were excellent, but hunting was discouraged on Sundays, to give their guides a rest!

Besides the steamer, one of the main inducements in the founding of Kawigamog Lodge was the construction of the Key Valley Railway, from Pakesley Station on the C.P.R. to Lost Channel. The new line, which extended a total of eleven miles, was undertaken by the Lauder, Spears and Howland Lumber Company, which, however, was soon bought out by the Schroeder Mills and Timber Company, who finished the job in 1918. At first, like most logging roads, the line was a mere skeleton track, without any kind of ballasting, so that trips over it were more than a little perilous and bumpy. The Key Valley Railway was built in conjunction with a large new steam sawmill at Lost Channel, also completed in 1918 and capable of cutting 140,000 board feet or 2,200 sawlogs per day. Along with the mill, the firm built a cook-house, bunkhouse, office, store and houses for its employees. In short, Lost Channel became another temporary lumber town. Before long the railway was carrying passengers as well as mill hands, in a homemade passenger car coupled onto its regular lumber trains. Later a combination passenger and baggage car was used.

The K.V.R. was highly beneficial to the tourist business as well as to lumbering. In the fall of 1919, a mere 40 hunters arrived to travel on the *Kawigamog*, but within a few years the total swelled to about 1,200. By then, the C.P.R. was dropping off one Pullman car from Toronto at Pakesley Station early every morning. Breakfast was served at the station. Then the visitors would embark on the K.V.R. for Lost Channel, board the steamer, and arrive at Kawigamog Lodge around noon. In 1922, Mr. Courtney was advertising that:

> Transportation between Pakesley and Lost Channel, an arm of Ka-Wig-A-Mog Lake, is over the Key Valley Railway, privately owned and not under the jurisdiction of the Canadian Railway Commission, hence assuming no liability for personal injury or loss of life. Fare, 50 cents each way. The trip between Lost Channel and the Lodge is by the Steamer Ka-Wig-A Mog, fare 50 cents each way, including baggage. For parties, the boat fare is paid by the Lodge and charged to guest's account.

Thus, early in the twenties, the steamer *Kawigamog* was central to an extensive and growing transport system, based on lumbering, freighting and tourism. Before long, Will Walton, who usually acted as engineer, purchased a 30 foot gas boat called the *Daisy* as a tender for the steamer.

Ka-Wig-A-Mog Lodge, on the Pickerel River.

S.S. "Kawigamog".

Older residents still recall the occasional incident aboard the *Kawigamog*. Right after the War came the very serious flu epidemic of 1919, which spread all across Canada and claimed quite a few lives. One of its targets was Will Walton, who became so ill one afternoon that he fainted at the engine controls while the steamer was docking at Bruce's Mill. With no one to reverse engines, the vessel ran right over the slab pile that served as a dock. No damage was done, but Arthur Walton ordered his twelve-year-old grandson Aubrey, who was serving aboard, to take over the engines. On the return trip the *Kawigamog* met the *Stanley Byers*, a tug owned by the Ellis and Haggart Lumber Company, and commanded at the time by Edgar Walton. Apprised of the situation, Edgar agreed to return to the *Kawigamog* as long as necessary, while arranging for a cousin to take charge of the *Stanley Byers*. Will Walton soon recovered his health.

Another time during the 1920s, the *Kawigamog* was pressed into an emergency trip. Having returned to Port Loring around 9:00 p.m. at the end of an unusually long day, the crew received word that a hunter had been shot near Toad Lake, and was being cadged out. His condition was very grave. The boatmen agreed to yet another trip to Lost Channel, amid fog so thick that some of the hands had to be stationed at the bow with pike poles to grop their way along. The steamer finally reached Lost Channel at 4:00 a.m., but the effort was in vain. The wounded hunter died in hospital at Parry Sound.

By this time the *Kawigamog* was sharing the waterway with several other steamers, all tugs. One of these, the *Douglas L.*, a 41 foot vessel listed at nine tons, was built at Port Loring in 1917 by a Parry Sound lumberman named James Ludgate, with some help from the Waltons. Most of the tugs, however, were imported from other waters. They included the *Stanley Byers* (9 tons); the *Arthur L.*, owned by the Empey Lumber Company; the *Nellie Bly* (7 tons), imported from Toronto around 1922; the *Norcross* (14 tons), owned by the Pine Lake Lumber Company; and the screw alligator *William C.* from Byng Inlet. All of these vessels appeared after the opening of the K.V.R., and some survived into the 1930s. All were sent regularly to Lost Channel and lined up for inspection, along with the *Kawigamog*. One summer's day in 1931 (which must have been a holiday!), the *Kawigamog* brought a crowd of 128 people, including most of the tug captains, into Port Loring for a baseball game. Someone in "Port", however, was busily selling "hi-wines" from Trout Creek, with the result that some of the passengers and most of the captains got drunk and were in a very sorry state for the return trip to Lost Channel.

The *Kawigamog* brought great benefits to the Pickerel River settlements, and for a time was highly profitable, but here, as elsewhere, conditions did not remain favourable to passenger steamers. The beginnings of decline set in around 1922, when the government undertook to improve the road from Trout Creek to Port Loring. Soon it was widened, graded, gravelled and relieved of its sharpest curves: in short, trucks and automobiles could now use it. Very gradually, freighting increased over this road, even as it declined on the steamer and on most other roads. Gas motorboats became available to bring tourists to Kawigamog Lodge, or hunters to their camps. Perhaps the steamer also lost its mail contract. Then came the Depression, reducing the tourist inflow drastically. The ship itself was wearing out and becoming shaky, after battering logs and deadheads so many years.

As it happened, Captain Arthur Walton did not live to see the end of the boat service he had founded. He remained active almost to the last, even taking the wheel at the age of 86, but finally in October, 1929, the old mariner began to fail. He died at his home on October 19, 1929, and was buried, by his own request, at Arnstein. Five years later, his devoted wife Becky was laid beside him.

His steamer, the *Kawigamog*, did not long outlive him either. She was bequeathed to his sons, but Will Walton promptly sold out his share, leaving the vessel to Edgar, who carried on with her for about another three years. Her last season was probably 1932, but after that the old ship was decommissioned and converted into a houseboat. Today her remains lie beneath a boat house at Port Loring. Captain Edgar Walton carried on with lumbering, prospecting and running boats on other waterways before his retirement and death in 1951. His brother Will, who had left the region, outlived him, but descendants of the Waltons still reside in the vicinity of Port Loring to this day.

The lumber trade, having exhausted all the local timber limits, moved on during the thirties. In 1933, the big sawmill at Lost Channel was closed and dismantled, leaving yet another ghost town, some of whose remains are still prominent: only the old Schroeder boardinghouse is still in use, as a summer lodge. As Lost Channel died, the Key Valley Railway died with it, though most of its roadbed still serves as a cottage access road. One by one, the local tugs that served the lumber trade either disappeared or were moved to other waters. Quietly and unobtrusively, steamboating died out on the Pickerel River.

S.S. "Sagamo" at the Natural Park (old wharf), 1924.

CHAPTER 6
The Muskoka Lakes Steamers During the "Roaring Twenties" (1920-1928)

On the south Muskoka Lakes, the Muskoka Navigation Company steamers were striving to cope with the accelerating tempo of the twenties. The War was over at last, and so was the brief depression that followed. People now felt entitled to indulge themselves a little in spending sprees, faster individual mobility, and livelier entertainment to celebrate the return of good times, and to compensate for all the privations of wartime and the uncertainties of the economy. Stock market speculations became an exciting pastime. Cigarette smoking flourished. Skirts became progressively shorter, clothing looser and more comfortable. Bathing suits ceased to resemble deep-sea diving gear. Chamber music gave way to ragtime, and the waltz to the tango. The radio superseded the record player; travelling shows succumbed to motion pictures, and faithful old Dobbin abdicated in favour of the Model T. Cities were paving their streets, and soon the principal roads between the cities were being paved too. Very gradually, passenger rail traffic declined, while the government was forced to consolidate thousands of miles of overextended and bankrupt railway lines into a new publicly-owned system called the Canadian National Railways, in the hope that they wouldn't lose too much money. On the whole, a lively and prosperous decade.

In Muskoka, it was a period of reorganization. The forest-related industries, especially sawmilling and shingle manufacturing, were rapidly dying out, while both tanneries at Bracebridge shut down before 1930, leaving only the Huntsville plant still operating. The emphasis was now on trying to save what remained of the forests. A few manufacturing industries helped to take up the slack, though it has always been a problem to persuade large companies to locate branch plants so far from the cities. The resorts, now recognized as fundamental to the district economy, continued to flourish as tourists spent more and more money in Canada, a trend that continued until 1928.

The Muskoka Navigation Company also prospered during the twenties, because times in general were prosperous. However, to the observant, a number of disquieting trends could be discerned. The lakes now swarmed with private motorboats, almost all of them gas powered. Many were built locally by such firms as the Duke, Minett and Ditchburn Boat Building Companies. Nor were motorboats limited to the well-to-do. Since 1906, a Swedish-American named Ole Evinrude had been perfecting and selling a new device known as the outboard motor, which democratized motorboating as surely as the Model T had democratized driving. Despite the state of the roads, automobiles were becoming more and more common. W.F. Wasley was once heard to comment that these contraptions would never succeed in taking much business away from the steamers, 'because it was impossible to build good roads in Muskoka', but this prediction turned more and more into a bitter joke among the Company employees.

Outside of the Muskoka Lakes, the trends in passenger steamboating were not encouraging. In Southern Ontario, where road and rail networks were much more extensive than in Muskoka, steamers on the inland waterways were becoming very rare. All but one of the steamboat companies on the Kawartha Lakes had gone out of business before the War; only the Stoney Lake Navigation Company still ran four small steamers from Lakefield. Only a single passenger steamer continued to sail from Lindsay during the twenties, and only one on the Rideau. All but a few of the big palace steamers on the Ottawa River were gone, while the last large excursion steamer on Lake Simcoe was laid up permanently in 1926. The remoteness of Muskoka and Stoney Lake meant that paved roads took longer to reach them. The resort hotels in both areas continued to rely on steamboats to bring in most of their guests and provisions, just as they both relied on superlative scenic attractiveness to lure thousands of city folk into a temporary escape to the country. For these and other reasons, steamboating survived and even flourished within the Shield, while it was wilting and dying out in most other parts of the province.

H.R.H. The Duke of Devonshire, Governor-General, boarding the S.S. "Cherokee" at Muskoka
Wharf, with his Duchess and W.F. Wasley (1918)
Courtesy, *Mrs, Irene Dickson*, Willowdale

At the start of the decade, the Muskoka Navigation Company still had six steamers in
commission: they were, the *Sagamo, Cherokee, Medora, Islander, Ahmic* and *Oriole*. Gone were
the *Kenozha* and *Charlie M.*, both destroyed by fire, while the *Nipissing* was immobilized with
ruined machinery. The only real competition in the passenger business came from Captain
Archer, who was now running the steam yacht *Llano*, primarily between Bracebridge and
Browning Island. Finding the *Llano* a trifle tippy, the Captain personally built false sides around
the hull amidships to broaden her out. Around 1920, Captain Archer teamed up with Bill Heintz,
a steam engineer by training, to found the Archer-Heintz Lake Service Company Ltd. of
Bracebridge. That same year they purchased the steam yacht *Mildred* from the daughter of the
deceased E.R. Woods and brought the 70 foot vessel down from Lake Rosseau to supplement the
Llano. Captain Archer then took charge of the *Mildred* (which could take about 40 passengers),
along with a hired engineer, while Mr. Heintz and Captain Joshua Kake, former Master of the
Oriole, operated the *Llano*; often running special charters to remote corners of the lakes where the
big ships did not call.

This pattern persisted until the spring of 1925. Then disaster struck. Early on the morning of
May 4, another waterfront fire at Bracebridge gutted four boat-houses, along with four launches,
one sailboat, various stores and equipment, and the steamer *Llano*. (The *Mildred*, fortunately,
had her own boat-house at Browning Island.) There was little insurance, but the *Llano* was not a
total loss: her steel frame and machinery were subsequently sold to J.A. Scriver, who rebuilt the
vessel as a workboat on the Huntsville lakes. Thereafter the Archers made do with the *Mildred*

Steam Yacht "Llano".

Steam Yacht "Mildred", on the Muskoka River.
Courtesy, *Mr. Ken Beaumont*, Toronto

alone. Before long, Captain Archer bought out his partner, who left to run a fishing boat at Port Elgin. Captain Kake, who had become a victim of tuberculosis, also left the area after the loss of the *Llano* and died about 1927.

Until 1921 there were four large supply boats on the Muskoka Lakes, but in that year the number dropped to three: the *Alporto*, *Mink* and *Newminko*. The *Constance* had also been sailing as an adjunct to a store in Rosseau, but then the vessel passed into receivership. Apparently the new owners engaged the Navigation Company to give her a thorough refit at the Gravenhurst yards; this was done, but the bill came to nearly $2,000, about three times what the job was expected to cost. Unable or unwilling to pay, the owners "sold" the boat to the Navigation Company, which thus involuntarily acquired another steamer. The Company kept the *Constance* for the next four years, using her to deliver freight and carry small groups of passengers, chiefly to smaller docks unfrequented by the larger ships. But there was little work for her in that line, and in 1927 she was sold to Captain James Campbell, who had recently worn out both the *Nymph* and the *Grace M.* Campbell used the *Constance* as a scow boat until 1934, when she passed to Captain Levi Fraser as the successor to the *Queen of the Isles*.

After the *Constance* ceased to serve as a supply boat, the Hanna Company more or less had the lakes to themselves, except for the *Alporto*. Soon the Port Carling firm began sending the *Mink* down to Lake Muskoka on a regular basis, leaving the *Newminko* to do the rounds on the upper lakes. William Hanna himself died on July 6, 1923, at the age of 75, active to the last, but his sons Fred and Wyman carried on the business with a few partners for the next two decades.

The steamer *Newminko* had a rather long life, which was quite remarkable, considering the number of scrapes and accidents she endured. We have already noted how she burned at Port Carling in 1915 and had to be rebuilt. About the year 1920, she experienced another mishap. She was returning home from Windermere one evening, with only a company clerk at the wheel: Captain McCulley was feeling ill and went to lie down, leaving instructions that he was to be notified when the boat reached the Indian River. Near the entrance to the river, the vessel ran onto a flat rock, heaved up and slipped off, only to ground on another rock. By the time the Captain reached the wheelhouse, it was too late. She was not damaged, but she could not clear the shoal under her own power. It required one tug, two scows and several beams to get her off. Later on, during the thirties especially, the accident-prone propeller was to repeat such incidents with depressing frequency.

The Navigation Company steamer *Islander* continued to have her share of adventures. One morning in early October, 1920, she left Stanley House as usual for Port Carling, under Captain A.P. Larson, with Captain Neil MacNaughton of Bracebridge acting as mate. MacNaughton was at the wheel when the vessel reached Port Sandfield. As she passed the swing bridge, he noted that there was mail to be collected, but no passengers. Accordingly he rang for "stop engines" until the mail bag could be thrown aboard, then signalled "forward". The engineer, however, became confused and replied with "reverse"! The steamer began to back up, as the bridge was closing behind her. MacNaughton again rang for forward, but now it was too late. With a grinding crunch the boat struck the bridge, snapping the rear flagstaff and several stanchions and splintering the end of the hurricane deck into matchwood. Needless to say, the *Islander* ran no more trips that season. MacNaughton, who had gained his Master's Certificate only the year before, decided to quit his post and enter the forestry service as a Provincial Game Warden. This was a year-round job that paid better than $40.00 a month, plus board!

From 1907 until his retirement in 1927, Captain Edward McAlpine was usually in charge of the *Medora*. During the 1920s he, too, has occasional trouble, both because the *Medora* was somewhat cumbersome, and also because the Engineer was rather elderly, and partially deaf. Swift, efficient teamwork between the Wheelsman and the Engineer is a 'sine qua non' in the safe operation of a steamship. Once, in 1921, the big ship approached the brand new wharf at Nepahwin-Gregory too fast, perhaps because the Engineer got his signals confused. The collision between boat and dock pushed the $1,000 structure several feet sideways off its cribwork. Who ended up paying for repairs is not certain. In 1926, the *Medora* was on her way downstream from Port Carling at half speed, and had just reached Foreman's Narrows on the river, when someone on the main deck rang the dinner bell. Hearing it, the old Engineer mistook it for a "full ahead"

Str. "Constance", around 1925.
The former supply steamer is now owned by the Navigation Company, whose symbol appears on the stack.

Supply Steamer "Newminko", leaving Ferndale House, Lake Rosseau.

S.S. "Islander", on Lake Joseph.

S.S. "Islander", on the Muskoka River.
Courtesy, *Mrs. Irene Dickson*

S.S. "Medora", at new Windsor Hotel, Bala.
Courtesy, *Tweedsmuir Women's Institute*, Bala

signal and reacted accordingly. To Captain McAlpine's shocked disbelief, the steamer gave a surge of speed and power: he wrestled with the wheel, but couldn't maintain control, and the steamer ran herself aground, bow first, in the mud below Foreman's Bay. It took the assistance of the *Cherokee* to drag her off.

The *Cherokee* became a witness to another dramatic event at Rossclair in midsummer of 1924. That season sizzled with heat waves, which was fine for tourists but left the bush as dry as tinder. One morning around 11:00 the steamer, now under Captain William Bradshaw, was leaving Beaumaris for Bala to connect with the noon trains, when smoke was seen in the distance, indicating a forest fire somewhere north of Rossclair. Despite the smoke, no one seemed concerned about it when she called as usual at the Rossclair wharf. Only a handful of guests at the hotel boarded the steamer, which resumed her run. Later, about 2:00 p.m., she left Bala on schedule, called at Bala Park, then continued past Pleasant View and Mortimer's Point without making any stops. With neither mail nor passengers on hand for it, there was no plan to call again at Rossclair either, but by now the smoke was getting pretty dense, and Captain Bradshaw decided that perhaps he'd better take another look before proceeding to Beaumaris. It was well that he did, because by 3:00 p.m. when he arrived, the scene looked very different from the morning. The hotel was now a mass of flames, and a large crowd had flocked to the wharf and the lawn between the hotel and the water, with whatever valuables they had been able to save. Almost everyone, except the proprietor, crowded aboard the ship, which backed away and set a course for Beaumaris; later the *Medora* arrived and took most of them to Gravenhurst. The evacuation was not really a very heroic affair, as neither the ship nor the people were ever in danger; the *Cherokee* just happened to be the first boat passing. Without any doubt, though, everyone was glad to see her.

Early in the 1920s, there was a considerable turnover of officers working for the Navigation Company. Old Commodore Bailey, who had started off as a deckhand on the *Wenonah* in 1867 and risen to be Master of the *Sagamo* in 1906, now reluctantly retired after the season of 1922, ending a brilliant career lasting 55 years. Captain Henry, now 70 and in failing health, was obliged to relinquish his beloved *Cherokee* to Captain Bradshaw. Both officers received a modest pension from the Navigation Company, which also saw fit to raise all the Captains' pay by 20% at the same time. Captain Henry survived less than four more years, but Bailey lived on for another sixteen. Often the devoted old man might be seen heading down to the Gravenhurst dockyards on a windy evening, cane and lantern in hand, to make sure his beloved steamers were safely secured for the night. What stories he used to tell his grandchildren around the fireside—stories about cold, dark nights out on the forlorn expanses of the Muskoka Lakes, facing fog, ice, logs, forest fires, snowstorms, wild animals and surly log-drivers, with only a few shivering fellow

Rossclair Hotel, Lake Muskoka.

Rossclair Hotel fire, 1924

Captain John Henry,
long time Master of the "Cherokee".

Commodore George Bailey,
first Master of the "Sagamo".

Captain Ralph Lee,
second Master of the "Sagamo".

crew-members for company. Muskoka had been but a forested wilderness when he first saw it. So much had happened since then. So many shipmates and fellow officers were gone. A few had taken up new careers. Captain William Board of the *Mink* had left the waves for the West in 1912, seeking greener pastures. Captain Parlett had left to go into the lumber business at Bracebridge, Captain MacNaughton had gone into forestry, and in 1915 Captain Jackson resigned to take up a new life as a farmer near Ziska, just west of Bracebridge. Most officers, though, were like Bailey; devoting their lives to steamboating, and never wishing for another job.

Fortunately, a rising generation of younger men was stepping forward to fill the shoes vacated by the old. Captain Ralph Lee, who had been Mate under Bailey since the loss of the *Kenozha*, now took over as Master of the *Sagamo*. He soon rose in rank to Commodore and remained on the flagship until the end of the Second World War. Bradshaw was now on the *Cherokee*: he was a smart, efficient officer, almost as good with the engines as he was with the wheel. In 1928, Captain Andy Corbett returned from the Huntsville lakes to follow McAlpine on the *Medora*.

Though detailed records are lacking, there is every reason to believe that, by 1924, the Navigation Company had recovered very nicely from the upset of the War. Though we cannot always credit the glowing testimonials of the period press, we cannot discount the generally prosperous times, the steady increase in the number of American visitors (until 1929), and the resumption of dividend payments by the Company. Perhaps the most convincing evidence, however, was the decision by Messrs. MacLean and Wasley that six steamers were no longer sufficient. Maybe the Manager also felt that a larger vessel than the *Islander* was needed for the run to Bracebridge. Whatever the reasons, it was decided to expand the fleet once more.

How to go about acquiring a new ship? Attention now reverted to the retired steamer *Nipissing*, idle at the Gravenhurst dockyards since 1914. The *Nipissing* was in sorry shape by now and her machinery was useless, but her sturdy old iron hull, and even portions of her superstructure, were still sound. What the Company wanted was another propeller steamer, but there was no reason why the old side-wheeler could not be remodelled that way, and in the fall of 1924 she was towed across to Muskoka Wharf, where she spent the winter. Two secondhand reciprocating engines plus a new stack and a brand new Scotch marine boiler were ordered, delivered and installed. The following spring the vessel was towed back to the yards and dry-docked. The pontoons and sidewalls were removed, two new propeller shafts installed, and most of the upper works rebuilt. Most of the two lower decks were retained, as well as the steering wheel and the wooden phoenix that Captain Bailey had carved for the old ship. What took form, after several months of work, was a handsomely proportioned steamer with two lounge cabins on the promenade deck, designed for daytime cruising. She was relaunched in June, and following trials, it was announced that she would make her first public cruise in July.

Originally the rebuilt craft was to continue to be known as the *Nipissing*, but the new version bore so little resemblance to the old that everyone agreed she must have a new name. (Old-timers were never in any doubt as to her identity, though: the old chime whistle of the *Nipissing* was unmistakable!) Since Indian names were a time-honoured tradition for Company ships, it was decided to call her the *Segwun*; an Ojibwa word meaning "springtime".

Re-registered at 168.39 tons, the *Segwun* set off for Bracebridge for the first time on July 9, 1925, with a crew of fifteen and a small party on board. She was greeted everywhere with applause and fanfare. Her first commander was the amiable Captain A. Peter Larson of Gravenhurst, son of Captain Hans Larson, who had retired in 1913. Though smaller than the *Sagamo*, *Cherokee* and *Medora* and much less ornate, the *Segwun* soon became very popular with the public. On short runs, she was probably the fastest in the fleet, planing smoothly through the water, in contrast with the *Cherokee*, which had a tendency to plow. The *Segwun*'s main defect was her tendency to wander, requiring continual adjustments of the helm to keep her on course: perhaps the propellers were set a little too far forward of the rudder. Despite this shortcoming, the *Segwun* proved a very useful vessel, easily capable of carrying 250 passengers.

The palatial *Sagamo*, meanwhile, was carrying on as usual every summer, receiving whistle salutes from all her sister ships whenever she met them. Since her maiden season of 1907, the "Big Chief" had missed only two scheduled trips, both in 1909, when she was dry-docked to repair a bent rudder shaft. On September 5, 1924, she was given the special honour of taking Governor

S.S. "Segwun", under construction in 1925.

S.S. "Segwun", on her maiden trip to Bracebridge, July 9, 1925.
The new ship still carries the phoenix inherited from the "Nipissing" on her pilothouse.

S.S. "Sagamo", docked at Rostrevor, 1924.
Courtesy, Mrs. Irene Dickson, Willowdale

S.S. "Sagamo", ablaze at her dock, Sept. 9, 1925.

S.S. "Sagamo", after the fire of 1925.

General Lord Byng and his entourage on a short cruise around Lake Muskoka, while Mr. and Mrs. Wasley acted as hosts. Until the end of the following summer, there was hardly a cloud in the sky.

Then it happened. Just over a year after Lord Byng's tour, and for the third time in eight years, fire struck. This time it was the *Sagamo*. It all started about 8:50, on the morning of September 9, 1925. The *Sagamo* had just finished for the season, and was tied up at the dockyards at Gravenhurst, where she was being laid up for the winter. Part of the crew was aboard, along with Captain Lee, the stewardess and the kitchen staff, and there was still a little steam up to run the pumps. During operations, one of the workmen put a container of cylinder oil on top of the stove in the galley. He did not realize that the stove was hot. The oil, unattended, boiled over and burst into flame, and by the time it was noticed, the fire was out of control. The alarm was raised, and everyone hastily got off, but there was little they could do. The Gravenhurst fire brigade rushed to the scene and turned on the hoses, but the fire, fanned by a stiff breeze from the south, rapidly engulfed the steamer. Except for the steel portions, the vessel was completely destroyed forward and amidships, and little remained of the wooden superstructure except the dining saloon. The damage was estimated at $75,000.

W. F. Wasley wasted little time with laments. He ordered the loose debris removed at once, and discovered that the engines and boilers were essentially unhurt. The ship, valued at $175,000, was partially insured, and the Manager called the principal shareholders of the Company the following day and got their approval to rebuild. A naval architect was hired to prepare plans, and a temporary cabin was built over the openings in the deck.

Reports disagree as to what happened next. Some say that two weeks elapsed without the architect having anything to show; others that tentative plans were drawn up, which didn't fit the hull. Whatever the reason, the Manager grew impatient, fired the architect, and sketched out his own rough plans on a piece of brown paper: these became the basis of the design of the new *Sagamo*. Perhaps secretly, Wasley may have regarded the fire as a blessing in disguise, in that it gave him the chance to incorporate something entirely new into the ship. He introduced fifteen stateroom cabins, enough for 40 patrons to sleep aboard the steamer if they chose, instead of being obliged to get up at 6:30 in the morning to board the boat, as before.

Work proceeded all winter, under the supervision of Yardmaster Charles Bonnis of Gravenhurst, who had lately fitted out the *Segwun*. A steel framework of angle-iron was used to support the new decks. Gradually the new upper works took form, and the *Sagamo* was ready to go again by the following July. She missed, in fact, only a few days of sailing in 1926, although minor work continued throughout the season. It took a little time, too, before tiny bits of charred wood stopped appearing all around the main deck!

The new *Sagamo* looked quite different from the old, and in some respects she was a little less attractive. The aft lounge and open spaces amidships on the promenade deck were now turned into staterooms, as well as most of the upper deck, giving her a rather boxy exterior. For a year or two after the rebuild, she continued to feature the small aft cabin at the stern of the promenade

R.M.S. "Sagamo", newly rebuilt after the fire of 1925. Note the small cabin, soon removed, on the aft end of the second deck above the dining room.
Courtesy, *Port Carling Museum*

Engine room, S.S. "Sagamo".
The view, facing the port side, shows the engine gauges (far right) and the reverse levers and a cylinder head on one engine (lower left).
Courtesy, *Mr. Brian Westhouse*, Parry Sound

In this view, facing aft, can be seen the engine-room telegraphs or chadburns (upperleft), and below them, the reverse levers for the engines.
Courtesy, *Mr. Brian Westhouse*, Parry Sound

S.S. "Sagamo", approaching Port Carling, 1928.

deck, which like the dining room below had survived the fire, but this was soon removed. The new rectangular pilothouse was mounted on top of the bridge, rather than in front of it as before, to offer greater visibility. Captain Lee did not appreciate the new arrangement, which eliminated the extra steering post set above the old pilothouse in the open air, where he and Bailey had preferred to steer in pleasant weather. Also, in an effort to decorate the new ship a little, the wooden phoenix carried by the *Segwun* was transferred to the pilothouse of the *Sagamo*, over the objections of Captain Bailey, who protested that he had carved it for the *Nipissing*. We might add that the new staterooms, featuring real beds with box springs, drop tables and toilet facilities, soon proved so popular that in the fall of 1926 the *Cherokee* was also equipped with them for the Sunset Cruise. This meant lengthening her upper deckcabin aft and removing the small cabin over the dining room at the stern.

The season of 1926 was another good year for the Navigation Company, which was again running seven steamers. The most memorable event for the boatmen was probably the violent wind and rain storm that lashed the lakes on the morning of August 21st, disrupting schedules for several of the boats. The *Sagamo* and *Cherokee* proceeded no farther than Port Carling that day, while the *Segwun* remained tied up at Bala. The others managed to complete their rounds, despite the weather.

By this time the little steamer *Oriole*, now the last survivor of the "second generation" steamboats of the Muskoka fleet, was reaching the end of her days. She had been operating faithfully since 1886, a total of 41 seasons (lately on the two upper lakes), under at least eight different captains, but now it was evident that her time had come, and after the autumn of 1926, Muskoka heard her familiar shrill whistle no more. She lingered in retirement at Gravenhurst for one more year, but by the spring of 1928, she had been broken up, the hull probably scuttled in Muskoka Bay, which has become the final resting place of many steamers. No one seems to know what became of the little wooden bird that perched on the dome of her pilothouse.

Meanwhile, a replacement was required for the *Oriole*, and the Navigation Company had already found one. With increasing public mobility around the lakes, and perhaps the opening of new stores here and there, the supply boat business was beginning to slacken, such that by

S.S. "Cherokee", (Second Version) at Foots Bay.
The Sunset Cruiser's upper deck has also been fitted out with staterooms.

S.S. "Oriole", last of the second generation Muskoka Steamboats.
Courtesy, *Mr. Bill Gray*, Port Sandfield

S.S. "Oriole".
Courtesy, "Public Archives of Canada" 129955

mid-decade the Hanna Company of Port Carling decided that one steamer would suffice. The firm then carried on with only its larger vessel, the *Newminko*; leaving the *Mink* tied up for a season or two at Port Carling. Thus, when the Navigation Company made inquiries about buying the *Mink*, the Hannas were happy to agree. In June of 1927, the shabby little steamer was towed away for a visit to the Gravenhurst shipyards, to be overhauled and remodelled into a passenger boat, chiefly by enclosing the amidships portion of the upper deck to create a new lounge cabin. Desiring to give the little vessel a new name, Mr. Wasley offered a free season's pass on the boats as a prize for anyone who could suggest a suitable Indian name, preferably not exceeding six letters and not easily abbreviatable (as in "Sag" for *Sagamo*), but the appeal failed, and the Assistant Manager, Robert Sleeth of Gravenhurst, had to rummage through a number of source books to find something. Finally it was decided to call her the *Waome*, an Ojibwa word meaning "water lily", and on May 28, 1928 the new name was duly registered.

The *Waome*, still listed at 60 tons, entered service in 1927. She was about the same size as the *Ahmic*, although a trifle less attractive, but within a few years the height of her stack was raised, making her more impressive. Like the *Ahmic*, the *Waome* was used as an auxiliary vessel, handling local calls except at the opening and closing of the seasons, when one of the two usually sustained the entire boat service unassisted. The *Waome*'s first Master was Captain Charles William Henshaw of West Gravenhurst, who had been a boatman since 1885; serving on tugs such as the *Kate Murray*, *Sunbeam*, *Rosseau*, *Bertha May* and *Grace M.*, as well as supply boats like the *Edith May* and the *Constance* and yachts such as the *Naiad*, *Priscilla* and *Willoudee*, and of course the *Oriole*. Though Henshaw would also command steamers like the *Segwun*, he felt most at home on the smaller boats. His career was destined to end, tragically, on the *Waome* in 1934, while the *Waome* herself turned out to be the last steamer built or acquired by the Muskoka Navigation Company.

The *Waome* was not spared the occasional misadventure before her demise. During the fall of 1927, she managed to pile up on a rock in the vicinity of Bala Bay. She slipped off again, with a hole under the bow, and the crew had to turn on the pumps and jam a blanket into the opening to keep her afloat. She returned to Gravenhurst safely, while the *Ahmic* had to be brought out of winter quarters to take her place. It was all part of the perils of steamboating.

The season of 1927 was also a bad one for the *Islander*. One spring morning, before the larger steamers were running, the little ship, commanded by Captain George ("Geordie") Stephen of Port Carling, had trouble as she was leaving the dock at Redwood on Lake Joseph. Just as she was reversing engines, there was a sudden jolt and the propeller shaft began burrilling. The lines were left attached while the purser and a deckhand borrowed a boat and took a look under the fantail. They found that the propeller shaft had broken, and the two of them had to row across the lake to Elgin House to telephone Gravenhurst. W.F. Wasley despatched the *Segwun*, which was then being repainted at the docks, up the lakes to bring the *Islander* home. As a result, the *Segwun* began the season ahead of schedule, while the *Islander* spent ten days in dry dock getting a new shaft.

Later that summer, the unlucky *Islander* got into another scrape; a minor one, though it caused a wave of anxiety at the time. The small steamer was calling at Clevelands House on a windy afternoon, and it happened that the wharf there had a protruding timber, sheathed with plate steel, intended to protect the side of the cribwork. Somehow, as the vessel strained at her lines at the wharf, the sharp edge ripped into her starboard sidewall, just in front of the aft gangway, and tore out four feet of planking. A gaping hole in the sidewall above the waterline did not prevent the steamer from completing her usual calls, but word spread rapidly around the lakes that the *Islander* had been holed on a rock in rough waters, and that no one knew what had happened to her. When the little steamer rejoined her sister ships at Port Carling that same afternoon, with nothing worse than a hole in her side, she caused quite a sensation. Captain Bradshaw, watching in disbelief from the bridge of the *Cherokee*, was heard to mutter, "Gol darn it! They said the ol' *Islander* had sunk and here she is!" Half the people of Bracebridge were out to see her arrive that evening, but Charles Bonnis and the yard crews, having been sent to the scene in the Company truck, had the damage repaired in less than an hour.

It was early in the twenties, shortly after assuming his new command, that Commodore Lee of the *Sagamo* made a very fruitful suggestion to W.F. Wasley. He proposed a one hundred mile

S.S. "Waome" (Original Version)

S.S. "Islander", during the 1920s.
Courtesy, *Canadian National Corporate Archives*, CP 6475

excursion cruise on all three of the lakes, to be conducted principally by the *Sagamo* for the special benefit of tourists. People should be encouraged to come to Muskoka, not just to stay at the resorts, but rather to take an all-day cruise on the steamers, or, if this were not practical, at least a half-day cruise. In short, boat trips should become an end in themselves, rather than just a means of transport to the hotels. Lee further suggested acquiring a piece of property, where passengers taking the all-day trip could go ashore and take a stroll for an hour, and proposed a site at the head of Little Lake Joseph, a large appendage to the rest of Lake Joseph. The property, then vacant, was only a stone's throw from a lovely little sheet of water called Slide Lake, so called because the lumbermen had once built a timber slide from this lake to Little Joe. Part of the shore of Slide Lake is a lofty bluff about a hundred feet high, offering a magnificent panoramic view of the sparkling little lake. Mr. Wasley came to see the site for himself, and agreed with the Captain's assessment. Following a meeting with the Board, the Manager arranged to purchase the property in 1923. A T-shaped wharf was provided, although it did not last long, and was soon replaced by a second one at the foot of an adjacent cliff. A network of broad paths and nature trails was also laid out. The site became known as the Natural Park, while Slide Lake was given the more romantic name of Mirror Lake. The new park became the midday docking point for the *Sagamo*, or any of her sister ships that might be substituting in the early or late seasons.

The new 'One Hundred Mile Cruise' (a name copyrighted by the Company) did not constitute a major disruption to the steamers' routes and services. All of the boats continued to carry freight and distribute mail as well as carry passengers. The cruise, more like 86 miles than 100, simply reflected the increasing importance of recreation as a source of profit, at a time when people had money to spend, and were often spending it on automobiles and motorboats, allowing them to get around the Muskoka Lakes independently of the steamers. Before long the '100 Mile Cruise' became famous throughout both the United States and Canada, and was one of Ontario's foremost summer tourist attractions. Eventually, as steamboating fell into decline, the Cruise became the sole reason for the operations of the boats.

As a rule, the summertime schedules for the Muskoka steamers during the 1920s were very similar to the previous decade. The flagship *Sagamo* still took the main route up the lakes, with all the other ships, except the *Medora*, acting as feeders. She left Muskoka Wharf daily about 7:00 a.m. and proceeded to Beaumaris, sometimes calling at Glen Echo Lodge and Walker's Point 'en route'. At Beaumaris, or sometimes off Horseshoe Island, at the north end of Lake Muskoka, she met the *Segwun*, coming from Bracebridge, and the *Cherokee* (and sometimes the *Ahmic*) from Bala Bay. Usually there was an exchange of mail, freight and passengers. The *Sagamo* then continued to Port Carling, where, as formerly, she connected with the *Medora*, coming down-lake from Rosseau, and the *Islander*, making her rounds on the upper lake. Passengers taking only the 'Morning Cruise' from Gravenhurst would transfer to the *Medora*. After locking through, the *Sagamo* proceeded to Windermere and the Royal Muskoka, then passed over to Clevelands House (sometimes stopping at the adjacent resorts on a flag signal), and then headed south to Port Sandfield. Once on Lake Joseph, she might call at Elgin House and Pinelands Lodge at the south

S.S. "Medora" at Rosseau.
Behind the ship is the Monteith House hotel.

end, then proceed to Redwood, Sherwood Inn, Foot's Bay, Barnesdale and other points, and finally sail past Chief's Island and Craigie Lea, at the entrance to Little Lake Joseph. At the Natural Park, she docked for about an hour. On the return trip, she might call at Hamill's Point before meeting the *Waome* at Lake Joseph Station. By late afternoon, she was back at Port Carling to connect with the *Medora*, now returning northbound. Those taking the 'Afternoon Cruise' from Gravenhurst, reversing the morning arrangement, would now transfer to the *Sagamo*. Later still, the *Sagamo* connected again with the *Segwun* and *Cherokee* (and perhaps the *Ahmic*) around Beaumaris, returning to Muskoka Wharf by 7:30 in the evening.

The *Medora's* route was to leave Rosseau at sunrise and provide a morning service down the lake to Port Carling, where she connected with the *Sagamo* and the *Islander*. Then she headed south to Beaumaris, met the *Ahmic*, and arrived at Gravenhurst around 12:15 to connect with the noon train. At 3:00 p.m. she began the 'Afternoon Cruise', made connections again at Beaumaris, rejoined the southbound *Sagamo* at Port Carling, and returned to Windermere and Rosseau. The *Cherokee* now spent the night at Bala, leaving after the arrival of the morning train and picking up passengers from the west arm of the lake, before meeting the *Sagamo* at Beaumaris. Then she returned to Bala by noon, and repeated the whole process in the afternoon. The *Segwun* was now on the *Islander's* former route from Bracebridge, and twice a day, she proceeded downriver to Beaumaris. If necessary, she also called at Milford Bay and Port Keewaydin to pick up any passengers waiting there, and met the other steamers off Horseshoe Island. By noon, she was back at Bracebridge, to repeat the run in the afternoon. The *Ahmic*, based at Torrance, looked after the local calls in that area, including Dudley, Whiteside, Mortimer's Point, Pleasant View and Rossclair, then headed for Beaumaris to meet the southbound *Medora*. She might also connect with the northbound *Sagamo*, as well as the *Cherokee* and *Segwun*. The little *Ahmic* also attended to some of the local stops around central Lake Muskoka, such as Walker's Point and Browning Island, while the slower *Medora* headed for Muskoka Wharf. The schedules were flexible to a degree: if at Beaumaris there were a hundred passengers bound for Bala, and only ten for Bracebridge, the *Ahmic* would exchange routes with the *Segwun*, so that the larger ship carried the largest loads. As a result, patrons at Bala or Bracebridge could never be sure in advance which steamer would call that day.

On the upper lakes the *Islander* now provided the local service on Lake Rosseau, and the *Waome* on Lake Joseph. The *Islander* docked overnight at Rest Harbour, near the Royal Muskoka, circled the lake to Clevelands House and Woodington House, and perhaps Gregory and Ferndale, then connected at Port Carling with the southbound *Medora* and the northbound *Sagamo*. She then made for Juddhaven and Rosseau, and other places off the route of the *Sagamo*; connecting again at Port Carling (or in mid-lake) in the late afternoon before returning to Rest Harbour. Finally, the *Waome*, based at Stanley House, would proceed down the west side of Lake Joseph twice a day, meeting the *Islander* at Port Sandfield or Woodington and the *Sagamo* usually at Barnesdale, much as the *Oriole* had been doing before her. It was quite common for the smaller steamers to exchange routes.

Let us pause for a few minutes to relive, in our imaginations, one of those sunny days when city folk, by the hundreds, converged at the great rotunda of Toronto Union Station, between ten and eleven in the morning, to begin their annual exodus from the heat and grime of the metropolis for a week or two of fresh air and relaxation on the Muskoka Lakes. Harried mothers with squalling youngsters, toting sand pails and fishing poles, jostle amid young dudes with stuffed valises and chattering girls carrying lunch baskets and dime store novels. Every so often, a young father pushes his way through the crowd waving tickets and looking for his family, or a youthful worm seller appears, peddling his wares in little tin pails. Suddenly, above the din the Station Master calls out "Muskoka Express!", and most of the throng starts flowing anxiously towards the platform gate. Huge piles of baggage—trunks, suitcases, perambulators, duffel bags, crated dogs—are being loaded onto the baggage cars by the porters. Finally, about half an hour late, the train pulls out, producing caustic comments about the C.N.R.'s 'rotten service'—not that the delay matters much, since the train doesn't arrive at Muskoka Wharf until after dark anyway, and the steamer doesn't leave until the next morning.

Dawn finds the 'Muskoka Express' at the Wharf, which now has a canopy running almost its full length for shelter. Today, however, is full of the promise of a lovely clear day. The passengers, directed by the porters, are sleepily filing off the coaches and heading across the quay; their tickets prepaid. Some of the local arrivals, getting out of their boxy little motor cars, have to file up to the station building to buy theirs.

Down at the dock, blowing off just a faint of whiff of acrid smoke, waits the *Sagamo*; her stack and pilothouse towering over the wharf canopy. During the 'wee hours' of the morning, yawning deckhands have been helping to wheel tons of coal into the cavernous stoke-hold, which the passengers never see: also, the ship has to be cleaned and tidied at the beginning of every trip. The Purser meets us at the gangway, checks the tickets, wishes us a pleasant cruise, and directs us up the grand staircase to the upper deck lounge. Here, there are plenty of seats set beside every window, but most of us choose to wander out onto the open forward deck. Exuberant youngsters elbow one another for places at the rail. Peering over the side, we watch the rest of the crowd file aboard, while the Red Caps are busy wheeling mountains of baggage and trunks up the gangplanks. Now and then, we cast a glance upwards to "B" deck, which is starting to fill with stateroom passengers who have spent the night on the steamer, and are travelling first class. Higher still, beside the bridge railing, stands the Captain in his white cap and navy blue uniform, intently watching the scene below. Presently he disappears into the pilothouse. A deep, rumbling, reverberating roar, seeming to come from the heart of the ship, shatters the quiet of the morning. A few quick kisses and farewell hugs, as the last of those taking the cruise part company with those not so lucky. The gangplanks are hauled aboard and the heavy hawsers 'cast off', under the watchful eye of the Mate. Another quick, deep-throated blast, and the *Sagamo* pulses with life as she backs majestically away from the wharf. People wave. Only a small cluster remain behind.

The steamer's stern begins to swing to starboard as she recedes from the wharf. We hear the muffled clang of the engine room telegraphs as the Captain signals for slow ahead on the starboard propeller. Slowly the big steamer pivots, swinging her bow around to the north. It's half ahead now, and the ship glides serenely forward across the bay. For newcomers taking their first cruise, the panorama of rocky, pine-clad shoreline is beautiful but bewildering. Two or three channels beckon, but which is the right one? As we pass Parker's Point to port and a few islands to starboard, an imposing complex of buff-coloured brick buildings crowning a rocky promontory comes into view. This, we hear, is the Gravenhurst Sanatorium, one of the first hospitals for consumptives to be built in Canada. Its founders felt that the cool fresh air of Muskoka would be beneficial to patients with respiratory ailments. Just beyond the Sanatorium are even loftier gray

Trains at Muskoka Wharf station.

S.S. "Sagamo", at Muskoka Wharf.

cliffs, at least 100 feet high, dropping sheer to the water. Passing them, the steamer abruptly erupts with another whistle blast, then swings sharply to starboard, entering a very narrow channel not 60 feet wide. We have reached the Gravenhurst Narrows. Quietly, with little space to spare, the ship glides through, passing a small island on which stands a handsome white wooden lighthouse. Beyond that, people gasp as they behold the wide open expanse of Lake Muskoka. We can see ahead for miles, from twenty feet above the water.

About a dozen gulls have joined us, expectantly circling the steamer; that small isolated island ahead is one of their rookeries. Some of the passengers, who have lunch baskets, try offering a little encouragement by tossing pieces of their sandwiches overboard. This, of course, is just what the birds have been waiting for, and not a morsel hits the water without a winged scavenger diving on it in a moment. The best place for watching this kind of show is, of course, off the fantail.

All this fresh morning air soon makes us hungry. Fortunately, the dinner bell is sounding now, and we troop aft through the lounge past some of the stateroom cabins to a wide, elegant stairwell descending gently to the dining room below. The doors at the bottom were closed earlier, but now we find them thrown wide open. Beyond lies a beautiful rounded wood-panelled room, glassed in with windows on three sides and set with three rows of tables with spotless white tableclothes. Pretty, attentive waitresses deftly cater to our needs. We order a full breakfast, with juice, cereal, bacon and eggs, and toast. Lingering over coffee, we watch the moving panorama of the passing shoreline.

Finally, breakfast over, we ascend to the upper deck. Some passengers have found a deck chair and a magazine or newspaper to peruse, but we are more entranced by the scenery. There are more islands now, at closer range, some bedecked with cottages. A sailboat lingers off to one side, waiting for a breeze. A motor launch drones past, leaving a white "V" in its wake. Presently the ship slackens her speed, sounds her whistle again, and swings to port, coming slowly to dock in front of a small green hotel with a red roof: it is Glen Echo. This place, we hear, is on an island: the only way to reach it is by boat. Nearly all the guests come down to the wharf to greet the ship. She pauses for just a minute to drop off the mail, then backs out again and heads away towards the open lake.

Rounding a point called Montcalm, its name painted on the rock, we follow the caped shoreline further. Another rumbling roar of the whistle as our ship turns to draw up to a small dock near a red brick house to pick up a few passengers: this time it's Walker's Point. There is a shoal adjacent to the wharf here, and the wheelsman has to be very careful. We continue past several long, narrow islands tufted with evergreens, planted mostly by cottagers. By now the sun is fully out, dispersing the morning mist and adding a sparkle to the rippling water. Cottages are more numerous now, and so are the small boats. An angler in a rowboat gives us a lethargic wave; excited speedboaters race one another, coming as close to the steamer as they dare. Off to our right now are Buck and Squirrel Islands, both adorned with splendid chateaux, ornate rock gardens and huge boat houses. We are passing the summer community known as "Millionaires' Row", composed primarily of wealthy Americans who have been coming to this area since the 1870s. Maintaining these mansions helps provide jobs for many local residents.

We are cruising past Tondern Island now, also studded with summer palaces, when suddenly a cove comes into view, containing a pretty little village. Another whistle blast, followed by a gradual swerve to starboard and a reduction in speed: obviously we are going to call here. The long concrete dock is alive with people, and the waters adjacent crawl with small craft, while to the right, crowning a grassy knoll, stands an impressive, three storey green-painted hotel. The sign on the wharf freight shed reads "Beaumaris". Another steamer, similar to our own but smaller, is waiting for us on the far side of the wharf. It's the *Cherokee*, lately arrived from Bala.

For about fifteen minutes, the waterfront scene at Beaumaris is animated chaos. Hotel guests mill around the wharf as travellers transfer from the *Cherokee* to our ship and vice-versa. Trunks and crates are loaded and unloaded, as the Purser checks his manifests. The *Segwun* should be here too, but the local agent reports that she has gone to pick up passengers at Milford Bay and Hutton House. The officers nod; that means another mid-lake transfer. The *Cherokee* gives a warning blast, then backs away from the wharf. About five minutes later, we follow. Cruising leisurely, we round the next point and find ourselves in an expanse of open water. Ahead of us, also idling, is the *Cherokee*.

We are not kept waiting long. A very small steamer, the *Ahmic*, we are told, flits into view off our port side, and heads in our direction. Meanwhile, from the inlet to our right comes a plume of black smoke, heralding the approach of the *Segwun*. Her decks are laden with a throng of people. As she draws closer, the *Sagamo* erupts with two quick blasts of her whistle. "Nothing for you today," she says. The *Segwun* replies with two of her own; she understands. Then she follows up

S.S. "Segwun", at Beaumaris.
Picture taken from aboard the S.S. "Sagamo".
Courtesy, *Mrs. Irene Dickson*, Willowdale

Cedar Wild Resort, Milford Bay (now Milford Manor).

Two sisters at a rendezvous
A mid-lake transfer betwen the "S.S. Cherokee" (left) and the "S.S. Segwun".
Courtesy, *Mr. Austin Wait*, Barrie

Mid-lake transfer on Lake Muskoka.
The Strs. "Ahmic" (left), "Cherokee", "Sagamo" and "Segwun" are gathering to exchange freight and passengers, around 1930.
Courtesy, *Mr. Austin Wait*, Barrie

Highlight of the Cruise.
In this view, the "Sagamo" is flanked by the "Segwun" (left) and the "Cherokee" and "Ahmic". Such dramatic exchanges were once routine on the Muskoka Lakes.
Courtesy, *Mr. Austin Wait*, Barrie

with four more quick blasts, meaning, "I have passengers for *you*, though." "Come alongside," replies the *Sagamo* in like manner, meanwhile telling the *Cherokee*, "You too."

The "Big Chief" now idles up to the *Cherokee*, along her starboard side. Lines are secured and the gangways aligned. A few minutes later, the *Segwun* eases up on the other side of the flagship, and the procedure is repeated. Meanwhile the little *Ahmic* is whistling in her turn: she then pulls up to the far side of the *Cherokee*. Now all four steamers are snubbed together, side by side in mid-lake, with the lordly *Sagamo* in the middle. For most passengers, this is the most dramatic moment in the cruise, as people, mail and baggage pass from one steamer to another. Some of us exchange greetings or even handshakes with those on the other ships. But the interval soon passes. The *Ahmic* has already disengaged herself and is pulling away. Now the gangplanks are removed, the lines cast off, and the *Cherokee* and *Segwun* both draw away from us. The *Cherokee* swings her bow to the west for Bala Bay, while the *Segwun* veers off to starboard and begins heading for Bracebridge. The *Ahmic* is already steaming south towards Walker's Point. The *Sagamo* now rings "forward", and we are again conscious of the familiar throb of her propellers as she pulses past tiny One Tree Island, leaving her sisters receding into the distance.

Before very long, however, the shoreline begin closing in on either side of us. At first it looks like a dead-end bay up ahead, but new vistas keep unfolding and the bay turns into a lovely, curving stream. This, of course, is the Indian River. It gets slowly narrower as we ascend it, then broadens out into a beautiful pond, only to contract again into a passage barely wide enough for our ship to squeeze through. We peer over the railing. We can see the bottom on both sides of us in places. How does the *Sagamo* manage to find enough water to keep going? Yet she glides along flawlessly, easily rounding each bend as it comes. The Purser appears now, and announces that we will soon reach Port Carling, and that those of us who are taking only the 'Morning Cruise' will have to transfer to the *Medora*. Then another rumbling roar as the *Sagamo* rounds a sharp corner and a village springs into view, filling both banks of the river. We have reached Port Carling, the "Hub of the Lakes".

As the steamer glides slowly up to the wharf below the lock chamber, we see the bridge master and his assistant cranking open the swing bridge. Just as they are finishing, our ship eases into the lock chamber, which is just barely large enough to hold her. On either side, there is only a foot of clearance. Dozens of villagers are on hand to welcome us: the steamer's arrival is a highlight of every summer's day. The lock gates swing shut behind us, and most of us decide to step ashore for a short stroll. A few youngsters scamper off to the ice cream parlour near the Navigation Company freight shed. Ahead of us, at the upper docks, awaits the *Medora*, and behind her the *Islander*. The *Islander* waits only until the pursers of the various ships have everyone and everything accounted for. Then, with a shrill blast, she bids farewell and turns away to resume her rounds on Lake Rosseau.

The lock chamber is full now, and the *Sagamo* gives a warning blast, bringing her patrons scurrying back. Then the big ship slowly glides forward, swinging her head to port. The men on the *Medora* wave to us as we pass. Proceeding upriver, we round Echo Point, giving it a wide berth, since there's a shoal in front of it, then weave our way around another bend. Soon the waters start to broaden out, and we find ourselves on Lake Rosseau.

It's full ahead now, as the '100 Mile Cruiser' sets off across another gorgeous expanse of water. We pass a cluster of little islands and then the southeast corner of Tobin's Island, beyond which stretches a four-mile vista of lovely lake scenery. Our attention is immediately focused on a big white hotel with a mauve coloured roof on the distant horizon. We appear to be heading straight towards it.

Suddenly we become conscious of a new dimension to the cruise: music! The strains of 'Danny Boy' are wafting on the breeze. Going aft to investigate, we find a regular five-man orchestra, including a pianist, violinist, xylophonist, drummer and saxophonist, gathered on the spacious after deck playing a medley of light classics and popular airs. The seats around are rapidly filling with passengers keeping time with their toes and applauding as each selection winds down. The musicians, who boarded at Port Carling, are quite happy to play any number requested, and their leader, violinist Joe Williams of Toronto, urges us to clap and sing along. Small boats are escorting us now, listening to the tunes.

Our concert is soon interrupted by another whistle blast. People jump up and crowd over to the rail to see what's up. No wonder! The distant white building which we saw earlier is now an imposing structure, crowning a grassy hilltop sloping down to a concrete wharf at which our ship is now docking. This is Windermere, one of the most popular resort-centres on the lakes. A second hotel, the Fife House, stands just off our bow to the right of Windermere House. As usual, people come flocking down, either to board the steamer or simply watch her come in. The *Sagamo* pauses here for perhaps five minutes, as freight is unloaded and people get on and off. Then the familiar warning blast, and again the lines are cast off as she backs away to resume her run.

As the cruise continues, people become spellbound and bewildered, almost mesmerized by "islands, islands everywhere". All sense of direction is lost as the *Sagamo* glides from one resort to

Windermere House, as viewed from the "Sagamo".
The small tug near the boat-house is the "Niska".
Courtesy, *Mrs. Irene Dickson*

another. She pauses at Waskada Lodge (later Wigwassan Lodge), perched on a rocky hilltop on Tobin's Island, then calls at Rostrevor, with its lovely lawns and beach, then cuts across to the majestic Royal Muskoka, crowning its lofty promontory. Ahead of us flits the *Islander*, heading up the north arm of the lake to Rosseau. The *Sagamo* docks briefly at the Royal, disembarks more passengers with their trunks, then continues westward, passing Rest Harbour, the Bluffs, and the familiar white Roman Catholic church at Morinus. She calls at Thorel House and Paignton House, then backs out and crosses over to Clevelands House wharf. This lovely spot is one of her most important calling places. From here she turns south, passing quaint old Woodington House on its lofty hilltop, and Nepahwin-Gregory. At last she slackens her speed again and approaches a narrow channel spanned by a lofty swing bridge. The whistle reverberates from the forested shores, home to numerous fine cottages. We have reached Port Sandfield, gateway to Lake Joseph.

As the bridge is slowly cranked open, the docks on both sides of the canal fill with people, watching the "Big Chief" waiting to pass through. The way is clear now, and the *Sagamo* glides slowly past the stubs of the roadway. Waiting motorists get out of their cars to watch us pass. Another lovely lake opens before us. Steaming across the bay, we pause at a wharf set at the end of a green, grassy point upon which stand the handsome buildings of Elgin House, then swing to the left down to Pinelands Lodge and Belmont House, which between them share the finest beach on the lakes. From here, we proceed northwards up the main channel of Lake Joseph. The islands here, we notice, generally seem loftier and more numerous than those on Lake Rosseau, and they rise more sharply out of the waters, which are themselves so clear that we can see way down into the depths. The Purser explains why. Lake Joseph, he says, is not fed by any tributary streams, and as a result its waters are sparkling clear. Sometimes, he insists, one can see straight down to the bottom!

On and on, the *Sagamo* continues her rounds; calling at Redwood, the Lantern Inn at Hamill's Point, and finally Foot's Bay. By this time we are hungry again, and it is good to go below once more to the dining room. While we are having tea, some truly spectacular cliff-like shoreline comes into view as we pass at close range. We are moving through the "back channel" on central Lake Joseph, past Pickerel, Bass and Perch Islands. This, we decide, must be seen from the upper decks. Reascending, we find we are passing tiny Bottle Island, off the south end of Chief's Island. Here we notice that the engines have stopped, though the ship is still moving. Peering over the side

The wharf at Royal Muskoka.
Courtesy, *Mrs. Irene Dickson*

Wharf at Clevelands House, Lake Rosseau.
Courtesy, *Canadian National Corporate Archives*, X 16758

S.S. "Sagamo" at Clevelands House.

S.S. "Sagamo" at Port Sandfield.

Lake Joseph station, Barnesdale, from the "Sagamo".
Courtesy, *Canadian National Corporate Archives*, X 10924

we can see the reason: there's a shoal about six feet below the surface, and the wheelsman is letting the stern glide safely over it.

The shores are again closing in to form a narrow channel. We pass Craigie Lea House, and, since there isn't a decent dock here, a young deckhand is dispatched in a small boat with the mail bag: not an unwelcome duty, actually, since Mrs. Croucher usually keeps a stock of cookies or doughnuts on hand for him as he waits for the steamer to return. Slowly we pass through the channel, into Little Lake Joseph, and within another quarter of an hour the ship eases up to a small dock alongside a steep rock. We are at the Natural Park. The Purser explains that we shall have about an hour to explore the Park, and cautions that the boat will sound a warning whistle about five minutes before departure time. In any case, he adds, if anyone should be left behind, just make yourselves comfortable, because the "Sag" will be back again tomorrow!

The Natural Park, we discover, is a lovely shaded spot. The big rock beside the wharf is about as high as the steamer's bridge. There is a wishing well, a small sandy beach at the head of the wharf, some broad, inviting paths beyond a tiny brook, and several ornate rock gardens shaded by the canopy of overhead trees. The whole scene resembles a sylvan cathedral. For those of us with surplus energy, the paths extend to the right, winding up a steep, rocky hill bathed in sunshine at the summit. Arriving there short of breath, we proceed a little further, directed by arrows painted on the granite, until we see Mirror Lake spreading below us, looking every bit as lovely as Lake Louise on a clear day. Treetops can be glimpsed far below us. A painted line near the edge of the bluff warns us not to proceed any farther, and few of us feel any temptation to cross it!

We would like to take more time to relax and explore the Park, but a glance at our watches indicates that we'd better be starting back. As people come filing aboard, the *Sagamo* sounds her whistle again. Then, when everyone seems accounted for, she gives a quick toot, casts off, and begins backing out into Little Lake Joseph for the return voyage. As she passes back through the entrance channel, several boys peering down into the depths exclaim that there's an enormous fish down there—"must weigh a hundred pounds at least!" Today there's a little time to spare, and the Captain decides to take the scenic route between Cliff and Chief's Islands. Officers obligingly name the points we are passing. The ship cruises across to Yoho Island, calls at the railway wharf at Barnesdale, where she meets the *Waome*, then turns south again to Foot's Bay. Within the hour, we are back at Port Sandfield. Again, the bridge obediently swings open in response to the steamer's whistle, then, she repeats her rounds on Lake Rosseau, with return visits to Clevelands, the Royal, and Windermere. The orchestra is piping up with Scottish dance music now, and playing "London Bridge is Falling Down" for the kiddies. Speedboats continue to buzz past us, and on the top of the mast a gull is perched; lord of all he surveys.

The music subsides as the steamer re-enters the Indian River and returns to Port Carling. It is now late afternoon, and the shadows are long. The lock chamber is ready to receive the ship, and below the lock the *Medora* is waiting for us on her return trip to Rosseau. The *Sagamo* locks through, makes the necessary exchanges, then blows her whistle and bids farewell to Port Carling. She weaves her way down the river until Lake Muskoka opens ahead of us.

The engines now start churning out "full ahead" as the *Sagamo* steams south for Beaumaris to rejoin the *Segwun* and the *Cherokee*. When the usual transfers are completed, the three ships back out from Beaumaris and disperse to their respective destinations: the *Cherokee* soon disappears astern of us while the *Segwun* parallels our course for a few miles past Millionaires' Row before veering off to our left for the far side of Eileen Gowan Island. Our ship takes the right-hand passage ahead for Gravenhurst.

Meanwhile, we have received the welcome word that it's our turn to have supper. Again we return to the dining room, where we make our selections from a menu offering several full course dinners. Towards sundown, we pass back through the Gravenhurst Narrows and finally return to our starting point at Muskoka Wharf. The crowd, tired but happy, slowly files off the ship to board the waiting train or rejoin their friends and families with the car. Another cruise has ended.

Some visitors, of course, have not taken the entire trip, but have disembarked or boarded at the resorts of their choice. Some have taken only a half-day cruise, by transferring from one ship to another. For others, a one-day cruise does not satisfy them, and they arrange to take a three-day or one-week 'Vagabond Cruise', combining trips on the steamers with rest and relaxation at the

Crew of the S.S. "Sagamo", posed at Natural Park.
This picture, taken about 1927, shows the "Big Chief" at the old wharf at the Park. Captain
Lee and Engineer Lambert are standing at the junction of the paths, to the right. Next to
the Commodore is Charlie Musgrave of Toronto, for many years the commentator and
orchestra leader on the Cruise.
Courtesy, *Mrs. Irene Dickson*, Willowdale

Royal. Still others prefer the overnight 'Sunset Cruise' on the spacious decks of the *Cherokee* as
she steams off into the twilight. There may be a romantic 'Moonlight Cruise' at night on the
Sagamo, when couples may choose to dance to the airs of 'Red Roses Bring Dreams of You' or the
'Blue Danube waltz', or simply sit peacefully by the railing, enjoying the pine-scented offshore
breezes as the steamer glides serenely past islands shrouded in darkness, with only the lights of
cottages and boat houses to compete with the stars.

The proud steamers of the Muskoka Lakes were truly in their element during the 33 year
interval from the so-called "Gay Nineties" to the "Roaring Twenties". Aside from the turbulent
dislocations of the First World War, life in Canada was, on the whole, prosperous during that
period. To many, it seemed that the good times had come to stay, and mercifully, few had the
remotest conception of the agonizing disillusionments in store. For Canadians generally, grim
years lay ahead, and Muskoka proved to have no immunity. When the steamers tied up in the fall
of 1929, no one knew that the best days were already over for them, and that, henceforth, a
desperate struggle for survival would have to be waged, almost unceasingly, against the
inexorably advancing forces of decline.

Mirror Lake, from the Bluffs of the Natural Park.

"The 100 Mile Cruiser", homebound from Port Carling.

"Your Hosts For The Cruise!"
Officers and Crew of the "Sagamo", posed on the bridge. Directly below the phoenix stand Captain Lee and Chief Engineer Lambert. To the left of the Commodore is First Officer Eric Wasley.

The fleet at Gravenhurst, 1930.
Shown, left to right, are the Strs. "Medora", "Segwun", "Waome", "Sagamo", "Ahmic", wrecked hull of the "Charlie M." beside the boat-house, and the "Constance". To the far right is the hulk of the "Muskoka". Absent are the "Islander" and "Cherokee".
Courtesy, *Public Archives of Canada* C 88103

CHAPTER 7
The Declining Years of Steamboating
(1929-1945)

On October 29, 1929, a date known ever since as "Black Tuesday", the bottom dropped out of the New York Stock Exchange, with reverberations soon felt all around the world. Stocks that had been soaring in paper value for several years suddenly began plummeting, as the enthusiasm of speculators turned into panic. Despite a few brief revivals in the months following, the deadly downward cycle spiralled on, sucking the entire industrialized world into the grim vortex of the Great Depression.

There had been drastic upsets in the stock markets in the past, of course, but nothing to equal this. Money abruptly became tight, as frightened lenders began foreclosing on their loans. This put intense pressure on businesses, and within weeks hundreds of shaky firms in the United States and Canada collapsed, putting their employees out of work. In a deadly chain-reaction the malady fed upon itself. As debtors defaulted, business orders fell off, dragging down other businesses and creating more unemployed for hard-pressed local authorities to house and feed. Wages fell, deficits rose, people rioted and sometimes governments collapsed. Even the wealthiest and most powerful corporations found their profits dropping as incomes declined or disappeared. The business community was sick, the jobless were everywhere, and in some regions, including the Canadian West, droughts deepened the misery by turning productive farmlands into dust bowls. The results were shock, hardship, despair and sometimes suicide. The exuberant vigour of the Roaring Twenties gave way to the harried desperation of the Depressing Thirties, as businessmen, politicians and ordinary people struggled with an invisible malaise they could not understand, which drove thousands to destitution and produced widespread poverty in the midst of plenty.

It did not take long for the shock waves of October 1929 to reach Muskoka. Small businesses closed, prices sagged, and summer tourists curtailed their visits or cut them out altogether. The luxury of a two week summer vacation was now beyond the reach of thousands of people. Even the unusually hot weather of 1930, 1933 and 1934 failed to bring them out: the annual inflow of tourists just seemed to dry up in the heat. This, naturally, put great strains on the resorts, and many of the smaller ones were forced to close. A few, such as the Milford Bay House and The Bluffs Hotel on Lake Rosseau, were destroyed by fire and not rebuilt. By 1937, W.F. Wasley noted sombrely that Muskoka then had fewer resorts than in 1922, with the number still declining.

Needless to say, as tourism waned, so did traffic by rail and steamer. Compounding the problems of the railways and the Muskoka Navigation Company was the steady proliferation of hard-surfaced highways now invading the resort regions. By 1929, for example, the road from Severn Bridge to Gravenhurst was asphalted for the first time, and a new coating applied over Highway 11 between Barrie and Orillia. In 1930, Bay Street in Gravenhurst was paved as part of a new highway to Bala, and so was the new approach to Bracebridge, as was the road from Bracebridge to Falkenburg, on the way to Huntsville. All this road upgrading, extending the already paved networks in Southern Ontario, reflected the growing preeminence of the automobile and the transport truck, although in part it was encouraged as a form of unemployment relief. In 1931, the Canadian National Railways announced that it was deleting one of its daily trains to and from Gravenhurst, complaining that it was being heavily taxed by the Province to help build new roads that only served to reduce the profits of the railways. The Muskoka Navigation Company might well have made the same lament.

By 1930, the Navigation Company held assets valued at about $530,000; all fortunately paid for. Its seven steamers were valued at roughly $255,000, its allotted share capital totalled $87,050, and it owned the Gravenhurst dockyards, the Natural Park, a few parcels of land at Rosseau and Port Carling, and the Royal Muskoka Hotel. Unfortunately the big hotel could hardly be called an "asset" any more. It was growing steadily older and more dated, and during the Depression it was impossible to keep it full. In fact, sometimes the staff outnumbered the guests, and throughout the thirties, any profits earned by the lake steamers were usually swallowed up by the hotel. Many times W.F. Wasley, Manager of the boat division, urged Major MacLean, the President, to sell the huge white elephant, but in vain.

Thanks to the recollections of a number of older men, we are afforded a number of inside glimpses of the steamboat scene during the thirties. One of these gentlemen is Mr. Gerald Leeder of Kearney. A son of Captain Albert Leeder, whom we have already encountered on the *Queen of the Isles* and the *Iroquois*, and a younger brother of the late Captain Reg Leeder, Gerald also caught the boating bug and would have made a career of it, except that his father, with more foresight than most during the 1920s, warned him to look for something better, because "these boats aren't going to be running forever". Consequently Gerald went into teaching, but this did not prevent his working on steamers on weekends and during the summers. For several seasons he served as a deckhand and wheelsman on the *Iroquois*, and in 1930, he joined his brother on the lower lakes as Purser: W. F. Wasley offered him a two week training period plus $30.00 a month and board. Only three days after he started, however, his intended teacher, Charlie Kelly, who was Purser on the *Ahmic*, was suddenly transferred to the *Islander*, whose purser had just been hospitalized. Gerald thus found himself promoted to full Purser, at $1.30 per day plus board. Thereafter he worked seasonally as Purser and Mate until the 1950s, usually shifting from boat to boat every season.

Mr. Leeder was back on the *Ahmic* in 1931. Over the winter, she had been fitted out with a large new lounge cabin amidships, which not only provided more shelter for passengers, but also made her more stable, since the winds were now less prone to build up under the bridge. She now looked almost like a twin to the *Waome*.

Purser Gerald Leeder, with his guitar.

S.S. "Ahmic" (Second Version), with S.S. "Segwun" at Beaumaris, 1930.
Courtesy, *Mrs. Irene Dickson*, Willowdale

S.S. "Ahmic" (Third Version).
The little steamer now has a new upper lounge cabin.
Courtesy, *Mr. Douglas Gray*, Port Credit

Sometimes the *Ahmic* took the Bracebridge run but with the Depression now in full swing, all too often she would leave town with almost empty decks, carrying little more than the mail. Distressed at this situation, Gerald began making a habit of calling on campers at the local motor park in the evenings, asking them if they'd like to take a cruise, and distributing folders. He would also offer a free ticket to anyone who would rustle up a party of ten, or two free tickets for anyone who could line up a group of twenty. W. F. Wasley was amazed to count 37 passengers getting off the *Ahmic* at Beaumaris one day. Hearing of Gerald's promotion work, the Manager remarked, "I only wish *all* of my pursers would make that extra bit of effort."

A Purser always had his hands full. He was responsible for all ticket returns, stateroom arrangements, dining room sales, mail sorting, and all articles of freight and baggage; making sure that everything was loaded and unloaded safely at the right place—to say nothing of keeping all the passengers happy. No sooner would one consignment of freight be straightened away than the next port of call would come into view. Detailed manifests were required for everything, and understandably the work was never finished before 11:00 p.m. Only on Sundays, when there were neither flag stops, freight nor mail to worry about, could the crews hope to relax a little.

Of course, for certain irksome but necessary jobs such as coaling up, everyone had to help, including the officers. Shortly after joining the *Ahmic*'s crew, Mr. Leeder prepared to take his first wheel-barrow load of coal (carried in sacks) from the hopper cars parked at Bala Park Station. Wheeling these loads aboard meant crossing the double spur to the wharf, but in so doing, Gerald's wheelbarrow suddenly flipped sideways and spilled the coal all over the track. The skipper, Captain Peter Larson of Gravenhurst, gave a knowing smirk, but the other hands expressed sympathy and helped clean up the mess. This was humiliating enough, but the next time the *Ahmic* stopped for coal the same thing happened again! However, after leaving Bala Park, the cook, a friendly Irish woman named Mrs. Rowley, confidentially offered "purse" a little tip; wheel the barrow across the tracks at right angles to the rails. That way, she said, the steel wheel

The other side of steamboating: the Coaling Crew.
The man in the centre is Eric Wasley.
Courtesy, *Mrs. Irene Dickson*, Willowdale

wouldn't skid. She also suggested that he not let the Captain see. Taking her advice, Gerald wheeled his load towards the tracks at an oblique angle the next time, pretending he hadn't caught on; then when Captain Larson wasn't looking he crossed at 90 degrees without any trouble. Nonplussed at first, the skipper afterwards felt compelled to admit that "that young feller Leeder is a heck of a lot smarter than I gave him credit for".

Gerald, of course, had heard all about Major Hugh MacLean, the President of the Line, whom he pictured as a tall, aristocratic-looking Englishman, complete with white gloves and a monocle. The Major, with all his other concerns, was seen only now and then in Muskoka, and Leeder wondered if the great man would ever make an appearance on the *Ahmic*. Early one evening in 1930, when the steamer was docked at Bala, the Purser was slightly amused to see a short, plump, stocky man with a big nose, about 64 years of age and dressed in a plain brown suit, come ambling up the gangplank. Gerald met him at the gangway and politely asked him for his ticket. The little man replied that he didn't have one. "Well in that case, sir, I'll have to sell you a ticket." The stranger looked indignant and retorted, "Look, in case you don't know it, I happen to be Major Hugh MacLean, President of this company!" Gerald was surprised, but he asked nonetheless for some sort of identification. The Major began searching his pockets but found nothing handy. Suddenly he announced, "Oh wait, I have a pass." Leeder asked to see it. The gentleman started hunting through his suitcase and finally produced it: stamped "No. 1". Gerald then apologized for doubting him, wondering all the while what would happen when Old Man Wasley heard about it.

Several years passed before Gerald heard anything more about the incident. Then one day while the *Cherokee* was cruising from Royal Muskoka to Clevelands, he met Major MacLean again. The Major at once hailed him and asked, "Aren't you the one who made me show a pass at Bala one time?" Leeder sheepishly owned up, and explained that he hadn't been able to believe that he had been talking to Major Hugh MacLean. The President, however, just smiled and confided that he had spoken to Captain Larson afterwards; complimenting him on having such a competent young Purser!

Another incident from that period helps to illustrate the mounting desperation of the times, and throw light on the character of Mr. W.F. Wasley. One day while the *Ahmic* was docked at Bracebridge, Leeder answered a telephone call from the Shier Lumber Company, inquiring whether the steamer could transport a couple of beams, 10 inches square and 40 feet in length, to Rest Harbour for a customer. Leeder checked with Ben Dewey, the Mate, to see if the *Ahmic* could handle timbers that size; Dewey in his deep drawling voice advised that it really wasn't practical, and Leeder repeated this over the wire. About half an hour later, the phone rang again; this time it was Wasley calling from Gravenhurst. He was furious with the *Ahmic*'s crew for turning away business in depressed times. He ordered them to accept the cargo, and carried on with his tirade

Captain Peter Larson.

until Gerald finally hung up. Somehow the immense beams, each half the length of the steamer, were stashed in the companionway, from the dining room forward, but even so the ends were left protruding through the gangway. They were then taken to Beaumaris, where they had to be transferred to the *Sagamo*. This was easier said than done, because the *Sagamo* was docked on the opposite side of the wharf, and the beams were so long that they became wedged under the support posts of the wharf canopy. The men from the *Sagamo* tried again and again to angle them around and get them on board. To Gerald's secret satisfaction, the Manager was present to witness all this, pacing nervously back and forth and glancing periodically at his watch. When the precious timbers were finally loaded aboard, the flagship had been delayed a full hour. W.F. Wasley was not very pleased.

Later that same afternoon, when the *Ahmic* returned to Beaumaris, Wasley met Gerry on the dock. "You thought you were pretty smart, hanging up on me like that, didn't you?" snapped the Manager, who then launched into another tongue-lashing. Leeder tried to defend himself, pointing out that the decision not to take the beams was Dewey's, and suggesting that Wasley take up the matter with those directly responsible. But the Manager was in no mood to see reason, and continued to heap abuse on Gerry. Finally Leeder decided he had had enough. "Mr. Wasley," he said, "you'd better have another Purser ready to take over the *Ahmic* in 24 hours. I'm leaving!" Then he turned and walked away.

The following afternoon, as promised, Gerald Leeder stepped off his ship at Beaumaris, carrying his suitcase. Again he met Wasley on the wharf, alone. "Where's the new purser?" asked Gerry. "He'll need these keys." Wasley replied that he had no new Purser. Leeder reminded him that he was quitting. Wasley wouldn't hear of it, and urged him to stay. Without directly retracting anything, the Manager insisted that they both had been angry the day before, and asked Gerry to forget it. Leeder wavered, then returned to his post. Relations between the two men were quite cordial after that.

Captain Andy Corbett of Bracebridge returned from the Huntsville lakes in 1928 to command the *Medora* and he proved to be her last skipper. One morning in 1930, he was bringing his vessel in from Lake Rosseau to Port Carling, as usual. The *Segwun* was in the lock chamber, while the *Sagamo* was waiting downstream of the locks. Captain Corbett's son Ted, then Purser on the *Segwun*, and his friend "Red" Stephen, a deckhand and son of Captain Stephen, both happened to be standing on the wharf near the lock gates, watching the *Medora* coming in, faster than usual, it seemed. Captain Corbett now rang for "reverse", but the Engineer, Adam Beck of Goderich, somehow misunderstood and gave him "forward". The big ship kept gliding straight ahead, while the skipper signalled twice again for "reverse." All he seemed to get was more speed! "Red" Stephen swore and shouted, "Let's get out of here. She's coming right through the locks!" W.F. Wasley, watching in alarm from the wharf opposite, grabbed a line and managed to wrap it around a snubbing post, but the other end wasn't secured and even if it *had* been, the rope would simply have snapped. Captain Corbett emerged from the wheelhouse, gripped the railing tightly and held on for dear life, and then, as an ultimate gesture of futility, slid his fingers through his hair without removing his cap. Then the crash.

Captain Andrew Thomas Corbett.

S.S. "Medora", beside the Navigation Company freight shed, Port Carling.
Courtesy, *Ontario Archives*, ACC. 9939, Roll 12A, #16

The bow of the big steamer struck the steel arm of the lock gate, rebounded, and struck the wharf itself, splintering the timbers and jamming the ship's forepeak in the gash. Fortunately, she missed the lock gates: had she hit them, the results might have been catastrophic for both herself and the *Segwun*. As it happened, because the arm was damaged, one of the gates could be opened only halfway afterwards, and the *Segwun* had barely enough room to squeeze past the *Medora* on her way to Lake Rosseau. The *Medora* remained jammed in place for about five hours, until jacks were used to pry her loose. The ship escaped with very little damage, but it had been a very close call.

The *Medora* also became involved in another collision in 1930; this time involving the little steamer *Constance*, now a tug commanded by Captain James Campbell. The big ship was preparing to back away from Muskoka Wharf when the *Constance* showed up behind her, heading for her dock near the Mickle sawmills with a scow in tow. Captain Corbett saw the *Constance*, but was not perturbed. She was still some distance off, and Jim Campbell usually gave him a wide berth. He blew the departure whistle, set the ropes on the spokes of the steering wheel to hold it steady, and signalled for reverse. Stepping out of the pilothouse, Corbett was greatly surprised to find the *Constance* broadside, directly off his stern. Campbell was trying to cut in behind him. Using the hand signals, Corbett frantically signalled "full ahead", then dashed back and began to swing the wheel, which was about five feet in diameter. It was too late. The rudder and the fantail of the *Medora* struck the scow that the *Constance* had in tow. The impact made the *Medora*'s wheel spin, and one of the spokes struck the Captain in the side of the face, fracturing his

187

Supply Steamer "Constance", at Port Sandfield.

jaw in three places and knocking him out of the wheelhouse: but for the railing he would have been flung overboard. He was at once helped to his cabin, while the mate, Captain Bert Campbell of Rosseau, took charge. Only after the ship was part way up the lake was the skipper's condition realized. W.F. Wasley, who was aboard, suggested giving him a glass of rye—which only made him feel worse. At Beaumaris he was taken off, driven to Bracebridge, and ultimately hospitalized at Toronto. Considerable controversy raged afterwards as to who was responsible for the accident, and who should pay for the damage done to the scow, but in the end, the Navigation Company agreed only to dry-dock the scow.

The *Constance* still had seven more years of active service ahead of her, but the *Medora*, though destined to outlast her, was already near the end of her cruising days. She re-entered service in July of 1931, but business had become so slack that around August 4th, Wasley reluctantly ordered her tied up again to await the return of better times that never came. The Depression simply intensified, putting even more people out of work. The year 1933 was the worst of all, with 1,227,558 Canadians (about 21% of the population) on relief or riding the rails looking for jobs. Ironically, that same season, the yard crews were ordered to get the *Medora* ready to go again. She was fitted up in drydock and relaunched, but she never turned a wheel. So it continued all through the thirties. Gradually, the stately old ship began to deteriorate, and steadily her prospects diminished. Finally, on the evening of June 1, 1940, a group of boys who had contrived to get aboard the vessel, accidentally started a fire in the hold, then fled. A passerby spotted the flames and phoned for help. The Gravenhurst Fire Brigade rushed to the scene and soon had the blaze under control, but not before the fire gutted part of the main deck and the interior of the aft lounge cabin. Though the ship's exterior showed little sign of damage, it was now a foregone conclusion that the old *Medora* would never sail again. Everything of value was stripped from her, and gradually she was ripped apart. By 1945, all of her upper works were gone, and the once proud queen had become an eyesore. Two years later, her hulk was sold for scrap yet the remains of the ship were still visible until 1952. Today only the steering wheel of this splendid steamer survives, in a Gravenhurst restaurant. A pathetic end to over 37 years of good service.

S.S. "Medora", in retirement at Gravenhurst.

The *Medora*'s retirement, of course, meant a retrenchment of service and a revision of schedules. The *Cherokee* took her place on the Rosseau route as running mate for the *Sagamo*. The *Islander* in turn was transferred to the Bala run, replacing the *Cherokee* and becoming more or less the running mate to the *Segwun*, which continued to ply from Bracebridge. The *Ahmic* continued to run from Torrance to Milford Bay, visiting cottages and local hotels and joining the *Cherokee* daily at Muskoka Wharf around noon. The *Waome* in turn replaced the *Islander* on Lake Rosseau. None of the steamers, except the *Sagamo*, operated regularly on Lake Joseph any more. Since the *Cherokee* was now the "noon boat" from Gravenhurst, orders from the office to the various captains and pursers were regularly dispatched on her. On one occasion in 1934, the Manager was startled to find the *Islander* cruising in to join the *Ahmic* and *Cherokee* at Muskoka Wharf, when she was supposed to be at Bracebridge. Her Master showed him a yellow form, on which the word "Bracebridge" was stroked off and "Muskoka Wharf" substituted. The *Islander* was immediately sent back, while the purser of the *Cherokee* was thoroughly bawled out for the error. During those years, we might add, Commodore Lee was always on the *Sagamo*, while Captain Stephen usually commanded the *Segwun*, with Captain Reg Leeder on the *Islander*, Captains Wesley Hill or Arthur Thompson on the *Ahmic*, and Captain Henshaw on the *Waome*. Captain Larson, whose nerves were getting bad, left the boats early in the thirties to work ashore. William Bradshaw remained on the *Cherokee* until the spring of 1931, when he suddenly took ill, wasted away rapidly, and died in a Toronto hospital at the age of 52. Captain Corbett succeeded him on the *Cherokee*, and remained her skipper to the end of her cruising days.

Andy Corbett was one of a rare breed of navigators who always seemed to know where he was, almost by instinct. One foggy morning he was embarking with the *Cherokee* from Stanley House on Lake Joseph and with him in the pilothouse were two visiting Great Lakes captains, who had come up on the steamer the evening before with their wives. The fog was so thick that visibility was restricted to about 50 feet, which from the helm, meant just a few yards beyond the bow. The skipper, however, set his speed at half ahead and steered by compass, meanwhile summoning his son Ted, the Purser, to the bridge and instructing him to stand at the port-side railing and listen for the sound of birds. "Birds?" asked young Corbett in surprise. "Yes, birds!" replied Andy. Within about fifteen minutes Ted reported that he could hear the twittering of birds. "Good. That's Sugarloaf Island," said the Captain, adjusting his course. "Now go over to the starboard side and listen for a cowbell." The Purser obeyed, and soon confirmed the sound of a bell. "Good. That's Fawcett's cow.* That bell means we're opposite Hamill's Point. You can go now," said the Captain, who could now make out the western shoreline. Before the steamer reached Port Sandfield the fog had cleared, revealing a lovely day. The two Great Lakes skippers, who of course always steered by compass, observed proceedings with casual interest, until one of them asked Captain Corbett, before the fog lifted, where they were going today? "Right where we went yesterday, only the other way around," came the reply. The Great Lakes captains were stunned. "What! Among all those *islands*?"

There were times, however, when the weather could upset the best laid plans of the most skilful navigators. One Saturday evening in mid-August, 1932, the *Cherokee* conducted an evening cruise from Rosseau to Port Carling for a dance, stopping at the Royal Muskoka, Wigwassan and Windermere on the way. The excursion started off in bright moonlight, but around 10:00 a thunderstorm was threatening, and by the time she was on her way back, the night was pitch black and the rain coming down in sheets. The searchlight was of little use: the beam merely magnified the raindrops so that they looked like driving snow. Despite this, the steamer returned safely to Windermere, Wigwassan and the Royal: that still left thirteen passengers bound for Rosseau. She left the Royal close to midnight and started for the north arm, but unknown to all, the gusty winds were blowing the vessel off course to the east. Suddenly there was a jolt and a crunch as the ship piled up on a small island close to Monyca. Purser Ted Corbett hurried forward and peered into the tiny front compartment of the hold, where the anchor chains were stored. Water was sloshing around up to the water level. One of the hull plates had been sprung by the impact. Furthermore, it was obvious that the vessel, though still rolling with the wind and waves, was firmly caught on the rocks. The men inspected the crew's quarters, in the second section of the hold. The steel bulkhead separating the two was watertight, but if the second compartment began flooding faster than the siphon could handle it, the ship would certainly sink. (She had four bulkheads altogether, but the aft three were *not* watertight.) Fortunately, when the floorboards in the second compartment were lifted, the bilges proved to be dry.

Captain Corbett came below to look into the situation personally. Ominous creaks and groans were coming from the hold. The skipper feared that reversing engines to back off might wrench the plates farther apart, and if that happened, the damage might be fatal. As long as the ship remained caught and the aft sections dry, she would be "safe", but outside the pitiless wind kept grinding her bow on the rocks. The Captain ordered full steam kept up and a close watch maintained on the leak. The mate and the engineer tried to fill the rent with sacks full of cinders.

The passengers, meanwhile, were very anxious, but the crew kept them calm and passed out life preservers. When it became clear that the ship would remain grounded for the duration of the storm, someone suggested disembarking in the lifeboats, but no one particularly wanted to leave in all that driving rain. The passengers were then offered the use of the staterooms, and since most of the couples aboard were unmarried, the ladies were assigned the starboard rooms and the gentlemen those to port.

Few members of the crew got any sleep that night. The wind did not abate, and eventually it blew the ship around nearly 180 degrees. The worried hands could only wonder: will she hold? It didn't look good. Captain Corbett made up his mind to run the vessel right back onto the rocks if she broke loose and the second bulwark began flooding, or, if time allowed, to try to beach her at Rostrevor, about two miles away. Finally, at about 4:10 a.m., the whole ship began to move. The shout went up: "We're off!" Immediately there was an additional rush of water into the bow, but the other sections remained dry. Once it was clear she was safe, Captain Corbett made for the Royal Muskoka and docked for a checkup, phoning Gravenhurst to alert the Manager.

* (The Fawcett family cow was well known to the boat crews, who were obliged to transport the animal to Bracebridge in the fall and back to Hamill's Point every spring. The cow was a very contrary creature, and frequently objected to boarding or disembarking from the boats. Sometimes it took half the crew to bring Bossy aboard or push her off.)

Crew of the S.S. "Cherokee", 1930.
In the second row, second and third from the left respectively, are Captain Bradshaw and Engineer Stanley Lambert, brother of Walter.

S.S. "Cherokee", at Rosseau, during the 1930s.

Dining room on the S.S. "Cherokee".

At Rosseau, meanwhile, the people felt alarmed when the *Cherokee* failed to return that stormy night. They wondered if the ship had gone down with their loved ones aboard. Many waited anxiously at the wharf and the relief was overwhelming when the steamer finally rounded Kawandag Point and arrived at Rosseau harbour about 7:00 a.m., safe and almost sound. Mr. Wasley meanwhile decided that there was no time to dry-dock the ship before the season's end, and since there was no likelihood of the damage getting any worse, he instructed the crew to finish the season as though nothing had happened. Few passengers afterwards were aware that the *Cherokee* had a flooded forepeak, though there were some who wondered why she sat a trifle down at the head!

Though Captain Corbett was an excellent navigator, he was also said to be a rather cantankerous man with a snappish temper. This showed up one afternoon in 1931 when he was bringing the *Cherokee* back north through Port Carling. Irritated to find the lock chamber filling with motor launches, Corbett moved the bow of his ship forward, so that the swing bridge could not be closed, and demanded that the launch owners move their boats out, since priority went to the passenger ships. None did. Meanwhile traffic began building up on both sides of the bridge, a crowd gathered, and impatient motorists beeped their horns. A policeman was summoned and tried to make the motorboat owners vacate the locks. They refused. As the tension built up to an unbearable height, Captain Corbett finally gave up and backed away, the bridge was closed, and the steamer had to wait until the next lockage.

A few years later, probably in 1933, the *Cherokee* had another adventure on the Muskoka River. This was not her regular route, but on this particular September day, two steamers were sent to Bracebridge to pick up passengers at the fall fair to return them to Port Carling. The *Segwun*, under Captain Stephen, entered the river first, with the *Cherokee* following about 300 yards behind. Three new hydro lines had just been strung across the river, close to the Parrett family farm: noticing them, the Purser, who was on the bridge, asked Captain Corbett if he thought the wires posed any danger? The Captain thought not. Ahead of them, the *Segwun* passed safely underneath, by a hair's breadth, and the *Cherokee*, after all, had a shorter mast. The point was soon demonstrated. As the *Cherokee* glided beneath the lines, there was a loud crack and a jolt—which made the Engineer think the ship had gone aground. For a moment the flash of the wires reflected green on the water. The vessel strained and hesitated as the lines went taut, then with a loud crack the mast snapped, dented the rim of the stack, and crashed onto the bridge between the skylight and a lifeboat. No one was hurt, partly because there were few passengers aboard, but it might have been a different story if the mast had jackknifed through the pilothouse. For the rest of the season, the *Cherokee* sailed without a mast, but W. F. Wasley promptly went after the hydro authorities to raise the wires. As it happened, the *Cherokee* made very few trips to Bracebridge after that.

S.S. "Cherokee", (left) meeting S.S. "Segwun" during the 1930s.

S.S. "Cherokee", after her encounter with the Muskoka River hydro lines. (Note the dent in the stack and the missing mast).

The *Segwun* had her share of adventures too. In the spring of 1931, Captain Henshaw was ordered to bring the vessel from Muskoka Wharf to the Gravenhurst dockyards. There was a wind blowing at the time, and Henshaw, unused to twin-screw steamers, soon found he was bringing the ship in at a bad angle. As the corpulent Captain hustled back into the wheelhouse, he tripped on the doorsill and fell flat on his face. Before he could get up, the steamer struck the wharf opposite the one intended, and ended up wedged diagonally between the two. It was some time before Captain Henshaw ceased to receive compliments on his "excellent docking".

Another unusual docking with the *Segwun* took place a few years later, while Ted Corbett and "Red" Stephen were deckhanding together. The two of them liked to clown a lot, much to the annoyance of Captain Stephen, who felt obliged to tolerate their pranks. They received their comeuppance one windy day when the ship was approaching the new wharf at Crusoe Island on Lake Muskoka. As the vessel came alongside, Corbett and Stephen jumped ashore and flung the mooring lines around three vertical posts on the dock. This, ordinarily, was the correct procedure, but unknown to them the "posts" were, in fact, just three blocks of wood that someone had left on the wharf, and since the blocks weren't attached to anything, they just flopped over. The ship began to drift away, leaving the flabbergasted pair stranded on the dock! The steamer executed a large loop by way of returning, and meanwhile the two managed to find attachments on the far side of the pier, to which they could safely secure the ship.

In the mid 1930's, there were several 'desertions' from the Huntsville Navigation Company, as several officers became dissatisfied with conditions there, or felt they had been badly used by C. O. Shaw. Captain Albert Leeder (Gerald's father) left the *Iroquois* to command Mrs. Sanford's yacht, the *Naiad*. Captain Tinkiss also left after a verbal dressing-down from Shaw, who raised a storm because the *Mohawk Belle* was late in leaving the Portage one day: he became mate on the *Cherokee* before taking over the Hanna steamer *Newminko* in 1934. Gerald Leeder also left the Lake of Bays at this time, as did Alvin Saulter, who had previously been Engineer on the *Iroquois*. Fed up with the Huntsville Line in 1930, and advised that engineers were needed on the lower lakes, Saulter phoned W. F. Wasley, who offered him a job on either the *Waome* or the *Segwun*. Saulter accepted, and soon reported at the Gravenhurst dockyards, not knowing what he was going to find. Meeting Walter Lambert, who was then Chief Engineer on the *Sagamo*, Saulter was directed over to the *Segwun*, but after taking just one look aboard he promptly stepped off again, ready to quit. Lambert asked him what was wrong. Saulter despairingly pointed at the *Segwun* and moaned, "That's a twin-engine ship. I can't handle that! I've never worked on a twin-engine ship in my life!" Lambert, however, gave him a reassuring pat on the shoulder, told him he would have no trouble, and then volunteered to come along himself for the first few days until Saulter "got the hang of it." Lambert did, in fact, sail with Saulter for one day; then, noting that the little man was rapidly getting used to the routine, he simply left him in charge, saying, "Okay, you can handle it all right." Alvin Saulter soon became one of the most efficient engineers the Company ever had, but when Captain "Geordie" Stephen, himself a former Lake of Bays man, heard who was going to be running the *Segwun*'s engines, he refused to believe it. "Hell," cried the little skipper, "it can't be Saulter! He's only a kid"—quite forgetting that he hadn't seen the "kid" for over fifteen years. Saulter remained on the *Segwun* only one season, then shifted to the *Cherokee* under Captain Corbett, with whom he worked very well, and eventually succeeded Lambert on the *Sagamo*. He found it pleasant to receive higher pay plus three hot meals a day, instead of sandwiches made at home.

At the time of Saulter's appointment in 1930, there was still considerable speculation as to whether the *Segwun*, admittedly a fast ship, could go as fast as the *Sagamo* in an open race. (It was certain that none of the others could.) There had already been a number of races between the two steamers, Saulter heard, in spite of objections from the management, and then the Navigation Company had recently placed larger propellers on the *Segwun*, alleging that the old ones turned too fast and let the engines run away. This might have been true, yet the *Segwun*'s partisans whispered that the real reason for the change was to slow her down, to make sure she couldn't outdistance the flagship on a parallel course. The men on the *Sagamo*, naturally, retorted that "there was never any chance of that!" As it happened, on at least one more occasion the issue was put to the test.

S.S. "Segwun", ascending the Muskoka River.

Captain Albert Frederick Leeder.

One afternoon in mid-season 1930, the *Segwun*, still commanded by "Geordie" Stephen, was docking at Lake Joseph Station, when the *Sagamo* arrived from the Natural Park to collect the afternoon mail. As the *Segwun* prepared to embark, her crew noticed that the men on the *Sagamo* were unloading their freight consignments with unusual haste! Both ships were due to head south, and everyone knew what that meant. Captain Stephen slowly backed out from the wharf and idled, while within minutes the "Big Chief" followed suit. A wave from Commodore Lee, answered by Stephen, and the race was on.

Belching smoke from their stacks, the two steamers surged forward, both heading for Crete Island, which they passed on opposite sides. Then they met, side by side, only 40 feet apart and churning along furiously. First the big ship would gain a slight edge, then the smaller one would catch up. On both ships, the stokers shovelled coal into the fireboxes as if their very lives depended on it. Aboard the *Segwun* the pistons pounded, while Saulter squeezed every ounce of steam he could get into the cylinders. Before long the two ships were kicking up such a wake that the swells from the *Sagamo* drenched the *Segwun*'s dining room windows. At times, too, the propellers of the *Segwun* flashed into view from the *Sagamo*.

Then the smaller steamer began to steal ahead. At this the men on the *Sagamo* seemed to go berserk and threw her engines absolutely wide open. For several miles, it was nip and tuck. Finally the *Sagamo* managed to cross the *Segwun*'s bow, and at the same time the smaller ship had to stop at Stainey Brae, near Foot's Bay, to drop off the mail.

An hour or so later, the *Segwun* steamed into Port Carling, to find the *Sagamo* in the lock. After docking, Saulter walked over to ask Lambert whether he had been running with his engines wide open? "Oh no," retorted Lambert casually, "she still had some left up her sleeve!" Saulter was crestfallen. "Well," he conceded, "I guess you've got the faster ship. I was running mine at full throttle." Only later did Saulter find out the truth, when Lambert's oiler confided that the men on the *Sagamo* were so scared of being beaten by the *Segwun* that they not only ran the engines wide open, but also opened the steam bypasses for the low pressure cylinders as well.

This playful little escapade had proved inconclusive, and there will never be agreement as to which of the two ships was the faster. Perhaps the truth is that the *Segwun*, with her splendid Scotch marine boiler, could marshal speed faster, and thus had an advantage on short runs, while the *Sagamo* could do better on longer hauls. Whatever the truth, the above episode was probably the last of its kind: Old Man Wasley put his foot down . . . . No More Races!!

As for the *Sagamo*, physically she seems to have sailed throughout the thirties with few difficulties (other than trying to keep ahead of the *Segwun*!) and few mishaps worse than the occasional broken bumper. At the start of one season, the '100 Mile Cruiser' sailed to Port Carling with a complete set of new bumpers. The big ship had little clearance in the lock chamber at the best of times, and the new bumpers were extra thick, so much so, that the steamer became wedged in the basin as she tried to pass through, unable to move until the fenders had been pried loose and hoisted clear, on both sides. Needless to say, the men at the Gravenhurst shipyards had a little job to do that night, after the *Sagamo* returned home!

Alvin Saulter and a few of his mates also experienced a whimsical incident one autumn during the early thirties, when the little *Waome* was docking at Bracebridge. It all started when Captain Reg Leeder, leaving the ship one day carrying a rolled up newspaper, was offered a lift home by Neil MacNaughton, the Game Warden, who had once been mate on the *Islander*. Discovering that the Captain was carrying a fish in the paper, MacNaughton drove straight back to the wharf and demanded to know who had been using nets to catch fish? Bill McCulley, the Mate (and former Captain of the Hanna steamer *Mink*), unsuspectingly owned up. He had long been in the habit of setting nets on Lake Joseph when the steamer went up on Saturdays, gathering his catches on Mondays. To his surprise MacNaughton confiscated the nets and imposed a fine. When McCulley protested, the warden told him it was against the law to use nets, and that he, MacNaughton, intended to put a stop to it. When asked how he knew that nets had been used, MacNaughton replied, "They always leave marks on the fish."

Later that day, the *Waome* met the *Ahmic* for an exchange at Beaumaris. Saulter was then running the engines on the *Ahmic*. McCulley came over and asked, "Did you know I got pinched today?" "No," replied Saulter. "Who pinched you?" "MacNaughton." "Oh, go on with you!" "No, MacNaughton pinched me," insisted McCulley, going on to explain what happened. McCulley

196

S.S. "Segwun", as she appeared during the 1930s.

Crew of S.S. "Segwun", 1930.
Captain Geordie Stephen stands, third from the left, with Engineer Saulter (hatless) in the centre.

The "Big Chief", locking through during the Thirties.
Courtesy, *Canadian National Corporate Archives, 31795*

S.S. "Waome" (Second Version), with a taller stack.
Courtesy, *Mr. Douglas Gray*, Port Credit

Four officers from S.S. "Cherokee", 1932.
Engineer Alvin Saulter (left), Captain Andy Corbett, Purser Norman Dickson, and Captain
C.W. Henshaw.

felt quite aggrieved, since he and MacNaughton had frequently used nets when the two of them went fishing together, until MacNaughton took up his new job as game warden. All the hands chipped in to help pay the fine, because McCulley had always been generous with his catches, but he never used nets again.

That did not end the affair, however. The suspicious warden was still convinced that the boat crews were fishing illegally, and a few days later, when the *Waome* was returning to Bracebridge, Captain Henshaw came down to the engine room and remarked to Saulter, "I see your friend is out there watching us." Sure enough, two men were keeping a close eye on the steamer from Neil MacNaughton's nearby boat house. This gave Saulter an idea. A minute or so later, he and McCulley were leaving the ship together with a suspicious looking wrapped up newspaper, held under arm, while Saulter, for good measure, threw a few furtive glances back towards the boat house. They had proceeded about 50 feet when a voice rang out, "Stop!" The game warden hastened forward, not wearing a badge, and demanded to see what was inside that newspaper. Saulter asked if he had any authority to inspect it? "Yes I do," said the Warden, producing his badge. "I hear you men have been netting fish and I'm putting a stop to it!" Saulter obediently handed over the package. It immediately went limp in the warden's hands. The inspector's jaw fell open, and before long all of Bracebridge was buzzing with the story of how the game warden had inspected one of Saulter's dirty shirts.

Mr. Saulter often sailed on the *Waome* in the early and late portions of the season. One time in 1933, he was at work in the engine room when the steamer, cruising near Birch Island on her way to Beaumaris, collided with something very solid. It proved to be an unchartered rock, which Captain Henshaw had judged to be only a log. Shortly afterwards the charts were duly rectified!

This incident was a minor one compared to what happened to the *Waome* on October 6, 1934. On that fateful day, the little steamer suddenly made headlines all around the province as the victim of Muskoka's worst marine disaster.

At the time, the *Waome* was the only ship in the fleet still operating, mostly to carry freight and mail. All the others were in winter quarters. The *Ahmic* might have taken her place that fall except that she was due for a shaft inspection at Gravenhurst. The crew of the *Waome* that day was a "scratch" crew, half of whom were captains, in keeping with the Navigation Company's policy of employing its officers as long as possible every season. Captain Bill Henshaw was in command, with Captain Arthur Thompson acting as mate, Captain Reg Leeder serving as cook, Alvin Saulter at the engines, George Harvey of Gravenhurst (who frequently worked for the C.N.R.) serving as Purser, and Robert Bonnis of Gravenhurst as fireman. Captains Lee and Corbett, who were senior, could have been aboard if they had wished but neither cared much for the bitter chill of the late season.

It was a cold, dark, overcast day as the *Waome* headed south from the upper lakes to Port Carling. Aboard was a single passenger, the Reverend L.D.S. Coxon, a Presbyterian Minister going from Hamill's Point to Bracebridge. At Port Carling Mr. Harvey advised him to take the Company's new bus service the rest of the way, but Mr. Coxon replied that he preferred the boat trip. Around 10:00 a.m. the little steamer left Port Carling and started for Beaumaris. Mr. Coxon went down to the engine room (the warmest part of the ship) to have a chat with Saulter, then proceeded up the stairwell to sit in the lounge cabin. Art Thompson meanwhile left the wheelhouse, exchanged a few words with Mr. Coxon in the lounge, then went below to call on Leeder who was peeling potatoes in the galley. By that time the steamer had cleared the Indian River and was passing One Tree Island, out on northern Lake Muskoka. Beyond the island stretches about a mile of open water, near the Seven Sisters Islands, with at least two more miles of open water off to the west. It was an excellent spot for an ambush by the forces of Nature. The weather was still overcast and a light rain was falling, but the winds were light and the waters fairly calm. There seemed no reason not to continue. No one on board was aware that a freak storm with hurricane-force winds was at that very moment ripping up trees and tearing down telephone lines just north of Bala.

The time was now about half past ten. The steamer was starting across the open water, north of Idylwild Island. Art Thompson stepped out of the galley and found Saulter and Bonnis standing in the starboard companionway, looking out the windows and the aft gangway. Both were eyeing a huge black cloud boiling up in the west, off the starboard side, which was

S.S. "Waome", 1934.
Reputed to be the last photo taken of the "Waome".

The loss of the "Waome", Lake Muskoka,
October 6, 1934.

unleashing a solid sheet of downpour. It looked almost like a waterspout. "That's a dirty looking piece of weather out there," noted Saulter sombrely. Thompson replied, "Yes, but it's going to miss us, Alvin."

Scarcely had Thompson uttered these words than a tremendous gust of wind shrieked across the waters, catching the steamer almost broadside. Instantly she began heeling over to port; so violently that Bonnis fell back against the boiler room casing wall, which was already underneath him. The window next to him was rising over his head. Without a second thought Bonnis smashed the window with his feet, then scrambled through. Thompson meanwhile dashed up the stairwell—which was nearly horizontal—to the lounge where Mr. Coxon was. Saulter sprang to the engine controls, for there was sure to be a signal from the pilothouse. Water was rushing in through the mooring chocks and around his feet. Just as he reached the controls the bell clanged to "stop engines", which he did. By now tons of water were spilling in through the port windows and gangways. Suddenly Saulter knew that the ship was not going to recover. She was going all the way over—and down.

The Engineer's first thought now was about the boiler. What if it should explode? But there was no time to do anything about it. Desperately, Saulter scrambled up the almost vertical deck to the aft gangway and climbed out. He found himself standing on the ship's side, but the wind was so strong that he could barely maintain his balance. Working his way forward, he found Bonnis loosening one of the bumpers.

Below, in the Purser's office—a tiny cubicle on the port side of the main deck tucked underneath the stairwell—Purser George Harvey was shaving. He had removed both his uniform coat and shirt, and above the waist was wearing only an undershirt. Suddenly he was pitched off his feet and out of the cabin. Recovering himself, he found the deck canting over sideways with water pouring in. Panic-stricken, Harvey scrambled up to the starboard side. There was no one in sight, and apparently no way out. Then the stairwell caught his eye. Impulsively he dashed through it to the lounge, which was filling rapidly. Art Thompson and the passenger were at the aft end, trying to force the door open. Mr. Harvey sprang to the forward port side door. It refused to budge. Water was now swirling around his legs. Suddenly the door swung open, freeing Mr. Harvey, but before the others could follow it slammed shut again. Outside, the water was rising over the port railing. Captain Henshaw was in the water, groaning; apparently flung out of the wheelhouse when the storm struck. Coming from the starboard stern he probably never saw it until too late. Harvey pulled the skipper back on board, but didn't notice Saulter and Bonnis on the other side of the bow.

Down in the galley, Reg Leeder had still been attending to his chores when suddenly, without warning, the room began to roll over. Dishes went flying, china tinkled and smashed, and water poured in. Tables and chairs were falling over one another in the dining room. Leeder hurried aft to find the dining room almost sideways and the lower half filling with water. Escape seemed impossible. Then a settee drifted by. Leeder stood on it, grabbed a floating chair, and smashed one of the windows over his head. The air pressure from the inrushing water acted like a catapult, pushing him through; he cut his right arm badly on broken glass but didn't even notice. Once out, Leeder saw no one around, but fearing suction he jumped off the wreck and into the water. Here he found the fender loosened by Bonnis and began swimming for his life.

The sinking steamer, still on her side, now began to roll back to an even keel. As she did so, Harvey and Captain Henshaw lost their grip on the rail and were washed into the lake. Saulter, too, lost his balance and got one foot caught in the forward mooring chock. Just then the stern went under, followed by the bow and the pilothouse, and Saulter found himself being pulled down into the depths. Finally he managed to jerk his foot free and rose to the surface, gasping for air. He was still wearing his baggy coveralls, which were a terrible handicap in the water, but Bonnis helped him onto one of the lifeboat saddles which had floated free. (The solitary lifeboat, still attached to one of the davits, had gone down with the ship.) The entire incident was over in barely more than a minute.

The men now began a desperate fight for survival. The waters were bitterly cold, the wind at its height was heaping up four foot waves, and there was no one around to help since practically all of the cottagers had gone home. It was now every man for himself, and Captain Henshaw lost his battle. The elderly skipper, then 63, swam a few strokes away from the wreck . . . . then the others saw him no more. Mr. Harvey, clinging to the stool from the wheelhouse, tried to make for a nearby island but the waves were too much. He and the others now groped towards Keewaydin Island, about half a mile distant, encouraging one another as best they could. Finally after an hour's struggle George Harvey, a strong swimmer, reached the shore and extended a branch to the other three men, who were helped ashore one by one. Reg Leeder was unconscious from exhaustion and loss of blood. Alvin Saulter's lungs rattled from inhaled water. Of Captain Henshaw, or Art Thompson and Mr. Coxon, there was no sign. The skipper had succumbed to a heart attack, while the other two had never broken out of the lounge.

The four survivors were spent and freezing. Leeder, they feared, was drowned. Bonnis and Harvey broke into a vacant cottage and managed to start a fire, and gradually the men began to recover their strength.

Back at Gravenhurst, W.F. Wasley was nervously pacing back and forth in his office while Sleeth, his assistant, tried to reassure him. Why had there been no word from the *Waome*? Local agents were supposed to report the comings and goings of the boats. Finally, the Manager could bear the suspense no longer and telephoned Beaumaris shortly after 11:00 a.m. The reply was not encouraging: "No, she hasn't come in yet." At last around noon a motorboat was despatched from Beaumaris to take a look. It returned with the four marooned mariners, plus the body of Captain Henshaw. The Company bus brought them to the hospital at Bracebridge. By this time news of the tragedy had preceded them, and a large crowd of shocked citizens was on hand when they arrived. Wasley grimly ordered the *Islander* out again to finish the season, and by the following morning she was steaming over the *Waome*'s grave.

A deep sea diver from Prescott was summoned to retrieve the bodies of Mr. Coxon and Captain Thompson. He found the *Waome* lying right side up in cold, dark water, on a gentle slope about 80 feet below the surface. The bumpers and the lifeboat (which he cut free) were all pointing upwards, while the chairs and tables were floating in the cabins. There, in the lounge, he found the two drowned men, and concluded that Thompson had met his death trying to save Mr. Coxon. Thompson and Henshaw were buried side by side at the Mickle Memorial Cemetery at Gravenhurst, before a large concourse of people. Captain Henshaw was eulogized as a careful, obliging and efficient navigator, always ready to share his many colourful recollections of the lakes, while Thompson was described by the Gravenhurst 'Banner' of October 11, 1934 as "a splendid type, happy with his family, contented with his lot, and . . . . devoted to his company's interest." As for the *Waome*, she still lies where she sank in Lake Muskoka, about two miles northwest of Beaumaris, the port she failed to reach. Divers visit the wreck every summer. They all say she is an eerie sight, still wearing her coat of white paint, her bottom now buried in the sediments of the lake. Lately, though, her corroding stack has fallen in, as little by little she disintegrates in her watery tomb.

The *Waome* disaster cast a pall over Muskoka and caused great apprehension among the officials of the Navigation Company. As a direct result, the Company ordered its two smallest vessels, the *Ahmic* and the *Islander*, to be remodelled in an effort to lower their silhouettes. Over the winter, the hurricane deck of the *Islander* was shorted at both ends. In addition, the lifeboats of the *Ahmic* were relocated at the aft end of the second deck, while the pilothouse of the *Islander* was lowered to the deck below. The larger ships, which could not easily be altered, were left alone. With the fleet now reduced to five active steamers, the *Ahmic* usually provided the local service on Lake Rosseau, leaving only the *Islander* based on Bala Bay.

In spite of her lowered profile, the *Ahmic* had at least one bad moment when she seemed likely to share the *Waome*'s fate. On a windy, overcast day in August 1935, the little steamer left Beaumaris for Bracebridge amid whitecaps and rough waters. North of the river estuary, a violent gust of wind made her heel over so much that several passengers lost their balance and began to panic: a girl tumbled down the stairwell, but was caught by the Purser. In the pilothouse, both Captain Hill and the mate had to wrestle with the wheel to keep the ship under control. Some of the people ashore also grew excited and stood ready to bring their launches to the scene if necessary. But the threat soon passed and to everyone's amazement, by the time the steamer reached the river, the water looked as smooth as glass.

By this time, the Navigation Company was becoming almost desperate. The firm had paid no dividends since 1929 and now it found itself barely able to break even. In 1930, its payroll, for

Fantail of S.S. "Ahmic" (Final Version).
The little steamer's lifeboats have been moved down to the promenade deck.

over 135 seasonal employees, was said to total about $73,000. Plant renewals and new equipment were costing about $27,000, provisions about $36,000, fuel at $17,000 (including 5,000 cords of slab-wood purchased from the farmers), insurance at $9,000, advertising over $7,500, and taxes near $1,900: the Line's expenses in 1930 came to about $171,400. Its steamers were reckoned to have travelled 61,110 miles that season, and to have carried about 40,000 passengers. In 1930, fares for the '100 Mile Cruise' were $2.50 for adults, at which rate the boats would have earned about $100,000: however, not passengers were adults taking the all-day trip, and it is more likely that ticket sales were closer to $90,000. According to the late Mr. Andrew D. MacLean, son of Major MacLean, the *Sagamo* and *Cherokee* each grossed about $6,000 a day for about twenty days a season, if the weather was fair, suggesting a total of $240,000 during the peak of the season. We are not informed about the profits from freighting, nor how much the Royal Muskoka made, but almost certainly the totals were declining. Nor is it certain how much the mail contract paid. In 1905, the mail service netted the Company $3,880 (not counting the Magnetawan division, which generated another $890), but this climbed to $6,240 in 1910 and $8,093.60 in 1916, the last season for which record has been found. Possibly the service was worth about $15,000 annually during the 1930s. In 1931 the Gravenhurst 'Banner' noted that the Navigation Company, by advertising in the daily newspapers of the big cities, was doing a great deal to promote the economy of the entire district, and concluded, "Muskoka must see to it that the Muskoka Lakes Line of boats are continued, because, to Muskoka, these boats are a national institution." The message was clear: the Navigation Company, which had always been such a great asset to Muskoka, was now in difficulty and deserved support.

The advertising, alas, seemed futile in the face of the sudden, brutal onslaught of hard times. Even the hot summer of 1930 failed to bring back the crowds of 1929. The season of 1931 was even worse. In the fall, with mounting desperation (resulting partly from the inroad of truckers), Mr. Wasley announced that freight rates for flour and feed were being slashed to 12½¢ per cwt. on one lake, or 15¢ per cwt. on two or three lakes, with comparable reductions on other items such as food and building supplies. Politely, he appealed to customer loyalty, asking Muskokans not to desert the Line. "For 60 years or more," he wrote, "the Company has operated, rain or shine, depression or no depression, and has appreciated your patronage in the past and respectfully solicits its continuance."

At the very time that Mr. Wasley was entering this plea, the Muskoka communities were bombarding the Ontario Legislature with petitions to extend paved and macadamized roads throughout the resorts regions. By 1931, plans were under way to pave the road from Gravenhurst to Bala. In 1934, the new Liberal government of Mitchell Hepburn agreed to pay the total cost of a new hard-surfaced road from Bracebridge to Port Carling and Bala and back to Gravenhurst, completely encircling Lake Muskoka; partly as unemployment relief. By 1936, this road was completed, and though parts of it failed to hold up well over the next few winters, the net effect was to simplify the task of truckers, and to allow motorists to reach the prime resort areas by land. In the summer of 1938, an estimated 2,000 automobiles drove through Port Sandfield and Minett by way of the Peninsula Road, which was being upgraded at that time. It was also possible to drive overland to Rosseau. Considering that almost all summertime traffic through these communities used to travel by steamer, it is obvious what all this meant to the Muskoka Navigation Company. It took the new highways barely three decades to eliminate both the railway and the excursion steamer from the recreation scene in Ontario.

In the face of these conditions, plus an economic climate that seemed only to get worse, W.F. Wasley strove unceasingly to keep alive the enterprise he loved. According to a former clerk at

S.S. "Islander" (Final Version) at Port Carling, 1936.

Muskoka Navigation Company Office, Muskoka Road, Gravenhurst.

Muskoka Navigation Company bus awaiting the S.S. "Sagamo" at Port Carling.
Mr. Fred Stafford, driver (right), stands beside his International.
Courtesy, *Mrs. Irene Dickson*, Willowdale

the Dominion Bank in Gravenhurst, the Navigation Company usually spent $75,000 to $80,000 every winter during the Depression: if the following summer were not too bad, the proceeds just barely erased the bills. Then the following winter, the Company would run up another overdraft of about $80,000. The season of 1932 was the worst of all, according to Mr. Ted Corbett, yet apparently even then, the Line made a slight surplus of $1,500. Conditions grew so tight that the Company was forced even to reduce the modest pension it paid to Commodore Bailey, who survived until 1938. As a rule, the steamers just about held their own during the Depression, but often one look at the receipts from the cumbersome Royal Muskoka were enough to make Wasley moan. The Manager worried constantly throughout the thirties and almost forgot how to laugh. Occasionally he was heard to mutter that if he could only make the *Sagamo* pay, the mail contract would sustain the other ships. Sometimes he considered tying up the *Sagamo*, which was very costly to operate, but he could never bring himself to do it.

Still the Manager refused to give up. In addition to his Bay Street office near the Company dockyards, he opened a new office on the main street of Gravenhurst in June of 1933, in the hope of intercepting tourists coming to town by car. He helped and exhorted the Muskoka Tourist Development Association to lure convention organizers and travel agency owners from various American cities to Muskoka (usually by way of the Gray Coach Bus Lines rather than the Canadian National Railway), to sample the delights of the resorts and the boat cruise at first hand. He cut costs by engaging motor launches to carry the mail to remote ports of call. In the spring of 1934, he decided to run two small buses and a truck to carry passengers and package freight from remote points to the main ports of call: this was in part intended to forestall rival operators from doing the same thing. One bus ran from Bala to Port Carling by way of Dudley and Whiteside, and then to Port Sandfield, Minett and Juddhaven, while the other operated from Port Carling to Windermere and Rosseau. The service was a great convenience to the resorts, speeded the delivery of the mail, and helped eliminate many a long wait for a steamer, but it failed to make much money. In time, the buses (which did not run during the winter) also extended their runs to Gravenhurst, Bracebridge and Lake Joseph. One slight ray of sunshine amid the gloom was the recruiting of Charles Musgrave, a Toronto pianist and band leader who used to spend his summers at Port Carling, to provide musical entertainment on the *Sagamo*. Mr. Musgrave, who started around 1931, offered a lively running commentary as well as music, and soon became the life of the '100 Mile Cruise'. He returned to the ship every summer until his death in 1953.

In spite of a slight upturn in the economy after 1933, the Muskoka Navigation Companay was soon teetering on the brink of collapse. By 1934 it would appear that the banks were dubious about lending it any more money. In January of 1934, MacLean and Wasley had to put their own personal property on the line as collateral to guarantee repayment of a Company bank loan of $35,000. Every ship in the fleet plus the Royal Muskoka were mortgaged. Both men specified in writing that they wished only to help the Company through difficult times, not to seize any of the Line's goods or chattels. (By this time Major MacLean had already bought out most of the shareholders in the firm in any case!) The mortgage was not officially lifted until 1946, though it

Major Hugh C. MacLean (left) and W.F. Wasley.
Courtesy, *Mrs. Irene Dickson*, Willowdale

had been paid off by then. By 1936, unemployment had diminished some, the summer was warm, and there was even a mild building boom in Bracebridge. Sluggishly, the economy was reviving. The faith of MacLean and Wasley proved justified.

Besides the six steamers of the Navigation Company fleet, about nineteen Muskoka yachts survived into the thirties, although several of them, including the *Adjie*, *Edith Ann*, *Hepburn*, *Izaak Walton*, *Rambler*, *Swastika* and *Willoudee* were one by one converted to gasoline or diesel engines. Several more, notably the *Elsa*, *Iona*, *Lotus*, *Phoebe II* and *Wanda III*, had been moved to other waters. Only the *Beaver*, *Ilderim*, *Ina*, *Naiad*, and *Mildred* were still cruising the lakes under steam at the close of the decade. The *Hepburn* was not converted until about 1938, sometimes running charter cruises from Glen Echo Lodge during this period.

The graceful *Mildred*, still commanded by Wesley Archer, also ran regular excursion cruises right through the Depression and into the War years on all three lakes. Captain Archer sometimes liked to needle the Navigation Company by advertising that his vessel also ran a one hundred mile cruise (until Mr. Wasley threatened court action to defend his company's copyright of the name), through some lovely scenery on routes never taken by the big ships, such as the Joseph River; sometimes making better time than the big steamers and charging much less. (In 1932 an all-day cruise from Bracebridge on the *Mildred* cost only $1.00 per person.) Another of Captain Archer's promotional efforts was the practice of selling or giving away postcards of the *Mildred*. Apparently he was always able to make his vessel pay.

One evening in 1937, the *Mildred* experienced a nasty moment near Mikado Island on Lake Muskoka, while she was on a charter cruise from Bangor Lodge to Cedar Beach. She piled up on a rock and put a hole through her bottom. However, the Captain's daughter Laura, who was serving as mate, stuffed her uniform coat into the rent, and soon the vessel was pumped out sufficiently to allow her to return home, where the damage was speedily repaired. Captain Archer continued to run the *Mildred* until the year of his death (1946) at the age of about 66, but even then the vessel's cruising days were far from over.

As we have seen, the towing fleet almost totally disappeared from the lakes during the 1920s. All that remained during the Depression years were a few steam workboats, some of which, like the *Edith Ann* and the *Ina*, were former yachts past their prime. The *Izaak Walton* was used from about 1933 onwards to peddle fruit, vegetables and supplies to cottagers around central Lake Muskoka, until she was crushed by snow near the Gravenhurst Narrows around 1942. The *Queen of the Isles*, which had been scowing on the lakes since 1895, continued to serve until 1934. For her last ten years she was owned by Captain Levi Fraser, who had already worn out three tugs. Finally the graceful *Queen of the Isles* also admitted defeat, at the ripe old age of 49 years, and was dismantled in the Muskoka River near Bracebridge. Fraser replaced her by purchasing the *Constance* from Jim Campbell in 1934, using her to scow timber. These exertions gradually exhausted the *Constance* too, and in 1938 she also went to the scrapyards. She had sailed the Muskoka Lakes for 40 years and fifteen owners.

Captain Fraser, who was a mere 65 years of age in 1938, and who had been sailing since 1893, was in no mood to retire yet, and accordingly looked around for another tug. He found one at the Locks, near Huntsville: the *Niska* lay idle at the Cottrill family sawmill, because trucks had eliminated towing on the North Muskoka Lakes. With two assistants, Fraser fitted out the little craft, ran her to Huntsville, and had her taken south on a flatcar. Thus the little tug completed her circuit from the Muskoka Lakes to the Lake of Bays, the Huntsville lakes and back again, although practically nothing now remained of the vessel built in 1897 except her whistle. The *Niska* served as Fraser's workboat for three years. She and the *Shamrock II*, still commanded by Captain Harry Croucher, were now the only steam tugs left on the lakes. In the spring of 1941, Fraser sold the *Niska* to Croucher and crowned his career by joining the Navigation Company as Master of the *Ahmic* for one or two seasons. Afterwards he commanded the *Mohawk Belle* on the Lake of Bays for a time.

The Muskoka supply boat business, already waning in the twenties, continued its lingering decline. The *Alporto*, as we have noted, last sailed from Milford Bay in 1934. Except for the small-scale operations of the *Ina* and the *Izaak Walton*, only the Hanna Company steamer *Newminko* survived the Depression and carried on into the 1940s. But the going was difficult. Every extension of the paved road network made it easier for cottagers to drive to town and buy

Steam Yacht "Naiad".
Courtesy, *Mrs. Joyce Schell*, Barlochan

Steam Yacht "Mildred", on the Joseph River.
Courtesy, *Ontario Archives*, Acc. 9939, Roll 12B, #26

their groceries whenever they liked. Matters were not improved when new stores were opened near Woodington House on Lake Rosseau, Gregory on the Joseph River, and Port Sandfield. The Hanna Company itself suffered heavily in the great fire that gutted much of the business section of Port Carling on the night of October 28, 1931; destroying the Duke Boat Works, the Bay View House hotel, the Sutton Ice Cream Parlour, the Navigation Company freight shed and telegraph office, plus nine other buildings.

Despite these and other setbacks, the hardy little *Newminko* carried on, primarily on the upper lakes. The year 1930 proved especially bad for her. That summer she ran over a rocky shoal while passing Chief's Island on Lake Joseph, holed her side, and sank in about eight feet of water. Her crew and passengers were picked up without difficulty, and most of her cargo removed. Later, Captain Fraser arrived with the *Queen of the Isles* and a scow to raise the *Newminko* and take her back to Port Carling for repairs. Later that same fall the vessel, still under Captain Jim McCulley, grounded again near Loon Island in Lake Joseph. Later still, she piled up on a reef in Bala Bay in foggy weather, heeled over to port, and spilled most of her cargo of oatmeal and baled hay into the water. The *Ahmic*, then on her way to Bala, was the first vessel to arrive at the scene. After the fog lifted, the *Newminko* was rescued by the *Alporto* and the diesel oil-tanker *Muskokalite*. Her remaining cargo was removed to lighten her, and gradually the craft was worked free.

Supply Steamer "Newminko", aground on Bala Bay.
Courtesy, *Mrs. Ruth Stanier*

Str. "Newminko", sunk at Port Carling, 1942.

This was not the last of the *Newminko*'s adventures. In 1934, Captain Reg Leeder was backing the steamer *Islander* out of Nepahwin-Gregory, when suddenly he saw smoke astern. Behind him was the *Newminko*, now under Captain Bill Tinkiss, bearing down on his own ship. Remembering his father's advice about what to do in a tight situation, Leeder paused to think for a few moments, while blowing the whistle several times. Then he slowly took his vessel forward, while Tinkiss responded by reversing engines on the *Newminko*. The two steamers slowly drew apart, and a collision was avoided.

The *Newminko* had a number of other close calls. One time during the 1930s she struck the Gull Rocks on Lake Muskoka, between Point Montcalm and Browning Island, and again had to be rescued. Another time she snapped off a propeller blade on a rock near Little Brackens Island on Lake Rosseau. Again, around 1941 she grounded near Craigie Lea, Lake Joseph, while under Jim McCulley's command. McCulley, by now 77, retired afterwards and the vessel was assigned to Walter Leeder, an uncle of Reg and Gerald, who often served as mate on the larger steamers. Apparently it was he who was running the *Newminko* when she piled up on yet another shoal across from Loon Island, and again she had to be brought home from Lake Joseph under tow. That, apparently, was the last straw. The War was now on, making it difficult to find qualified engineers and wheelsmen. Merchandise became both more limited and more expensive. The Company was also changing hands at the time, and apparently the new owner was uninterested in the boat division. Shortly afterwards the *Newminko* took in water through her seams with the onset of winter, and sank in the Port Carling locks. Refloated and taken back to her regular mooring below the locks, she again filled and grounded. Fred Hanna, finding her thus, slackened her lines, which only caused the vessel to cant over. It cost $600 to board up her windows, pump her out and refloat her. The little *Newminko* never sailed again, though she lingered on at Port Carling for another twelve years. With her died the supply boat business on all the Muskoka Lakes, after more than half a century.

The Navigation Company was still struggling along. Though the national economic scene was gradually getting better, that simply allowed more people to buy motorboats and automobiles. Trucks, too, continued to cut deeper and deeper into the freighting business. New roads were opened to various ports of call, such as Walker's Point, Barlochan and Mortimer's Point, previously almost inaccessible by land. Snowplowing was first undertaken during the 1930s too, breaking the winter's annual siege of isolation: consequently, local residents no longer felt the need to stock up provisions for the cold season. As a result, the seasons for the steamers became shorter. In 1936, the *Islander* left the lakes for winter quarters on October 23rd, which to old-timers was a far cry from the days when the boats plied as late as December.

Still, despite all these trends, the Muskoka Lakes Navigation Company survived, still running five fine steamers at the end of the decade. It was one of the few steamship lines in Canada that did. The last passenger steamer on the Rideau Canal tied up for good in 1935. The Stoney Lake Navigation Company still had two vessels left in service by the beginning of the forties, but it was now a mere ghost of its former self and would soon be out of business. Only one passenger steamer, the *Modello*, still plied on Lake Nipissing, from North Bay to the French River, and there was still a steamer operating on Lake Temagami: otherwise steamboating was a thing of the past in Northern Ontario. The Huntsville Navigation Company was reduced to two ships still in commission during the thirties. The Muskoka Navigation Company was the largest and healthiest survivor of them all.

1939 started off much the same as previous years, across Canada, but soon there was a difference. Introverted and isolationist though the nation's general outlook had been for twenty years, the country was about to be shaken out of its complacent slumber. Events in Europe were again shaping up ominously in a way that not even Canadians could ignore. The insatiable, ruthless aggressiveness of a rearmed Nazi Germany thirsting for vengeance over the Treaty of Versailles was becoming obvious to even the most dyed-in-the-wool pacifists. To most it was merely a matter of time before the world would again be at war. On September 1st, 1939, Hitler's panzers and dive bombers blitzed their way into Poland, and ten days later a reluctant but resolute Canada followed Britain and France into war. Factories at once began receiving almost unlimited orders for war materiél, and started gearing up for the job. Men volunteered for service. Farmers were urged to produce all the food they could. The railways were soon running at full capacity, pressing every available piece of rolling stock into service. Practically the entire economy was soon geared for war. Luxury items, including automobiles and tires, were almost unobtainable. Gasoline was rationed, and roads received only minimum maintenance. The military disasters of 1940 in Europe merely intensified the pressure: everyone now had a job, and soon over 700,000 men were in uniform. Even a local firm like the Greavette Boat Building Works in Gravenhurst was doing its share by building sub-chasing Fairmiles for the Navy. Despite its terrible costs, the War put an end to the Depression and gave a listless country a new faith in itself.

There was little that the Navigation Company could do to assist the war effort, except to provide the occasional cruise for soldiers on furlough, or to conduct special charity trips, with the proceeds going to such agencies as the British War Victims' Fund. Nonetheless, the Company was still vital to the local economy, and hence it was not denied oil and coal. In fact, the Line became a major morale booster for thousands of Canadians undergoing the privations of wartime, in that it offered one of the few avenues of recreation left in Ontario. In spite of regulations, restraints and rationing, there was nothing to prevent citizens from boarding a train at Toronto to take the 'One Hundred Mile Cruise'. Most of the larger hotels in Muskoka were still in business, while vacations in Europe were out of the question. The *Sagamo* and her sister ships continued to ply faithfully every summer.

Given all these incentives, people again began flocking to Muskoka Wharf in droves to escape the heat of summer. Sometimes over a thousand would arrive at a time, requiring both the *Sagamo* and the *Segwun* to handle them. One double cruise by the Gravenhurst Oddfellows and the Bracebridge Rotarians on June 30, 1940, drew about 1,200 participants, travelling on four steamers. Even Moonlight Cruises were often sold out. On Labour Day, 1940, the whole fleet, plus a record crowd, were on hand at Port Carling with whistles and streamers to bid farewell to the *Sagamo* at season's end. Suddenly steamboating was back in style. The 1941 season was said to have seen the heaviest trade the Line had experienced in 36 years; even the Royal was busy. In 1945, the Gravenhurst 'Banner' was claiming that "traffic had tripled on the lake steamers since 1940, and that between 40,000 and 50,000 people were vacationing at the resorts."

Thus the War years, by curtailing trips by car and motorboat and sharply restricting other forms of recreation, were kind to the Muskoka steamers and afforded them a genuine, though fleeting, prosperity: the last they were ever to know. All debts from the Depression were wiped off the slate; the worries of the thirties vanished. In 1940, the *Sagamo* was fitted out with a set of seven loudspeakers, each individually controlled, which added a whole new dimension to Charlie Musgrave's music and commentaries. Except for the *Medora* fire of 1940, the Navigation Company suffered no real setbacks at all during the War, barring the occasional accident. The worst seems to have been the cost of a new $400 propeller for the *Segwun*, when she managed to shear off part of one of her old ones near Birch Island on Lake Muskoka, around 1943.

The upturn of wartime, unhappily, did not come soon enough for W.F. Wasley's constitution. Nervous, high strung and excitable, the 66 year old Manager had never spared anyone, himself included, in his efforts to promote the well-being of his Company, and the resulting strain had driven him to almost incessant smoking, and then to ulcers. Though he always seemed as sharp and clear as ever, the ordeal was slowly destroying him. During the winter of 1939-40, Wasley contracted a bad cold and sprained a nerve in his throat, which made his coughing worse. Unwillingly, he was confined to bed, and even when he "recovered" he became forgetful and absent-minded, and soon it was clear that he was having a nervous breakdown. In March of 1941, he was officially relieved of his duties as Manager, although continuing for a time as Secretary-Treasurer. It was assumed that he simply needed a good rest, but instead he only grew worse, and was finally committed to a hospital at Guelph. Eventually he was released, but though he sometimes returned to Gravenhurst, he always remained at home and avoided the limelight. He died in Toronto, on June 24, 1964; a broken remnant of the vigorous, watchful, plain-speaking William Franklin Wasley who had conducted and guided the affairs of the Muskoka Navigation Company for a total of 34 years.

There was never much doubt about who would succeed him. William Eric Wasley, his only son, had been born and brought up in Gravenhurst before continuing his education at Trinity College School in Port Hope, and later at Osgoode Hall in Toronto. In 1938, aged 28, he was called to the bar, and shortly afterwards opened a law office in Gravenhurst. Although trained as

S.S. "Sagamo", with a shipload of Air Force Cadets, Muskoka Wharf.
Courtesy, *Fry's Photo Shop*, Gravenhurst

S.S. "Sagamo", on the Marine Railway at season's end.
Note the four carts for loading coal.
Courtesy, *Mrs. Irene Dickson*, Willowdale

Coaling up at Bala Park!
Eric Wasley lends a hand.
Courtesy, *Mrs. Irene Dickson*, Willowdale

Assistant Manager Robert Sleeth.

a lawyer, Eric Wasley had been smitten with steamboat fever, (a potentially dangerous malady), ever since his youth, when he began working on the boats during the summers. The young man came to know the lakes very well, and deep down, he really wanted to be a ship's captain. It was probably family pressure that induced him to train as a lawyer, but he also obtained his mate's ticket. For five years Eric worked seasonally as purser or mate, or as office assistant to Robert Sleeth, who left the Line in 1942. Assisting them both was young Wasley's friend, Norman Dickson, for many years Purser on the *Cherokee*: later he would marry Eric's sister Irene. Eric in fact became Acting Manager in 1940, and when the elder Wasley had to step down, his logical successor was waiting. Like his father, Eric Wasley — "Hornblower" to his intimates — had a lively, excitable temperament and was an avid curler. He was also a lot more affable than his father, and had many friends in Gravenhurst.

Just about the time that Eric Wasley stepped into the Manager's shoes, the immediacy of the War was brought home dramatically to the people of Gravenhurst. In 1940, the government leased the old Calydor Sanatorium property fronting on Muskoka Bay near the modern Ontario Fire College, and turned it into a prisoner of war camp to house captured German officers and servicemen. The camp held over 400 prisoners, who from the compound had a clear and unobstructed view of the Bay. They were even allowed to go swimming in it during the summer, although naturally there was barbed wire out in the water to make certain they didn't swim too far! Every so often the wail of the Rubberset Brush Company whistle in Gravenhurst alerted nervous townspeople that enemy aliens had slipped out of the camp and were perhaps right in their midst, although none were ever at large for long. From the camp, the Germans could watch the *Sagamo* passing every morning and returning at night. What were the thoughts of the prisoners as they beheld the graceful little ship cruising past every day, laden with sightseers and proudly flying the Union Jack at her flagstaffs? Did she remind them of peaceful scenes in Germany, of, perhaps, steamships cruising up and down the Rhine as in happier times? Or was she just a hateful symbol of the detested British Empire? Probably the latter. Charlie Musgrave, with his impish sense of humour, could not refrain from ordering his orchestra to play patriotic airs every time the steamer passed the camp (for the prisoners' benefit of course), usually finishing up with 'Rule Britannia' or 'There'll Always Be an England'. The Germans, we are told, objected and complained of harassment. It is said that the Canadian authorities requested Eric Wasley to put a stop to this, and that Eric flatly refused to forbid such tunes in wartime, least of all to avoid ruffling the feelings of the Germans! It is also said that vague threats were made to burn the *Sagamo* during the War, and that the Company, taking no chances, kept a watchman on duty every night. Meanwhile the ship's orchestra soon began to play a discreet distance from the camp, and in any case the prisoners soon organized their own band, which could drown out the offending airs.

Shortly after the onset of war, the Line lost one of its best officers. Captain "Geordie" Stephen, the quiet little man once known as the "little red squirrel" because of his complexion, took the wheel of the *Segwun* for the last time in 1940, before suffering a stroke which led to his death in Orillia the following year, at the age of 76. The result was a shakeup among the captains. Reg Leeder now took over the *Segwun*, while "Nipper" Hill replaced him on the *Islander*. Levi Fraser, who had been working on the tugs longer than most people could remember, now briefly took over the *Ahmic*, with Ben Dewey as his mate, though it is said that Fraser left most of the actual steering to the easy-going Dewey.

Captain Leeder once found himself in a difficult position at Port Carling, thanks to Fraser. On this particular day in 1941, Leeder happened to be at the wheel of the *Sagamo*, coming upstream from Lake Muskoka. Though the downstream boat legally had the right of way, it was customary for the other ships to defer to the *Sagamo* at Port Carling, since idling in the river current was dangerous for her. Hence the Captain was not very pleased to discover the *Ahmic*, under Fraser and Dewey, already in the lock chamber as the *Sagamo* approached. The chamber had already been partly drained. The choice for Captain Leeder was not an enviable one: either anchor in the river, insist that the lock chamber be refilled so that the *Ahmic* could back out, and then wait for the lock to be emptied (which might take an hour or more), or else try to manoeuvre the *Sagamo* sideways to the west side of the lower harbour and tether her there without crushing any of the docks or the parked steamer *Newminko*, so as to let the *Ahmic* pass. The latter alternative raised another unpleasant question: what if there were rocks in that portion of the river? Captain Leeder grimly decided to take the risk. Gingerly, he alternated his engines forwards, trying to coax 152 feet of steamship over to the side of the basin. Eventually he succeeded, though it taxed his abilities as a ship handler to the utmost. Leeder always considered Fraser to blame for putting the *Sagamo* in such a risky position: Dewey, he felt, would have known better.

Captain Fraser did not remain on the *Ahmic* very long. By 1943 the little steamer had been assigned to the amiable Captain Hector Hatherley of Gordon Bay and Toronto, who had trained as an engineer before joining the Navigation Company. That same season, the *Ahmic* experienced a mishap that put her out of service for nearly a week.

It happened on the morning of July 7th, when the *Ahmic* was cruising downriver from Bracebridge on her way to Beaumaris. At that time a number of sharpened logs had purposely been driven into the lake bottom near the mouth of the river to carry lanterns and serve as buoys. One of these planted deadheads, almost out of sight, happened to be pointing directly at the bow of the oncoming steamer. She struck the lurking menace head-on and harpooned herself, splintering one of her hull planks, though initially no one noticed. Within a few minutes, however, the Engineer, Jack Simpson of Gravenhurst, complained that water was building up in the hold. Only then was the damage discovered, and the pumps couldn't begin to cope with the inflow. Captain Hatherley at once made for a cove off the south end of Birch Island, a mile or so away, and beached the vessel in shallow water, sounding the whistle repeatedly with four quick blasts as a distress signal.

Just about that time the *Sagamo* was on her way north up the lake, and was in the act of docking at Walker's Point when the *Ahmic*'s shrill cries for help echoed across the water. Captain Lee at once steered in that direction at full speed, and soon found the little ship, listing badly to port, with the freeboard of her main deck partly under water. The stranded passengers were picked up, and later the *Ahmic* was rescued by Captain Harry Croucher with the *Niska* and two scows, which were placed on either side of her. Quite a few motorboats gathered to watch as the *Ahmic* was raised and towed back to Gravenhurst. After a few days in drydock, she was ready to go again.

S.S. "Ahmic", beached at Birch Island, Lake Muskoka, on July 7, 1943.

The following year (1944), the *Ahmic* had another, less serious adventure on Lake Joseph while cruising south from the Stanley House. It was an extremely foggy morning, and before long Captain Hatherley became unsure of his bearings and asked one of the hands if he knew where they were? The crewman recognized a tall pine above the fog, advised that they were near Elsinore Island, and that they'd better swing around to port to avoid hitting Johnson's shoal. Then—crash! The steamer abruptly grounded on said shoal, and could not be backed off. All the men could do was whistle for help. In time, some local boys appeared in two small motorboats. Pulling directly backwards proved futile, but then the lads were instructed to try pulling sideways. At last, around noon, the steamer rolled off the shoal, bade farewell to her rescuers, and made for Foot's Bay, where she was inspected and pronounced all right. The *Ahmic* completed her rounds that day about three or four hours behind schedule.

A similar incident befell the *Islander* around 1941, also on Lake Joseph. It was late in the season, on another foggy morning, when the steamer, commanded by Captain Hill, was assigned to deliver six bags of cement to Governor's Island, where a new dock was under construction. As the vessel approached the wharf, the caretaker asked the crew if they would please leave the cement at a new makeshift dock a short distance away, to save wheelbarrowing it through the woods. The crew obliged, although it meant manoeuvring in unfamiliar waters. A line was secured to a tree and the bags thrown ashore without touching the flimsy little dock. It was in pulling away that the fun began. Right behind the steamer was an undetected rock, barely a hundred feet off the main channel. The *Islander* backed right onto this shoal, heaved up at the stern, and was left stranded with part of her propeller out of the water. There was no way that she could move by herself, so she blew her whistle periodically and waited for help. After about an hour, a motorboat emerged from the fog with the contractor on board. Attempts were made to drag the steamer off, but in vain. Meanwhile two more boats arrived, and all three began pulling the *Islander* sideways. Gradually they swung her around, about 180 degrees. Suddenly the steamer slipped off the rocks undamaged, then returned to Port Carling about two hours late. Word of the incident had already been telephoned around the lakes: Captain Lee for one refused to believe there was a rock only a boat's length off the *Sagamo*'s daily route on Lake Joseph. By the time the *Islander* got back to Gravenhurst that evening, however, it was a different story. By then all of the other boatmen had always known there was a rock off Governor's Island. How could the *Islander*'s crew have been so stupid as to pile her up?.

Commodore Lee remained with the *Sagamo* almost until the end of the War. Gerald Leeder sailed with him for one season as mate, but relations between them were not cordial. Captain Lee was a bit pompous as Commodore (Captain Bradshaw had once dubbed him "Admiral") and he was not very helpful about pointing out possible hazards, although this may have been a symptom of old age: the Commodore was 72 in 1944. Gerald was shocked to find out in later years that Captain Lee had been allowing him to take the *Sagamo* right past a gigantic sunken rock near Chief's Island, Lake Joseph, on a regular basis, without warning him about it. In another instance Leeder was invited, for the first time, to try docking the *Sagamo* at Clevelands House. Unknown to him, recent dredging operations had created a mud flat opposite the wharf. Gerald grounded the bow in the mud and had to back out and try again. Captain Lee bawled him out afterwards. This put Gerald on edge. He replied that he hadn't been aware of the mud flat. Lee told him it was his duty to know; whereupon Leeder retorted that it was the Captain's duty to *tell* him these things! Leeder finished the season with the Commodore, but none too amicably.

At least once, though, Gerry Leeder had to admire the skipper's nerve. During that season, the proprietor of the Stanley House, W.F. Bissonette, complained that the *Sagamo* (for lack of business) seldom called anymore. The mail for the hotel was then being left at the Natural Park, just a few miles away, and transported overland: that way it always arrived sooner, but Bissonette wasn't satisfied. Wearying of these complaints, Eric Wasley asked Lee to call at the Stanley House and reason with Bissonette. The result was a violent scene in the pilothouse. Both men lost their tempers. Then the proprietor, who was quite a big man, threatened to give Lee a black eye. The spunky little Captain instantly whipped off his glasses, handed them to Gerald, and said, "Try it!" Bissonette didn't. Nor did the *Sagamo* increase her calls.

Another time that season, a deplorable incident occurred on a windy afternoon at Port Carling. The *Sagamo* was returning from Lake Rosseau and preparing to enter the lock chamber, when Captain Lee spotted a beautiful big mahogany motor launch illegally parked at the wharf adjacent to the lock gates. The steamer needed that space for manoeuvring. Captain Lee dared not reverse engines and wait, because of the wind, and therefore blew the whistle several times as a signal to move the launch. Nobody reacted. Then he stepped out onto the bridge and shouted for someone to get that launch out of the way. No one moved. The result was inevitable. The big ship slowly swung in towards the lock, and, in passing, squeezed the launch against the wharf. The cambered mahogany deck heaved up and splintered; then, as the steamer glided past, the launch, crushed like a basket, slid into the deep. Only the lines kept it from sinking completely. How the matter was ultimately resolved is not known, but without a doubt, Ralph W. Lee refused to take the blame for it.

Towards the end of August, the "Big Chief" ran into trouble at the Gravenhurst Narrows. She was returning from a Moonlight Cruise around 11:00 p.m. when a strong southeast wind sprang up. As she approached the channel, a gust began to blow her sideways, and Captain Lee decided he'd better back out and take another try at it. As the ship idled, the wind carried her closer to Lighthouse Island. Then the starboard propeller glanced off a rock and sheared off two blades. The big ship backed far out in a semicircle, manoeuvring on one screw, until finally the wind abated a little and the Captain decided to make another attempt at the passage, this time successfully. The *Sagamo* completed her few remaining trips of the season, running mostly on a single screw, until the broken propeller blades could be replaced.

Captain Lee returned to the *Sagamo* in 1945, but by then his health was failing and the years were catching up with him. Too weak for his duties, the old man made a number of bad dockings; then, without waiting to be asked, he walked off his ship at Muskoka Wharf, purposely leaving his uniform jacket behind. He had been working on the steamers since 1891, and in the course of half a century had carried over a million passengers safely. He was also credited with rescuing five people from drowning. Another twelve years elapsed before the jaunty old Commodore passed away at his home in Toronto, just short of his eighty-fifth birthday, and only a year short of the end of steamboat operations in Muskoka. Reg Leeder succeeded him on the *Sagamo*.

The new Captain experienced one of the closest calls of his career during his first season on the *Sagamo*. It happened one afternoon in August on the upper Indian River, as the *Ahmic*, under his uncle Walter Leeder, was approaching the second bend above Port Carling, followed by the *Cherokee*. The whistle of the *Sagamo* was heard, returning from Lake Rosseau: the *Cherokee* sounded a reply, but apparently the *Ahmic* did not. She met the flagship right at the hairpin turn (the worst possible place), but even so, all would have been well, except that Walter Leeder impulsively decided to pass on the starboard side. This entailed cutting across the big ship's bow, which forced Reg to reverse engines in mid-turn to avoid a collision. The *Ahmic* managed to squeeze past but the *Sagamo* was now effectively blocking the entire channel, with the *Cherokee* bearing down on her. Fortunately, Captain Corbett also kept his head and reversed one engine. Then, with a mudflat tugging at the propeller, he put his ship into forward, while the *Sagamo* was still in his path. But Corbett knew what he was doing. The *Sagamo* was also moving, and moments later she and the *Cherokee* passed each other, port to port, with a scant few feet to spare. The passengers cheered and waved to one another, quite oblivious of the danger. Surprisingly, no one ever mentioned the incident again, least of all Walter Leeder, who was fully aware of the magnitude of his blunder.

In the summer of 1945, the Armageddon of the Second World War at last came to an end, and once again the Dominion had to readjust to a peacetime economy. This time, unlike 1918, the transition was almost painless. As for the Muskoka Navigation Company, it had now completed a total of 64 years of active service and had just survived two world wars and a disastrous depression, emerging solvent once again. It was, in fact, the oldest line of passenger steamships in the country. "With all the difficulties of the war years to contend with," observed the Gravenhurst 'Banner' in 1946, "the company still continued to give first-class service, both as regards accommodation and cuisine. No trouble was too great for them to go to, to satisfy their many hundreds of patrons . . . . The Muskoka Lakes Navigation Company is one of our great tourist assets and we trust it will continue to be so for many long years to come." Thirteen, as things turned out.

Officers of the S.S. "Sagamo", 1940.
Commodore Lee (white cap) and Chief Engineer Walter Lambert appear at the centre. Eric Wasley is second from the right.

S.S. "Segwun" at Bracebridge, 1940.

Steamboat time at Port Carling.
This picture, taken in late afternoon around 1945, shows the "Cherokee", (left) in the lock, the "Ahmic" docked above the lock, and the "Sagamo" (right), awaiting her turn.
Courtesy, *Thatcher Studio*, Bracebridge

S.S. "Algonquin" (II), meeting the Portage Railway train at North Portage (July 1946).

Crew of the S.S. "Iroquois", 1932.
Gilbert Thompson, deckhand (left), Ernie Thompson, Bill Murray, Engineer, Captain Edward
Pink, and Purser George Rutherford.

CHAPTER 8
The Decline and Fall of the
Huntsville Navigation Company
(1929-1953)

We left Muskoka's other navigation company just at the end of the prosperous twenties, after the launching of its new flagship, the second *Algonquin*, the last new steamer the Company would ever acquire. Thereafter, the experiences of the North Muskoka line were to prove very similar to those of its South Muskoka counterpart. In 1929, the Huntsville Navigation Company still had four passenger ships; the *Mohawk Belle* and the *Iroquois* on the Lake of Bays, and the *Ramona* and *Algonquin* on the Huntsville chain. The ferry *Bigwin* had recently been assigned to the Bigwin Boat Livery Ltd., which, like Bigwin Inn, was legally a separate entity from the Navigation Company, as was the Portage Railway: no doubt C. O. Shaw found it advantageous to keep the books separate. As of 1930, the Navigation Company had 2,000 shares fully subscribed, for a total value of $20,000, plus real estate valued at $6,150, and no outstanding debts. To the outward eye it seemed as prosperous as ever.

The Depression changed all that, drastically. In 1930 the crowds who had flocked to Bigwin Inn and the other resorts just didn't appear. Trains arrived at the Huntsville Station with the coaches half empty. Towing for the steamers was almost a thing of the past: at best, two small towboats remained on the lakes during the 1930s. Each succeeding season seemed to get worse. Even more disheartening for General Manager Moore was the relentless demand by cottagers for better roads, so that they could drive all around the lakes and get to their cottages by land. The excursion business suffered because the steamers were tied to the railway, and had to wait faithfully at the station whether the trains were on time or not. Sometimes patrons boarding the *Algonquin* for a 2:50 p.m. cruise to the Portage were exasperated to be kept waiting as late as 6:00 p.m. for the arrival of No. 55 tourist train from Toronto. Even worse, No. 55 might not stop at the wharf siding, but only at Huntsville Station itself, and often passengers had to wait for a passing freight to go by before they could cross the tracks and head down the ramp to the wharf. This only increased the delay. Reputedly, C. O. Shaw used to make furious phone calls to the C.N.R. to demand better service (sometimes successfully), but otherwise there was little the boat line could do about these problems except tighten the belt wherever possible and hope for better times.

We have noted elsewhere how several officers quit the Company around 1930; usually because they resented the attitude of the management, or because they felt unjustly treated by C. O. Shaw. Captain David Langford of Huntsville, a "rustabout" wheelsman who commanded steamers all the way from the Niagara River to Lake Nipissing for over half a century, grumbled to Alvin Saulter in 1929 that the Huntsville Navigation Company seemed to feel that it was the only firm in the world where a man could work. Saulter felt much the same way at the time, and both men left that season. The following year Shaw lost the services of two more captains, Albert Leeder of the *Iroquois*, and William Tinkiss of the *Mohawk Belle*, in each case because he lashed out at them publicly for things they or their crews couldn't help: both left for the Muskoka Lakes. Happily for the Huntsville Line, the steamer *Armour* had recently burned at Burks Falls, freeing her former master, Captain Edward Pink, who soon took over the *Iroquois*. Pink got along very well with Shaw, and remained with the *Iroquois* to the end of her cruising days.

Shortly after assuming his new command, Captain Pink had one of those hair-raising experiences not unusual for steamboatmen. He was docking the *Iroquois* at Bigwin Inn as usual, on a windy summer day, when most of the 200 passengers crowded over to the wharf side of the ship. That, in addition to the wind, made the vessel heel over alarmingly. The Captain at once appeared on the bridge and ordered some of the passengers to move over to the other side, but the result was that they 'all' did, and the ship lurched the other way. Down in the engine room Bill Murray, the Engineer, nearly lost his footing, wondering what on earth was going on. Finally, Captain Pink and his crew were able to restore order, and got the steamer on an even keel again.

Another little incident, harrowing to the victim, occurred on the *Iroquois* during the mid-thirties. One of the deckhands, Gilbert Thompson of South Portage (a cousin of Lou Thompson, Superintendent of the railway), was busy polishing the whistle one day as the steamer was approaching Norway Point. Captain Pink, forgetting this, blew it and nearly cooked Thompson, who luckily escaped with a slight scalding. Thompson, understandably, raged at the Captain for his carelessness, forcing the Captain into a posture of surly defensiveness. Afterwards Thompson left the ship and joined the Portage Railway crew as Brakeman and Engineer.

As for the railway, it carried on much as it had during the 1920s, but with minor differences. Freighting was in decline, and most remaining consignments were usually groceries bound for Bigwin Inn. Generally, only a single mixed train was formed now, using two coaches, both boxcars and both locomotives. Furthermore, since tourism was becoming the mainstay of the little line, the season became shorter, with usually eight crossings each way per day. Also, by the 1930s, the old enclosed coaches had been replaced by another pair of open coaches with steps on the sides, obviously suitable only for the warm season. Of these two cars, the smaller was obtained from the Toronto Street Railway, while the larger came from a radial line at Preston, Ontario. (A third car was also purchased but never used.) Parties of campers could cross with their canoes for $5.00. A succession of superintendents ran the railway, including Captain Elder, Thomas Barnes of Toronto and Huntsville, Captain St. Amond, David Miller of South Portage (an ex-tannery man) and Lou Thompson.

As a rule, the purser on the *Algonquin* also had to act as conductor on the Portage Railway: after the coaches were replaced he might have to collect his fares and transfers from the running-boards, holding onto a pillar to keep from losing his balance and falling off, since the trains were frequently moving before all the tickets were collected.

One afternoon in 1940 the purser-conductor had a vexatious experience with a haughty Huntsville lady who arrived at North Portage by car for a run on the railway. She was irritated to hear that the fare was 30 cents return. "Young man," she declared emphatically, "I have never paid more than fifteen cents on this railroad and I have no intention of paying more!" She was not mollified to be told that the rates had been 30 cents for quite some time. Without further comment, the purser calmly collected the fares from all the other passengers, then returned and politely asked the Huntsville lady to please get off the train and make way for another traveller who could not find a seat. Grudgingly, the lady reached for her purse, but instead of paying the 30 cents she handed him a fifty-dollar bill; then a very hefty sum of money. Without batting an eyelash, the purser, who had plenty of cash with him, proceeded to count out all her change, in one-dollar bills; to the intense mortification of the lady and the delight of all the other passengers.

The Portage Railway had an enviable accident free record, but dramatic incidents were not unknown. One time a flatcar loaded with tanbark broke loose from a train at North Portage and ran off the end of the wharf into the lake. The flatcar disappeared from sight, leaving a heap of tanbark floating in the water. Another time in 1942, a cow had the misfortune to be caught on the tracks at one of the terminals when the train showed up. With piles of cordwood flanking the line on both sides, there was no way for the poor animal to escape. She was overtaken and killed and the locomotive derailed. This, however, was the only fatality in the Line's 54 year history.

As for the passenger steamers, their fortunes seemed only to go from bad to worse. As the Depression deepened and the competition from trucking intensified, the boats had to curtail services. Gradually they reduced the number of calling-places; to the quiet satisfaction of the crews, since extra calls, especially to out-of-the-way places like Grassmere, simply made a long day even longer, at a time when overtime pay was unknown. Around 1933, the handsome little steamer *Ramona*, now the Line's main freight carrier, was withdrawn from service and boarded up at the Huntsville tannery, to await the return of better times, which never came. Slowly the vessel deteriorated, until finally, in the spring of 1941, she was stripped of everything of value, towed into Lake Vernon, soaked with oil and set on fire, in the expectation that she would soon join the *Empress*, the *Sarona* and the old *Algonquin*. The plan miscarried, however. The attachment line itself burned through, and the wind carried the blazing boat over to the mouth of the Big East River, where she settled into the mud. No effort was made to move her.

This did not end her story. About seven or eight years later, Mr. E.G.R. ("Ted") Rogers, owner of Puck's Lodge near the Canal, was taking some of his guests for a cruise on Lake Vernon

Portage railway train, backing down to the wharf at South Portage.
The "Mohawk Belle" (left) and the "Iroquois" are at the dock, but only the latter is still in service.

Crew of the S.S. "Ramona", 1928.
John Forbes (left), Joe Cookson (deckhand), Captain Arthur Thompson, Engineer Archie
Ennest, and John Lewis (fireman).

S.S. "Ramona", passing the Mountain at Huntsville.

S.S. "Ramona", boarded up at Huntsville Tannery.

S.S. "Mohawk Belle" at South Portage.

S.S. "Iroquois" (Left) and S.S. "Mohawk Belle" at Dorset.
The "Mohawk" has been demoted to a scow.
Courtesy, *Mr. Brad Robinson*, Dorset

in his motor launch, when the boat suddenly piled up on the protruding steel ribs of the *Ramona*. The launch was holed and sank. No lives were lost, but Rogers was infuriated and threatened to sue the Navigation Company. In the end the matter was settled out of court.

About the same time that the *Ramona* was tied up, the *Mohawk Belle* was also retired and boarded up at South Portage, where she lay idle for several years. With her died the passenger service to Dwight; henceforth a motorboat brought in the mail. The *Mohawk Belle* was used again during the 1940s, but only as a self-propelled scow between Bigwin Inn and Norway Point. The Huntsville fleet was now effectively reduced from four to two active vessels, whose main duties were to run freight and passengers to Bigwin Inn.

Amid all these symptoms of decline, there was, surprisingly, an increase in the number of steam yachts on the Lake of Bays. In the summer of 1930, C.O. Shaw purchased the *Wanda III* from Lady Eaton, and had the 94 foot craft imported from Lake Rosseau to Huntsville, and across the Portage behind a tractor. Here she became the hotel launch for Bigwin Inn, and officially part of the holdings of the Bigwin Boat Livery. She was usually commanded by Captain Elder; in fact Shaw objected to anyone else taking her wheel. Captain Elder quite liked the *Wanda III*, even though once she almost gave him heart failure. One afternoon while the yacht was out cruising near Britannia, a plane happened to buzz overhead. Back in the 1930s, this was rather a novelty, and the passengers all crowded over to the starboard side to get a better look, not a wise idea on a vessel as narrow as the *Wanda III*, which immediately began to roll over. The Captain turned white, and frantically rushed about, shouting to the people to move back and redistribute themselves, which they did, avoiding disaster. Nonetheless, the authorities themselves were dubious about the *Wanda's* limited beam, and in 1944 her passenger certificate was revoked. For the next few years, she remained inactive at her boat house at Bigwin Inn. The *Bigwin*, meanwhile, continued her monotonous rounds usually under a succession of elderly skippers nearing retirement: Captains May, Elder, Tinkiss, "Nipper" Hill, Reg Leeder, and even Kawartha Lakes

Steam Yacht "Wanda III" on Lake of Bays.
Courtesy, *Mrs. Allan Fraser*, Bracebridge

Steam Ferry "Bigwin" at Bigwin Island.
Courtesy, *Mr. Cecil Goodwin*

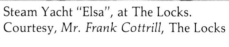
Steam Yacht "Elsa", at The Locks.
Courtesy, *Mr. Frank Cottrill*, The Locks

Steam Yacht "Phoebe II".
Courtesy, *Mrs. Allan Fraser*, Bracebridge

Captain Bill Scollard, a veteran from the Stoney Lake Navigation Company, all finished their careers on the *Bigwin*.

In the meantime, the boat fleet on the Lake of Bays was steadily growing larger, thanks entirely to one man. David Cameron Peck of East Evanston, Illinois, had been summering on the lake almost all his life, first at Fox Point Inn, and later at Bigwin, thanks to his very wealthy father, who owned the Bowman Milk Company in Chicago. Later the Pecks purchased Langmaid's (Burnt) Island near Baysville, where they built a large cottage with elaborate grounds. If ever a man was born with a silver spoon in his mouth, it was Cameron Peck. Only rarely did he ever have to do a day's work. Mr. Peck happened to be an avid boat enthusiast, and since money was no object with him, he felt free to indulge his hobby to the full. Over the years, starting around 1930, he amassed a fleet of 50 vessels, including 42 gas launches and seven steamers, plus an eighth which he kept at Bronte on Lake Ontario. Peck also had a marine railway built at Baysville, and contemplated a marine museum on his island. Needless to say, he also employed quite a few people to groom and run his boats.

One of Peck's first acquisitions in the steamboat line was the *Clermont*, a small showpiece oil-burning craft, about twenty feet in length, with a varnished hull, a fantail stern, a large stack and an open cockpit. This vessel, like many of Peck's boats, was always kept immaculate but seldom sailed. During the 1930s Peck also purchased the steamer *Elsa*, once of Beaumaris and lately on the Kawartha Lakes, renamed her the *El Cid*, and relaunched her at Port Sydney; sometimes engaging Captain Langford to operate her. In 1939, Peck obtained the *Phoebe II*, formerly Professor Brashear's yacht at Beaumaris, and also put her on the Huntsville lakes. She usually wintered at the Locks. In 1940, he bought the graceful *Naiad*, the Sanford family yacht (then 50 years old and lately inactive) and had her transported on heavy sleighs over the snows from Gravenhurst to Huntsville behind a large tractor. The *Naiad* was placed on the Lake of Bays, and was sometimes lent to Bigwin Inn for charter cruises after the *Wanda III* lost her certificate.

Peck's flotilla continued to grow. Around 1947, he purchased the aging steam launch *Beaver* from Lake Joseph and transferred her to the Lake of Bays, reviving her original name, the *Scudder*. Then in 1949, he crowned his collection by acquiring *Wanda III* from Bigwin Inn. He also picked up the machinery from the yacht *Ahteamec* at Port Sydney, and even the old alligator *John Bull*, which had been placed on skids at Dorset and the boiler removed after the lumber trade petered out. No doubt he would have purchased the entire Huntsville Navigation Company, had he been able.

Cameron Peck's fantasy world was suddenly wrecked on the rocks of reality around 1954. Apparently, his father decided to discontinue funding all these expensive frivolities. In addition, the Canadian revenue authorities were after him for taxes in arrears. Peck abandoned everything and fled to Arizona "for health reasons", and never returned to the Lake of Bays. His entire collection, except for the *Wanda III*, which reverted to the Bigwin Boat Livery, was seized and sold at auction in 1955. All of his other steamers were taken from the District. The *Naiad* went to the Ontario Northland Transportation Commission, and spent her last years as a dieselized passenger boat on Lake Temagami: only in 1965 was she finally cut up and burned. The *Scudder* and the *Phoebe* both went to the United States; the latter to the Finger Lakes region of New York State, though recently she has found her way back to Kingston, Ontario, where she was originally built in 1907, and where she still continues to cruise periodically, under steam.

The Huntsville Navigation Company, meanwhile, staggered on through the Depression years, sustained partly by the mail contract, which it assumed even during the winter. For many years one of W.J. Moore's sons drove the mail truck around the Lake of Bays for the company; later (after 1941) the task was sublet by tender to a local trucking firm, usually Middleton Transport of Huntsville, which also took the mail from the railway station to the post office, and then to the wharf for the *Algonquin*'s crew.

Then came the Second World War, and with it a temporary revival in prosperity for both the railways and the boat service. Gasoline was rationed, and both automobiles and tires were hard to find. People could no longer go abroad for their vacations. Charter buses were unobtainable. Again tourists began coming to Huntsville by train (though not on express trains, alas: those were forbidden in wartime) and to the adjacent camps and resorts by steamer. Once again the *Algonquin*, still commanded by Captain Parsons, was sailing with up to 300 passengers every

S.S. "Algonquin" (II) on Hunter's Bay, Huntsville.

trip. The steamers were back in their element once more.

Captain Parsons ran the *Algonquin* so long that he was sometimes known to boast that he could take her safely across Hunter's Bay to the river entrance in his sleep. This claim was put to the test one foggy August morning in 1943. The steamer left the station dock as usual and groped her way toward the river, with the purser and a deckhand acting as lookouts at the bow. Suddenly they noticed weeds and water-lilies ahead and raised the alarm—too late! The keel of the *Algonquin* grounded in the soggy clay bottom near the north shore. She could not be dislodged, and meanwhile all the passengers came forward to see what had happened. The skipper ordered all freight and passengers to be moved aft to lighten the bow, and soon induced the *Algonquin* to slide backwards and resume her run. That, however, was the last time Robert Parsons was ever heard to comment on his unerring skill at locating the river channel!

As might be expected, the boat crews were persistently pestered to call at out-of-the-way stops (often for trivial reasons), where the docks, if they existed, were often unsatisfactory. One of these was at Balinor Heights, opposite Deerhurst. The wharf was sturdy but small, and Captain Parsons didn't like it. One day, however, he gave in to the urgings of a group of passengers (no doubt encouraged by the proprietor) and agreed to try docking at Balinor. Unluckily, the dock had no facing timbers, and as the steamer came alongside a fender brushed against the ends of the top planks, ripping them loose one by one as it passed and leaving them in a pile. Seeing this, the Captain backed out again and later managed to let the people off at the Canal. Not surprisingly, the *Algonquin* was never invited to call at Balinor Heights again.

Despite the wartime revival, two of the passenger steamers disappeared from the scene early in the 1940s. One was the *Ramona*, which was scuttled in 1941. That same year, the shabby old *Mohawk Belle* was stripped down and converted into a single-decked self-propelled freight barge, used to carry trucks, cement, cordwood and other bulk supplies to Bigwin Inn. In November of 1946, the *Mohawk Belle* was formally sold to Bigwin Inn, whose owners no longer had any direct connection with the Navigation Company. She always wintered in the drydock at the rear of Bigwin Island, but the drydock never worked well, being impossible to keep dry.

Finally, in the winter of 1949, the ice pulled the oakum out of the seams of the *Mohawk Belle*, which then filled with water and sank in the chamber. The hulk was then sold to a marina owner from Port Cunnington, who removed the engine and boiler and left the rest of the wreck there. It still lies in the abandoned Bigwin drydock, itself now in ruins.

One by one, the men who had been the mainstays of the Huntsville Navigation Company were also nearing the end of their days. Charles Orlando Shaw was one of them. Seemingly indestructible, the little tannery tycoon had battled and bulldozed his way through every obstacle in life for 84 years. He had severed his ties with the Leather Company in 1931, but he had kept his hotel, the laundry service and the boat line going, despite the Depression, with little diminution of his formidable energies. Now Nature claimed her forfeit. On December 4, 1942, Shaw, with his usual quick step, marched past the Huntsville Town Hall, stopped briefly to chat with a man shovelling snow, resumed his errand, then collapsed a few hundred feet away. He was carried

Charles Orlando Shaw.
Courtesy, *Mrs. Barbara Mills*, Georgetown

into a nearby house and help was summoned, but there was no pulse, and the verdict of the doctors was death from heart failure. He was buried beside his first wife at Mount Pleasant Cemetery, Toronto. According to a local legend, however, Shaw still managed to get in the last word. At his own funeral, so we are told, he suddenly popped his head out of his coffin and demanded of the foreman, who was presiding, how many men were engaged in carrying the coffin? "Six, Mr. Shaw," came the reply. "That's too many! Fire two of them!" snapped C.O., who then reverted to a state of decease. No doubt there were extremely mixed feelings around Huntsville at the time of his passing, but no one could deny that things would never be quite the same again.

The Navigation Company and Bigwin Inn still carried on, both under the headship of Mrs. Pauline Gill of Brockville, one of the two daughters of C. O. Shaw. Mrs. Gill directed most of her energies to the hotel and left the boat line almost entirely in the hands of W. J. Moore, whose authority was, if anything, increased. Nonetheless, she succeeded in enticing Captain Bill Tinkiss back as mate on the *Iroquois*, which for a time was liberally endowed with deck officers, since Tinkiss, Captain Pink, and George Rutherford, the Purser, all had Masters Certificates. Tinkiss, unfortunately, did not get along well with Captain Pink, perhaps because both were accustomed to supreme command, and so he was not sorry to be transferred to the *Bigwin*, sometime later. Meanwhile Captain Elder, Mr. Moore's assistant, died early in February, 1943 at his home in Huntsville from the effects of a stroke, active to the last.

Though the War years dealt kindly with the Huntsville Line, the postwar years were a different matter. Bigwin Inn, already sliding during the thirties, now became a serious liability. After the War, people were again able to buy cars and gasoline, and along with these, mobility. Many resumed their vacations in Europe or the Caribbean. Besides, tastes were changing. The older plutocrats, who liked a quiet, dignified holiday were dying off, and the younger set demanded noise, and excitement, and bars, and found them in some of the newer, more adaptable resorts. It was no longer possible to isolate Bigwin from these influences, and even the older clientele soon stopped coming. Fuel bills alone sometimes exceeded $10,000 a year, and the cumbersome big hotel required a staff of about 300. In the postwar slump, the staff sometimes outnumbered the guests.

By 1946, Mrs. Gill had had enough, and arranged to sell Bigwin Inn and the boat livery to Vernon Cardy of Toronto, who headed a syndicate that owned several city hotels, including the King Edward Hotel in Toronto. The Cardy interests tried to run Bigwin using the methods of modern big business, adding such amenities as a new cocktail lounge and transforming the atmosphere in ways that would have horrified C. O. Shaw. Those methods failed (largely because the season was so short) and the great hotel passed into the hands of Frank Leslie, a Toronto stockbroker, who had long been enthused with Bigwin. But Leslie had no better luck than his predecessors. Service deteriorated, and few guests came. Finally the hotel's creditors decided to convert it into a giant summer condominium, with indifferent success. Bigwin Inn remains almost indestructable, but today it is empty, and falling into ruin.

Captain Bill Tinkiss (left) and Captain Levi Fraser, with the "Wanda III" at Bigwin Inn.

Wharf, boathouse and dance pavilion at Bigwin Inn. The S.S. "Iroquois" is the dock.

The ferry steamers also disappeared by the wayside. In 1948 the *Wanda III* was sold, then abandoned by her new owners at Baysville and allowed to sink: happily she was afterwards raised and taken away to Dwight. As for the *Bigwin*, she carried on as the hotel ferry until quite recently. In 1956, following a number of small fires, the vessel, by then an oil-burner, was converted into a diesel, with a noisy General Motors No. 671 engine, giving her speeds of twelve miles per hour. Thus re-equipped and ballasted with rock, she carried on until about 1970, when Bigwin ceased to be a hotel. Today she is still languishing in the Bigwin boathouse.

The passenger steamers did not last nearly that long. All of the pre-war trends that were slowly killing the boat services were resumed and accelerated during the prosperous postwar years, as the country entered a phase of phenomenal growth and development. Road construction was resumed. People who had made good money in wartime without being able to spend it, now indulged themselves with automobiles and speedboats. The elegant little passenger steamers now seemed antiquated and out of style. No longer were they needed as part of the transport routes to the resorts: buses and motorcars were now the norm. There was, in fact, little for them to do now except carry mail and run excursion cruises during the short two month season.

In 1948, Carl R. McLennan of Brockville took over the reins as General Manager. (W. J. Moore carried on as Secretary, handling the book work and freight orders, which were now very few, thanks to the competition of trucks.) McLennan, a former trumpet player in the dance band at Bigwin Inn, had met Mrs. Gill's daughter there and married her. He had all sorts of ambitious schemes, among them a new boat livery at Huntsville to compete with the Blackburn Marina. He also wished to convert the *Algonquin* into an excursion steamer and discontinue the service on the Lake of Bays completely.

McLennan soon put his plans into practice. First, he demolished the old office building and had it replaced by a new structure containing an office, a waiting room and a freight shed. He also built a new boat house and imported canoes and punts for rent. As for the *Algonquin*, the aft lounge (usually known as the "ladies' lounge") was removed and an expensive hardwood deck laid down for dancing. The stairwell, which had hitherto opened into this lounge, was removed and a new one built near the bow. At the same time, the pilothouse was replaced by a new one that looked too big for the ship.

The results were disastrous. On wet or chilly days it was now impossible to find a warm, dry place anywhere on the *Algonquin* except in the pilothouse (which was off limits to passengers), the forward smoking lounge, and the main deck at the stern. She was now, in effect, strictly a fair weather boat, and whenever the weather wasn't fair, there were a good many unhappy passengers. McLennan also hoped to revive the old tradition of weekly moonlight cruises, which had declined to only about three charters per season, but the idea failed to catch on; partly, no doubt, because of the occasional wet weather. In 1949, the Manager also decided to convert the *Algonquin* into an oil-burner, using a jet blowing device designed for the purpose by a local blacksmith. It did not work well. The burner was noisy, dirty and inefficient. On the vessel's maiden trip of the season, she consumed two thirds of her fuel supply before she reached the Portage, and was forced to put in at Deerhurst and wait for a truck to arrive with more oil. That in itself was costly, but worse were the complaints from patrons who found their clothes getting smudged with oily black soot belching from the stack. Some improvements were effected before the season was over, but finally McLennan conceded that the move was a mistake, and by 1950, the *Algonquin* was burning wood again.

In the meantime, the boat livery plan also met with disaster. As qualified officers for the inland lakes became scarce, McLennan was obliged to look for them elsewhere. In 1951, following the retirement of Captain Parsons, he recruited Captain A. N. ("Archie") Hogue, a hearty Great Lakes skipper from Owen Sound, to run the *Algonquin*. Unfamiliar with his new charge, and unaccustomed to manually-steered ships, the Captain ordered "half astern" on the

S.S. "Algonquin" (Final Version), passing Hi-Lo Lodge near Huntsville.
Courtesy, "Ontario Archives", Acc. 9481, Bos 4, #14-H-72

engines while leaving Huntsville one day, but his new engineer, likewise unused to bell signals, gave him "full astern". The aft line snapped, and the steamer backed right in among the small boats of the livery. Some were crushed, some shoved aside, and some pushed under the wharf, while the enraged McLennan could only shout and curse from the dock. In effect, the boat livery had been wrecked at one stroke, and even though McLennan cleaned up the mess and carried on, the rented boats were often returned in damaged condition. In short, the livery scheme was not very successful either.

Another time, Captain Hogue was approaching Deerhurst wharf in foggy weather. He came in just a little too fast and at the wrong angle. The vessel struck the wharf and rebounded, forcing a second try, but even then she bumped the pier quite hard. Mr. Maurice Waterhouse, the proprietor, witnessed all this, and was not amused: it seemed as if the steamer, having failed to demolish the dock the first time, had then backed up and taken another run at it! The *Algonquin* seldom if ever called at Deerhurst again.

Rounding the curves in the river below the Huntsville swing bridge always required great care by the *Algonquin's* crew. One day in 1951, Captain Hogue met a fast-moving steam launch right at the bend: apparently it had not heard the warning whistle. To avoid a collision, the Captain ran his ship into the bank, while the launch also swerved away. Neither boat was damaged, except that the *Algonquin* lost her bowsprit amid the shrubbery. It was never replaced.

On yet another occasion, Captain Hogue had an embarrassing mishap near Grassmere. Calling at this spot always added an extra 40 minutes to a cruise, and one day the skipper was irritated at being obliged to detour all the way to Tally-ho Inn to drop off some passengers who hadn't boarded there on the outgoing trip. He vented his displeasure by throwing his vessel hard astern after docking; forgetting that there was a rock off the wharf. The ship struck the rock and rebounded her entire length, throwing most of the passengers off balance. Thanks to her steel frame, the tough little *Algonquin* survived the mishap without injury. Much sobered, Captain Hogue brought her home without further incident.

As for the *Iroquois*, her days had already come to an end. This handsome little composite had been refitted with a new tube boiler around 1945, replacing her old pipe boiler, at a cost of more than $20,000, but her timbers were aging badly. She continued to ply from the Portage to Dorset daily until the fall of 1948, despite the fact that there was no longer much business east of Bigwin Inn. (Captain Pink and his crew were not exactly overjoyed about having to spend the nights at Dorset either: the hotel would have suited them much better.) By 1948, however, Bigwin Inn no longer had any connections with the Navigation Company, and Carl McLennan decided that the sensible course was to retire the *Iroquois* and get a large new motor launch to replace her. The *Iroquois* was left idle for a year at South Portage dock, under the watchful eye of Lou Thompson, the railway Superintendent. Then, during the winter of 1949, her hull planking began to shrink around the caulking in her seams. On Christmas Eve, Thompson phoned McLennan to report that the steamer was leaking badly, and that the pumps would soon be unable to cope with the situation. It was, of course, a bad time to phone. The Manager hedged, and implied that he would send some men over the day after Christmas, but by then it was too late. The sturdy little ship, now 42 years old, sank on the Yuletide and never rose again. The wreck was soon stripped down to the main deck. Efforts were made to extract the machinery, but these met with only partial success. For years afterwards, the hulk lay at South Portage. Today her remains lie buried beneath landfill at the site.

Her gas-powered replacement, known as the *Iroquois II*, was another mistake. A 60 foot cruiser with a cedar hull and two Chrysler marine engines, the new vessel was built at Orillia and looked like a water bus. She was quite speedy, but she was built to handle only 100 passengers. Sometimes the little railway train would arrive at South Portage with twice that number aboard, and naturally those excluded from the cruise at the Lake of Bays resented it. After the *Algonquin* stopped running, the *Iroquois II* was moved back to the lower lakes on a float and began plying from Huntsville to the Portage. Thus ended the boat service on the Lake of Bays.

The little *Algonquin* still had a few more years left. She still carried the mail, but was otherwise dependent on excursion cruises, which in turn depended on warm, sunny weather over a peak period of little more than a month in midsummer. It was not enough. Every year the little packet grew shabbier, and it was clear that her days were drawing to a close. It appears the

The retired S.S. "Iroquois" at South Portage, with her successor, M.V. "Iroquois", July 1, 1949. Photo by *J.D. Knowles*

citizens and business community of Huntsville were largely indifferent to the fate of the Navigation Company which had served their community and the North Muskoka tourist industry so well for over half a century. Even in the 1940s the local merchants would seldom bother to advertise or support the Company, while the citizens confined their help to coming down to the electric swing bridge and watching the steamers pass. Rarely would they take a cruise. Mr. John Laycock of Huntsville, who pursered on the *Algonquin* for several years and kept a tally, noted that a total of 31 adults and 22 children from Huntsville actually paid fares to travel on the steamers during the 1945 season, even though the rates had not gone up in over twenty years. The warm community acceptance the Company had enjoyed in the days of Duperow and Captain Marsh seemed to have disappeared. Cruise ships do not flourish amid indifference, and soon the deep-throated whistle of the *Algonquin* was to become a memory. She sailed for the last time in 1952, but then Carl McLennan decided that there was no point in running her any longer with rising expenses and diminishing patronage. In September 1952, she was tied up for good at the Bigwin Laundry Company wharf, almost directly opposite the spot where she was launched, 26 years before. Shortly afterwards she canted over and sank, with only her lines preventing her from capsizing. For years the hulk lay there, an ugly, rotting eyesore, until finally a wrecking crew moved in, winched the remains partway back to an even keel, and cut them up for scrap metal. The ship's fog bell was mounted on one of the Portage Railway locomotives. Today nothing remains of the flagship of the Huntsville Navigation Company except a door fragment, now in the Huntsville Pioneer Village. (In 1954, W. J. Moore died, following his retirement the previous year, after about 47 years of devoted service to the Line.)

This was not quite the end. Cameron Peck's lovely launches remained on the local lakes for another year or so after the *Algonquin* ceased, while Captain Hogue took command of the *Iroquois II*, which was now on the Portage run.

The Portage Railway, by now a local institution, outlasted the steamers it was meant to complement, by seven years. In 1947, its two aging saddletankers failed to pass a boiler inspection, and Carl McLennan sold them to Cameron Peck. They later found their way into the Pioneer Village Museum in Minden, Nebraska, where they remain to this day. Two new locomotives were imported from the coal mines of Cape Breton Island. Unluckily they weighed 15 and 21 tons respectively, about two to three times as much as the originals, and showed such a

South Portage terminus, Portage Railway, 1948.

Portage railway locomotive No. 1 watering up at South Portage, 1947.
Courtesy, *Mr. Gilbert Thompson*, South Portage

tendency to spread the tracks that the larger one was, in fact, never used. Even worse, they proved to have a gauge of 42 inches, instead of the 44½ inches of the little railway. At that point, a decision almost unprecedented in railroad history was made: the entire line was regauged to fit the new locomotives, including the tracks and the other rolling stock, except for two of the three flatcars, which were simply left parked on a siding. (Railways have changed gauges for other reasons, but seldom for the sake of the engines; usually it works the other way around!) The work was completed over the winter, in time for the "Portage Flyer" (as it was now dubbed) to enter service in 1948. As late as the 1952 season, it was said to have carried 15,000 passengers and 500 tons of freight; not bad for a tiny operation in decline.

The railway carried on until the late fifties, but gradually the maintenance work on it slackened and soon the roadbed, once so well groomed, was sprouting grass and weeds. Towards the end, the supply of soft coal ran short, but the Manager declined to order any more, despite the busy season. In desperation, the crews decided to try using some Brazzo Briquets, a new product made of coal dust and oil for use in stoves. These seemed to work, but once they were fired and the throttle opened, they disintegrated in the heat, and the first blast of air triggered by the exhaust blew the entire fire out the stack: the engineer was shocked to find the grates empty. As a result, the Portage Flyer ran no more that year. After 1958, the *Iroquois II*, which had been developing endless engine troubles, ceased making connections from Huntsville. This left the tiny railway isolated, except by circuitous gravel roads. It staggered on for one more season, but then in September 1959 it was shut down for good. Again, the reaction of the Huntsville community was apparently one of indifference. No one lifted a finger to save what had been one of Muskoka's foremost tourist attractions, despite Carl McLennan's attempts to sell it.

By now the unfortunate boat line Manager had had enough. Having tried so hard for years to make excursion cruises pay, and having lately lost his own personal residence at Huntsville by fire, Mr. McLennan now threw in the sponge. In 1960 he sold the *Iroquois II*, which was removed, re-engined and converted into the cruise boat *Miss Kingston*, plying among the Thousand Islands of the St. Lawrence River. The office and boat house at Huntsville went to the Blackburn Marina, and the McLennan family moved back to Brockville.

For several years the remains of the little Portage Railway were left to rust and moulder amid the woods and weeds. Finally, someone took an interest in them. In the fall of 1961, a semi-retired C.P.R. fireman from London, Ontario, named Percy Broadbear (along with his son Donald, also a railway-man), bought all the assets of the Line and removed everything, almost down to the last spike and tie, to St. Thomas, itself a noted railway town, and arranged to reassemble it there in Pinafore Park. Gradually they succeeded in restoring most of the rolling stock, including a coach and one locomotive. The Pinafore Park Railway first opened in 1964, and became a tourist attraction for the town: a much worthier fate for the little line than being consigned to the scrapyard.

At the Portage today, the railway lands have reverted to private ownership, and today it takes a keen eye to discern the old track beds used for 55 years by the world's shortest railway line. Do the people there miss it? Very much indeed. Even today tourists continue to arrive from distant parts, always asking the same question: "Where's the little railway?"

Of late, a group of railway buffs has been working to bring back the Portage Railway, at a new site along the Oxtongue River, near Dwight. In October of 1984 they triumphantly arranged to bring the two locomotives back to Huntsville, and have since obtained a coach as well. Work is proceeding at the new site, and it is to be hoped that one of North Muskoka's leading attractions will soon be re-established where it belongs — more or less!

And the lake steamers? Vanished almost without a trace today, having served the communities of North Muskoka well for a total of 76 years. The Huntsville Navigation Company, the second most successful inland steamboat line in Ontario, officially wrapped up its affairs in 1965, and was formally dissolved in January 2, 1967. There is no need to repeat again the reasons for this demise. Blunders and mistakes had certainly hastened the end, and determinists may argue that the disappearance was inevitable. Perhaps it was. But the old lake steamers and the hardy men who ran them probably did more, in their time, to open up North Muskoka and set it on its feet than any other influence. Modern times have made the steamboats redundant. But the memories still remain.

Portage Railway new locomotive and coach.
(Refurbished as the Pinafore Park Railway, St. Thomas, Ontario.)

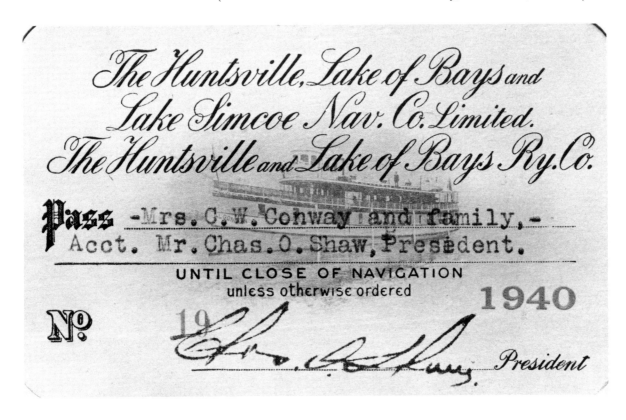

The Huntsville, Lake of Bays and Lake Simcoe Nav. Co. Limited.
The Huntsville and Lake of Bays Ry. Co.

Pass -Mrs. C. W. Conway and family,-
Acct. Mr. Chas. O. Shaw, President.

UNTIL CLOSE OF NAVIGATION
unless otherwise ordered

1940

N⁰ 19

President

S.S. "Sagamo", backing out from Windermere during the 1950s.
Photo taken from Windermere House.

CHAPTER 9
The Last Years of the Muskoka Lakes Steamships (1946-1958)

The holocaust of World War II came to an end on September 1, 1945. While it left millions dead, millions homeless and whole nations ruined, ravaged and exhausted all around the globe, it left Canada industrialized, wealthy and prosperous as never before. A return to depression was feared as the demand for wartime products abruptly ceased, but instead the national economy switched almost painlessly to peacetime production. Citizens had been earning good money during the War (despite high taxes), without having many outlets for spending it. They now had the means of paying for consumer products, lately in very short supply, and soon industry was rushing to meet the demand. Real earnings, despite inflation, were more than double those at the end of the Depression, and the country was able to absorb not only the "baby boom" of the postwar years, but also hundreds of thousands of refugees from war-torn countries abroad. During the late forties and fifties, it was good to be a Canadian.

Good times nationally had hitherto meant good times for the inland excursion steamships. Not now. People no longer wanted to while away their leisure hours on a quiet, sedate passenger ship. They wanted noise, speed, novelty and high individual mobility, and therefore began transforming their new affluence into automobiles, trailers, and motorboats, or vacations in Europe and Florida. Canadians bought over 10,000 motorboats in 1950 alone. Meanwhile, highway construction was resumed with a vengeance, as if to make up for lost time. By 1953, there were about 5,600 miles of paved roads plus 7,813 miles of highway in Ontario, as compared with a mere 1,055 miles in 1923. By 1956, the highway from Toronto to Gravenhurst, plagued with the worst traffic jams in the province, was widened or supplemented to four lanes, complete with bypasses around Barrie, Orillia and Washago. Along with the new roads appeared the motel and the roadside snack bar, and soon the highway from Severn Bridge to Gravenhurst was lined with them. In part, the new thoroughfares had the effect of funneling travellers right through Muskoka, straight past the lakes and the local centres. Hence many visitors missed the best of what the District had to offer, while local businesses lost the revenue.

As superhighways and internal combustion engines combined to reassert the primacy of land travel everywhere, Ontario's surviving steamship lines began to wither away. In 1947, the last steamer on Lake Nipissing was withdrawn from service. In 1949, the steamship service between Toronto and Port Dalhousie, on the Niagara Peninsula, lapsed. The Huntsville Navigation Company was dying, and the Georgian Bay steamers cruising the Thirty Thousand Islands were in trouble. None were destined to outlast the fifties.

The Muskoka steamships, too, were becoming anachronistic in this new, rapidly changing, fast-moving world, struggling to make up for the wasted years of the Depression and the privations of the War. Having become so deeply rooted on the local scene, it is not surprising that the Muskoka steamers held out longer than all the rest. Perhaps the surprise should be that they held out as long as they did.

As with the Huntsville Line, the Muskoka Lakes Navigation Company went through a major readjustment in 1945. At the end of that season, Major Hugh C. MacLean, who had reached the age of 79, at last decided it was time to retire, and accordingly sold his 90% interest in the Company for a modest $110,000 — without consulting the Wasleys. Four years later he died in Toronto. For the Navigation Company, one result was the disappearance of its main outlet for advertising, through the numerous publications of the MacLean empire.

The new owner was Gordon Douglas Fairley, a self-made Toronto businessman and speculator who had spent parts of many summers on Lake Rosseau, to which he sometimes used to fly in his own private plane. Well acquainted with Muskoka, although no boatman, Mr. Fairley was interested mainly in the Royal Muskoka, now dusty and faded, and badly in need of a face-lift. Many people around Lake Rosseau urged Fairley to "take on the Royal", and indeed the hotel seemed worth a gamble: its patronage had increased substantially during the War. The lake steamers had not been doing badly either. In fact, their freighting receipts alone had come to about $24,000 in 1945, but that end of the business Mr. Fairley proposed to leave in the capable hands of Eric Wasley. A new Board of Directors was sworn in, consisting entirely of Fairley's friends and backers from Toronto and St. Catharines, plus Eric. Commenting on these developments, on May 9, 1946 the Gravenhurst 'Banner' announced that "Last year the MacLean interests sold out and the new holders are putting up considerable funds to make the company's hotel, the Royal Muskoka, and the steamers, more attractive than ever."

As far as the Royal was concerned, the new syndicate was as good as its word. The entire building was given a massive overhaul, and many of its antiquated furnishings replaced. Another imaginative idea of Fairley's was to link the operations of the Royal (which was limited to a season of four months) to those of another of his projects, the Fort Montagu Beach Hotel at Nassau in the Bahamas. Previously a military convalescent hospital for servicemen, the Fort Montagu had been left empty and vandalized after the War until Fairley, with a sharp eye for opportunity, bought it at a low price and renovated it, just as the wartime restrictions on tourist travel were lifting. The proposal was that the staff of the Royal Muskoka should commute to the Bahamas and run the Fort Montagu in the winter.

Nor were the steamers ignored. In the winter of 1946-47, the *Segwun* was remodelled and fitted out with seven carpeted staterooms on the upper deck. This entailed the removal of her aft or gentlemens' lounge (which already had two small staterooms at one end) and enclosing the amidships section. The oak panelled forward lounge was incorporated into the new cabin. Perhaps it was at this time that a second steel bulkhead, extracted from the wreck of the *Medora*, was installed in the forward hold to create a dormitory for the crew, who had previously slept around the tiller flats at the stern. The new arrangements for the *Segwun* worked quite well, though they tended to increase the mass of her silhouette in the face of the wind.

As for the *Sagamo*, Mr. Fairley proposed all sorts of innovations for her, including variable-pitch propellers for greater efficiency, and moving the engine controls to the pilothouse. He also considered installing a shortwave radio to help her keep in touch with Muskoka Wharf. None of these proposals were actually carried out, but the 'Big Chief' did undergo some renovations in 1947. Two extra staterooms were added to "B" deck, commonly called the "boat deck" because the two lifeboats had been carried there. The new cabins filled the space occupied by the lifeboats, which were now transferred to the bridge and two more added. At the same time,

S.S. "Sagamo" approaching Royal Muskoka Hotel, from a Company brochure cover from the postwar years.

S.S. "Segwun", on Bala Bay, around 1945.

S.S. "Segwun", (Final Version) at Beaumaris, 1956.
The "Sagamo "(Final Version) is approaching at the left.
Photo by *Henry Fry*, Gravenhurst

S.S. "Sagamo" (Final Version), around 1950.
The '100 Mile Cruiser' now carries four lifeboats, all on the bridge. The Union Jack with the white border, flown from the forward flagstaff, is the Royal Mail flag.

the sidewalls at the aft ends of the cabins on both the two upper decks were embellished with rakish curves, giving the ship a jaunty air. On the whole, the *Sagamo* was now a much more handsome vessel. In 1950, the forward end of the promenade deck cabin was extended a little to make room for a tuck shop and snack bar on board. The colour scheme for all the steamers, which had varied from black to grey on the lower hulls during the Depression, was now firmly set as follows: orange or red at the waterline, green up to the main deck, white upper works with green trim, gray decks, and orange (or red) stacks with a band of metallic silver and black on top: quite an agreeable combination.

The result of all these efforts, on the whole, proved disappointing. The Royal Muskoka succeeded in attracting a number of conventions, as, in the past, but seemingly not enough business to make it really profitable. The 'Fort Montagu', on the other hand, proved a great success and was soon sold for three times the purchased price! As for the steamers, their profits diminished in direct proportion to the increase in the number of cars and trucks on the roads. Even the lure of special excursion rates failed to attract the crowds who were seeking their pleasures elsewhere. The same applied to the Canadian National Railways' Muskoka Express, which was resumed after the War. Steadily, one train after another to Muskoka Wharf was cancelled. The steamers meanwhile were getting old, and so were some of the men who ran them.

As of 1946, Captain Andy Corbett, now 76, was still Master of the *Cherokee*, while Reg Leeder had reluctantly taken over the *Sagamo*, on condition that his brother Gerald would sail with him as mate. That way, said the Captain, he could go down to the dining room for a coffee now and then, feeling perfectly confident that he had left the helm in good hands. (Eric Wasley objected that it was contrary to Company policy to allow close relations to serve together on the same ship, but finally agreed.) Alvin Saulter succeeded Walter Lambert as Chief Engineer. He and Captain Leeder were responsible for many of the accident-free years enjoyed by the big ship.

Captain Wesley David Hill
of the S.S. "Segwun".

Captain Jack Ariss of Rosseau, who had left for Toronto during the 1920s, now returned to resume command of the *Ahmic*. Hector Hatherley was now usually on the *Islander*, while Wesley Hill followed Leeder on the *Segwun*.

"Nipper" Hill had quite a sly sense of humour. Sometimes, to the fury of his fellow captains, he could not resist edging his ship forward a bit during mid-lake transfers, with the result that the approaching steamer, instead of coming alongside the *Segwun*, would find herself at right angles. If this brought the other captain out onto his bridge in a rage, Hill would shrug and shout back something about a "puff o' wind". At least once, Andy Corbett, fit to be tied, shouted over the waters, "Puff of wind nothing! I saw you put yours into forward!"—to which Hill blandly replied, "That's right. I was only trying to help."

Practical joker or no, Captain Hill was a superb ship handler. Once in 1946, he was bringing the *Segwun* into Bala around mid-day, when suddenly a strong gust of wind from the west caught the steamer broadside, threatening to carry her away from the wharf and onto the beach. Hill reacted instantly. Instead of trying to dock on the right-hand side, as usual, he brought the ship in on the left, letting the bow jam against the shore. The wind meanwhile blew her hard against the wharf, with the stern protruding past it. He then sat it out until the wind subsided.

That same season, the *Segwun* experienced a close call of a different sort. She was on another Bala trip, waiting for a train to cross the bridge at Bala Park Island, and since there was a wind blowing and idling was out of the question, the Mate, Gerald Leeder, decided to pass the time by circling around Coulter's Island. Everything proceeded uneventfully, but afterwards Captain Hill quietly commented on a certain big rock off the southeast end of the island, about four feet below the surface: the ship had just missed it. Leeder was startled. "Wait'll we're on another trip, and I'll show you," volunteered the skipper. He did, and there it was, lurking in the depths. Leeder, shocked, asked why there wasn't a buoy to mark it? "There used to be one," replied Hill, "only the ice took it."

There were times, of course, when docking a steamer could be ruined despite the wheelsman's best efforts. A serious problem in wartime, and afterwards, had been finding suitable engineers. In 1944, Captain Hill was bringing the *Islander* in to Glen Echo on Lake Muskoka in midsummer, but when he signalled for "reverse", the Engineer, Alfred Whitehead of Muskoka Township, gave him "forward" instead, sending the bow of the steamer straight onto the mud bottom and part way up on shore! Captain Hill, coming out on deck to survey the situation, muttered, "I'll bet that durned old farmer was asleep again!" All the guests at Glen Echo gathered to watch as the grounded steamer churned her propeller uselessly in reverse. Someone telephoned for the *Cherokee*, then in the vicinity of Beaumaris; she came, and attached a line to the stern of the *Islander*. Using the power of both vessels' engines, the small ship was dragged safely back into the water.

The *Islander*'s troubles were not entirely the fault of the engineer. By about 1947 her stern was beginning to droop a bit with age, despite her steel frame, and Whitehead was having a lot of trouble with the propeller shaft. Occasionally she was known to go aground in the Port Carling lock, because she was drawing more water than any of the other steamers. Consequently the Navigation Company had her put in drydock, where the entire stern was rebuilt. This was the last refit the little *Islander* was destined to get.

S.S. "Islander", preparing for a mid-lake rendezvous with S.S. "Cherokee".
Courtesy, *Canadian National Corporate Archives*, X 12959

The Sunset Cruiser, calling at Royal Muskoka wharf.
Courtesy, *Canadian National Corporate Archives*, X 16745

Captain Corbett sometimes had troubles with his own engineers in the late forties, after Saulter left to work on the *Sagamo*. One time when the *Cherokee* was returning to the Royal Muskoka from Rosseau, the Engineer got his signals confused during docking, and the ship's nose grounded in a sandy space between two rocks. There she was stranded for about two hours until the *Islander*, returning the favour at Glen Echo, arrived and swung her fantail towards that of her sister ship. Two lines were secured, and the *Islander* pulled, and the *Cherokee* pulled, until finally the larger ship slipped loose, undamaged. The same thing happened again at the Royal, about 1949, and for the same reason; only this time the *Cherokee* rebounded from the wharf and sheared into a boat house, slashing a big hole through the building. By that time, Captain Corbett was so disgusted with the engineers he was given that he declared he would not be back the following season. Only at the last minute did Eric Wasley manage to persuade him to stay.

Captain Leeder took charge of the *Cherokee* only once, late in the season of 1947, when Corbett left for a few days to attend the funeral of a son. Leeder found the *Cherokee* a good ship to handle, although heavy at the bow. During those few days Reg amazed his uncle, Walter Leeder (who was serving as Mate), by the ease with which he disembarked the ship from the wharf at Beaumaris. When Walter asked how he did it, Reg explained the technique: simply put the propeller nearest the dock in forward, turn the rudder towards the dock, and let the other propeller idle. The result? The propeller generated an eddy that rebounded from the cribwork and pushed the stern neatly away from the pier.

The *Sagamo* also had the occasional mishap with her propeller shafts during this period. One day in 1948 the "Big Chief", under Captain Leeder's command, was approaching the dock at the Natural Park when the cotter pin on one of the shafts slipped loose, allowing the shaft and the screw to slide backwards. With one engine now useless, the ship grounded in the sand at the head of the dock. Water gushed in around the loose shaft. While the hands gaped in confusion, wondering what to do, the Captain ordered them to stuff some old potato bags or anything handy into the gland to stop the inflow. There was no chance that the loose shaft would slide all the way out, nor was it touching the rudder, but the ship was now firmly grounded on the beach. Since there was no telephone at the Park, Captain Leeder decided to call on a nearby cottager whom he knew, and the cottager at once drove him to Rosseau, refusing any remuneration. There he phoned Gravenhurst and explained the situation. Eric Wasley proposed sending a small boat, but Leeder insisted on a large vessel with more power, and suggested the *Segwun*. The *Segwun* arrived within a few hours and with much swaying from side to side, she managed to help draw the *Sagamo* loose. When asked if he needed a tow, Captain Leeder replied that he felt he could get his vessel back on her own power.

Gingerly, on one propeller, he started to take her home at half speed, avoiding all narrow channels. Fortunately it was a bright, clear day with hardly a ripple on the water. At Port Carling, the Captain let the wharfingers tow the crippled ship into the lock chamber. The Indian River proved difficult to manoeuvre, but the "Big Chief" steamed back to Muskoka Wharf before dark. A diver at once went to work on the shaft, and the *Sagamo* was running again in a day or two.

In the meantime, Eric Wasley had been growing more and more uncomfortable with the Company. He seemed to be the only member of the Board of Directors who cared much about the boats, and apparently he did not get along well with some of Gordon Fairley's cronies. Acrimonious incidents occurred. It is said that the Company bus was used to shuttle employees from the Royal Muskoka to Florida, to work at the Fort Montagu, but after one such trip the bus failed to return. It took a special, emphatic long distance phone call to the President to get it sent back.

Before the spring of 1949, Eric decided to try forming his own company to run the steamers, independently of the Royal Muskoka. It can only be conjectured that he did not like the way the affairs of the Navigation Company were being conducted, and that he felt impelled, with more heart than head, to try and save his beloved steamers from what looked like an inevitable demise. Fairley allegedly advised him not to take on the boats alone, but finally agreed, though the terms were stiff: $150,000 for the fleet and its accessories, with a cash down payment of $50,000. Eric sank all of his own personal funds into the venture, and lined up a number of friends and backers to raise the balance of the capital needed: his own mother, Mrs. Laura Wasley, offered to provide some collateral. By April he had incorporated the Muskoka Lakes Line, with himself as President. His friend and brother-in-law Norman Dickson became Secretary-Treasurer.

S.S. "Islander" leaving Bracebridge, 1948.
The "Niska" is blowing off smoke at the left.
Courtesy, *Mr. Ken Beaumont*, Toronto

The fledgling operation started on a sour note. On May 1, 1949, the very day that Eric Wasley was getting married in Toronto, a group of men from the Navigation Company arrived at Gravenhurst and virtually ransacked his office, making off with stacks of records. They then proceeded to the dockyards, commandeered one of Eric's trucks, and helped themselves to all the linen belonging to the boats and the Royal. Puzzled, and much disturbed, Alvin Saulter telephoned Dickson, who arrived at the scene just as the truck was about to leave. A heated argument broke out, and someone called the police. Dickson snatched the keys to the truck and hurried uptown to try to reach Eric, but in his absence, the men crossed the wires of the truck and made off. With no one to lay a charge, the constable felt powerless to stop them. Eric was in New York City when he heard about the incident, and he was later informed that the linen had been sorted, and that he could come and collect his own at the Royal! The documents, apparently, were never returned.

Despite this little episode, the Muskoka Lakes Line commenced operations in 1949. The schedules were much the same as before. The *Sagamo*, as always, ran the '100 Mile Cruise' north from Gravenhurst. The *Cherokee* was still based at Rosseau, the *Segwun* at Bracebridge, and the *Islander* at Bala. The *Ahmic* provided a twice-daily service from Rosseau to Port Carling by way of Minett and the west side of Lake Rosseau. The traffic, however, proved disappointing, and at season's end Eric Wasley reluctantly decided that there was no longer enough business to keep all the boats going. As a result the *Ahmic*, the "baby of the fleet" as the crews liked to call her, was beached at the Gravenhurst dockyards. She had been sailing the Muskoka Lakes since 1896, and had carried hundreds of thousands of passengers. The shabby little vessel lingered on for two more years, but was scrapped in October 1951 because she was not large enough for current operations and was too large to be moved elsewhere. The process began on October 22nd with the removal of her pilothouse, then was briefly delayed when the *Sagamo* was dry-docked beside her. Within a few more weeks, however, it was all over, and today only a few minor relics of the *Ahmic* survive. Her master, Captain Ariss, now took charge of the *Islander*, while Captain Hatherley became mate on the *Sagamo*.

246

S.S. "Ahmic", coming into Port Carling, 1949.
Courtesy, *Canadian National Corporate Archives*, X 16755

The end of the road for the S.S. "Ahmic"
The little steamer undergoing demolition at the Gravenhurst dockyards, while the "Big Chief"
gets a new propeller shaft, October 1951. The pilothouse of the "Ahmic" has already been
removed.

"Remember When...?"
The '100 Mile Cruiser' locking through Port Carling during the 1950s.

S.S. "Cherokee", preparing to pass the Port Carling Swing Bridge.
This picture was taken from aboard the "Sagamo", whose flagstaff can be seen at the lower left.

The 1950 season started auspiciously enough. The *Segwun* opened the '100 Mile Cruise' on June 19th, followed by the *Sagamo* on June 22nd. The *Cherokee* continued to take the 'Sunset Cruise', spending the nights at Rosseau. The *Islander* sailed as usual from Bala, connecting at Beaumaris or in mid-lake with the *Segwun* from Bracebridge and the *Sagamo* from Gravenhurst. In June alone, eight conventions and special charters were lined up, some combining cruises with a few days at Windermere, Wigwassan Lodge, Clevelands House, Elgin House and the Royal.

The follow-up was not the best. The summer of 1950 proved one of the coolest and wettest on record. Perhaps as a result, caterpillars blighted the landscape everywhere. Costs for fuel and supplies were rising. Outside of Canada, tensions from the outbreak of the Korean War again discouraged tourist travel. Yet all these worries were trivial compared with the aftermath of an incident that occurred on September 17, 1949. From that date, one might say, the Muskoka Lakes Line was already doomed.

The 'coup de grace' was delivered, not in Muskoka, but in Toronto. On the evening of September 16th, the S.S. *Noronic* of the Canada Steamship Lines, laden with tourists mostly from Cleveland and other American cities, steamed into Toronto harbour for what proved to be the last time. Hours later, in the dead of night, fire broke out aboard the 7,000 ton vessel, which soon turned into a roaring inferno. Most of the passengers were asleep in their staterooms at the time and a total of 118 were asphyxiated, burned to death, or in one case, drowned. Hundreds more were hurt and had to be rushed to hospital. By the following morning the ship had been gutted from stem to stern, and news of the tragedy was making headlines all over the United States and Canada.

Though terrible in itself, the *Noronic* fire was also a disaster for passenger ships in general throughout Canada. The Ministry of Transport began reviewing and revising all its regulations on safety and fire prevention on steamships. Almost overnight, ships and their owners were confronted with exacting new rules demanding all sorts of expensive new equipment, sometimes entailing major restructuring of vessels. Many firms could not meet all these new regulations and several ships were tied up after the season of 1949, never to sail again. Among the victims were the S.S. *Kingston* of the Canada Steamship Lines, last passenger ship on the Toronto to Prescott run; the S.S. *Manitoba* of the Canadian Pacific's service between Georgian Bay and Lake Superior; and the S.S. *Manitoulin* of the Owen Sound Transportation Company. The Georgian Bay Tourist Company, which was operating the famous ex-steamship *Midland City* between Midland and Parry Sound, now found its operations in jeopardy. On Lake Ontario, only the S.S. *Cayuga*, on the Toronto to Niagara run, still remained in business, though not for long. Everywhere, Canadian passenger ships were being driven out of existence.

The Muskoka Lakes Lines was in the melting pot with all the others. In 1950, the Company was obliged to spend about $8,000 on hoses, hydrants and fire extinguishers for its vessels, to say nothing of fireproofing decks and bulkheads. This was not enough to satisfy the Ministry and in February 1951, Eric Wasley and his friends received the paralysing news that three of their steamers would have to be outfitted with the very latest modern fire fighting equipment to keep operating. At the very least, the *Sagamo* would have to have a complete sprinkler system, along with automatic valves on all the fire pumps, two annunciator boards (one in the pilothouse and the other in the engine room) to pinpoint the locations of possible fires, plus sirens and an automatic bell system. The estimated cost: $45,000. Already burdened with liabilities totalling $127,496.42, the Muskoka Lakes Line just could not afford that outlay. Eric did not question the wisdom of the new regulations, but he argued that the Muskoka steamers could always be run ashore quickly in case of an emergency. The plea cut no ice. Groping desperately for a way out, he tried to interest Cameron Peck, the millionaire steamboat buff from Chicago who owned the flotilla of antique boats on the Lake of Bays, to invest in the firm; but Peck demanded at least 66% of the Company's stock in exchange, which was unacceptable. More appeals to Ottawa failed as the Ministry adamantly refused to modify its demands. By May 1st Eric knew it was "game over", and on May 11th he filed papers of voluntary bankruptcy at Osgoode Hall. In doing so he was leaving himself practically penniless, but such was the measure of the man's character that he voluntarily paid back some of his leading fellow investors from the proceeds of his legal practice, as soon as he could. The bankruptcy, however, imposed a great strain on his marriage, and eventually his wife left him. Eric began drinking a great deal and his health deteriorated. Meanwhile, Muskoka received word that the lake steamers might never sail again.

The result was an uproar. Many citizens had bought stock to help keep their steamers going. Businesses were alarmed at the prospect of the District losing one of its foremost tourist attractions: the boats were still known to carry over 50,000 passengers per season. Letters and phone calls poured in to the local Member of Parliament to do something. The Muskoka Tourist Development Association called the new rules "catastrophic", and offered its help to the Company and its creditors to try and solve their problems.

Though nothing could save the Muskoka Lakes Line, there was still a chance that the Muskoka Lakes Navigation and Hotel Company might step into the breach and pick up some of the pieces. Automatically the old company repossessed the steamers, and by mid June activity was noted aboard the the *Sagamo* and *Segwun*. It was also reported that the unyielding Ministry was taking a second look at the Muskoka steamships, noting that they never had to operate more than a mile from shore at any time. By June 21st it was definite. The *Sagamo* and *Segwun* would sail in 1951, with the *Islander* (too small to be affected by the regulations) placed on standby, perhaps to re-enter service at the season's peak. The Government had agreed to allow the *Sagamo* to run for one year with only two thirds of the required equipment. The *Segwun* was fitted out with new hoses and hydrants, but was henceforth licensed for only 100 passengers instead of 243. The *Cherokee* would be tied up to await future developments. Such drastically curtailed operations meant that several routes had to be abandoned, and that the boats would no longer sail from Bracebridge or Bala. Fortunately the mail contract still applied and the steamers continued to carry freight. A new Manager, Arnold Warren of Toronto, was hired to run the boat division, but Eric Wasley remained as his assistant. Precariously, Canada's oldest steamship line was still in business.

The sprinkler system, when completed, added about eight tons of weight to the lordly *Sagamo* and cost approximately $35,000. It was installed by a Montreal firm and tested on June 26th. One day earlier, the *Segwun*, now commanded by Captain Ariss, re-opened the season with two whistle blasts but few passengers. She now assumed the *Cherokee's* old run to Rosseau. Reg Leeder was no longer on the *Sagamo*: believing that the Muskoka steamers would never sail again, he had left to work on the ferries between Prescott and Ogdensburg, New York, and his place was now taken by Captain Hill. Andy Corbett briefly assumed command himself, but the task was too much for an ailing man of 80 and before the year was out, he died in Toronto. Alvin Saulter remained Chief Engineer.

He soon began to wish he hadn't. Morale was not high aboard the Muskoka steamers at this time and the Company, with its financial difficulties, was in no position to pay attractive wages. One night in 1951, the deckhands, oiler and two firemen on the *Sagamo* mutinied and handed Saulter a paper demanding substantial increases in pay. Unable to mollify them, Saulter telephoned Eric Wasley. The Assistant Manager arrived to find a council of war in the crew's quarters. "What's the matter, boys?" he asked. The men told him, and handed him their terms. Eric looked them over, and told them their demands couldn't be met. Finding them adamant, he then ordered them all off with their belongings. Wasley, Saulter and Arnold Warren now had to find some new hands, fast. Two deckhands were recruited, but Saulter refused to sail without an oiler and fireman and Wasley agreed with him. Warren managed to find someone to fire but Saulter, after meeting the fellow, sized him up as useless. Somehow enough hands were found for a curtailed cruise, but Saulter was forced to act as his own oiler. Furthermore, he had repeated difficulties trying to keep a dependable engine room staff. The ship had no fewer than thirteen firemen in fifteen days during that unhappy season, and many were no better than tramps. Most accepted a free meal and a night's accommodation, only to vanish by daybreak: Saulter soon ceased hiring at night. He also found it very difficult to get even the most essential supplies. Finally, the "chief" had had enough and gave the Company nine days notice. Gordon Fairley himself came down to the ship to ask why Saulter was leaving. The little Engineer explained why, and showed the President the turnover list of firemen. He refused to castigate anyone or assign blame, but insisted that "Either I go ashore or go to the nuthouse. This is not steamboating!" Fairley finally promised to get another engineer from Toronto, while Saulter speedily found a freighter sailing from Owen Sound whose skipper was glad to have him. He had scarcely taken his new position when a wire came through from Sarnia, urging him to call Gravenhurst, collect. Saulter did and asked what the trouble was? "There's no trouble," replied the voice on the line. "We just want you to come back." Saulter refused, feeling quite content with his new job, although he did return in

Chief Engineer Alvin Saulter, with granddaughter.
Courtesy, *Mrs. Zella Saulter*, Gravenhurst.

the fall to help lay up the *Sagamo* for the winter, without even getting a firm promise that he would be paid for his trouble. (In the end, he was.) The ex-chief was urged to return in 1952, but was offered only $350 a month, whereas he insisted on $400. Later it came out that the offer was supposed to have been $400, or even more if necessary. This attempt at chicanery by one of its personnel cost the Company dearly, in that less experienced hands than Saulter's failed to drain the piping system of the *Sagamo* properly one winter, resulting in a repair bill of nearly $10,000! Saulter never worked for the Muskoka Navigation Company again.

The year 1951 was unfortunate for the Line in other respects as well. Once again there was a lot of wet weather. Muskoka Wharf station was ransacked by vandals that spring. In July, a Company employee robbed the Purser's office on the *Sagamo* of $735.05, another indication of the calibre of men the firm had been hiring. Another day that summer, while the flagship was docked at the Natural Park and the passengers had all disembarked for sightseeing, a freak storm blew in and carried the ship towards the beach, dragging most of the pier with it. Luckily, Captain Hill, the Engineer and a few hands were still aboard. They reversed engines, backed the ship out of danger, and managed to cast off the lines. After the winds subsided, Captain Hill brought her gently back to the beach and engaged the local boats to load the people aboard. The wharf, unfortunately, was a shambles.

Even this was not the most costly incident. The worst luck of all came in mid September, when the *Sagamo* was completing her final trip of the season. A propeller shaft broke and disappeared into the depths of Little Lake Joseph, taking the propeller with it and leaving a hole through the housing. Captain Hill beached the ship at Natural Park until the hole could be plugged, and then took her home on a single engine. The *Sagamo* was dry-docked for a week while a new shaft was forged and machined. The bill exceeded $1,000, but things would have been much worse had it happened earlier in the season. The *Segwun* and *Cherokee* were also inspected, with the result that the *Cherokee*'s outside shafts were condemned. The 44 year old 'Sunset Cruiser' was forbidden to sail again until they were replaced. They never were, and the *Cherokee*'s cruising days were now at an end.

So were the *Islander*'s. By 1950, this handsome little vessel was 50 years old, and a close look revealed a disturbing amount of dry rot in her timbers. In 1953, after an inspection in drydock, she was officially condemned as unfit to carry passengers. The unkempt little craft was then tethered by the shore close to the highway, canted over in the mud. Late that summer, she was sold to an O.P.P. constable from West Gravenhurst, who refloated her with the intention of beaching her as a pavilion. The following year she was back at her wharf, ballasted but without her engine and boiler, and was even given a fresh coat of paint on her stack. But her owner soon decided to give her to a local contractor at Torrance, who offered him a scow in exchange

S.S. "Cherokee" at Lake Joseph station.
Courtesy, *Canadian National Corporate Archives*, X 12962

S.S. "Islander", last of the Muskoka woodburners.
Courtesy, *Canadian National Corporate Archives*, X 12961

(which the constable found more suitable for his purposes). The little *Islander* now completed her last cruise; in tow of a motorboat to Torrance, where she was stripped down to the main deck and converted into a barge. By 1958, however, trucks had taken over practically all the bulk-transport business, and even the barge was broken up. Today, except for a few relics, nothing remains of the vessel save her propeller and pilothouse. She had served the Muskoka communities for over half a century.

Also in 1954, the *Newminko* completed her last trip, under tow. Somehow, the aging supply steamer had survived a dozen years of neglect at Port Carling. Finally, she was sold to Francis Fowler of Milford Bay, who found her sunk and canted over at her dock. He bailed her out, using a raincoat and a pike pole to plug a hole in her hull, and towed the grimy old steamer off to Milford Bay. He had vague notions about restoring her but his neighbours, especially the cottage community around Beaumaris, objected to the old derelict as an eyesore and one day in 1955, some of them poured gasoline on her and set her on fire. For good measure, they taunted Mr. Fowler when he tried to put the fire out. Afterwards, he cut the hulk in two and turned the two halves upside down to shelter two boat house slips. They are still there, though probably not for very much longer.

The fortunes of the Navigation Company generally continued to wane. In the spring of 1952, shortly before the onset of the tourist season, it suddenly lost its greatest asset. On May 18th, at about 2:00 o'clock in the morning, fire broke out in one of the enormous dormitory wings of the Royal Muskoka, and within minutes the flames flared up into a roaring blaze that swept through the great hotel like a hurricane, generating its own wind. Flames visible all around Lake Rosseau shot hundreds of feet up into the night skies. Word spread quickly and people began speeding to the scene in their motorboats. No effort was made to fight the fire, but countless individuals risked their lives running in and out of the doomed building, grabbing china, furniture, or anything else they could lay their hands on. Within a few hours it was all over,

Steamboat time at Royal Muskoka!
Courtesy, *Canadian National Corporate Archives*, X 16746

Royal Muskoka Hotel, viewed from the Golf Course.

though the coals continued to smoulder for days. Nothing remained but the chimneys and a few twisted pipes and radiators. No lives were lost.

What caused the Royal Muskoka fire? The answer will probably never be known. Investigators at the scene immediately afterwards had nothing to go by except a vast heap of cinders. The hotel had not been making much money since the War, despite the massive renovations, and it is said that it had ceased to advertise towards the end, which of course is fatal. Yet the season seemed to be unrolling as usual, and several conventions had already been booked. For the insurance companies involved, the case must have been a legal nightmare since the hotel's replacement value was estimated at the time at $2,000,000. For hundreds of cottagers and long time local residents, the fire meant the loss of a prestigious social centre where people could go for haircuts, movies, dancing and the like, though few could afford to stay. To the Navigation Company, according to almost all the available testimony, the fire meant the end of an enormous and embarrassing white elephant, but once it was gone, many of the remaining shareholders relinquished their stock for whatever they could get. Now that the Company was reduced to a few excursion steamers and a little real estate, it no longer seemed a worthwhile investment.

Today, the headland once occupied by the Royal Muskoka is studded with many fine cottages, reached by service roads bearing the names of several of the old steamers. The peninsula itself is still known as Royal Muskoka Island. But of what was once Canada's largest summer resort, host to statesmen, politicians, millionaires and other celebrities, nothing still stands except its aging water tower; a lonely, tottering memorial to a past that is gone.

In spite of the troubles of the Navigation Company, the 100 Mile Cruise remained a pleasant and agreeable experience, thanks largely to the devoted efforts of faithful hands. Charlie Musgrave returned annually to entertain on the *Sagamo*, though towards the end his health was failing and he was reduced to playing by himself on the piano, without his orchestra. Captain Ariss remained on the *Segwun*, and Captain Hill, despite periodic frustrations, stayed with the *Sagamo* until Saturday August 24, 1952, when the air pump on the ship began to misbehave at Port Carling. The Engineer, quite properly, refused to go any farther, and Hill decided there was nothing for it but to curtail the cruise and return home. His decision was sensible, but he neglected to telephone Gravenhurst first. Gordon Fairley was surprised, then angry, when the *Sagamo* returned at midday without authorization. A heated exchange followed, and Captain Hill was dismissed. Eric Wasley, who had ceased to be active in Company affairs, stepped in once more as a deck officer until a replacement Captain could be found.

The new Captain proved to be none other than Reg Leeder, who had not cared much for the job on the Prescott ferry. Learning from Fairley that the *Sagamo* was still sailing and in need of a master, Captain Leeder applied for his old position and was welcomed back. He stayed with the *Sagamo* until the end.

A number of attempts were also made in the early 1950s to lure some of the former officers of the vanishing Huntsville Navigation Company. Although several boatmen served on both waterways, there was a tendency for the Muskoka mariners to belittle the Huntsville lakes as mere set of mill ponds, requiring no particular navigational skills, just as some Great Lakes seamen despised the Muskoka Lakes until they were called upon to try to navigate them! (One visiting Great Lakes Captain was invited to take the wheel of the *Cherokee* on Lake Joseph during the 1940s, only to lose control of her within five minutes.) A few North Muskoka mariners did move to the lower lakes, though few stayed long. Captain Parsons, late Master of the *Algonquin* and now pushing 77, served as Mate on the *Segwun* in 1952, but he did not get along well with the rather caustic Captain Ariss and soon left. Engineer Charlie McArthur of Burks Falls, who also ended up on the *Segwun*, was another veteran. He died of a heart attack in his own engine room in 1957. In 1953, Captain Edward Pink and his wife took a cruise on the *Sagamo* as special guests of Captain Leeder, with the full approval of Eric Wasley who hoped to recruit him, but Pink died suddenly the same year. Around that time, too, the ailing Charlie Musgrave died in Toronto; an event that drew commentary on CJBC Radio at the time. A born showman of irrepressable good humour, Charlie had been the life of the cruise for about 22 years. Captain Leeder noted that the atmosphere aboard the *Sagamo* seemed to turn drab and dismal without him: passengers became restless and the crew more sullen. Leeder was no musician, but he had heard Charlie's commentaries so often that he knew them almost by heart, and soon the

Captain himself was pointing out places of interest and repeating some of Charlie's stories over the p.a. system, to the distinct satisfaction of the public.

The year 1953 was the first in which the Muskoka District began promoting its dazzling autumn scenery as the 'Cavalcade of Colour', a tradition that has since been allowed to wane. The Navigation Company joined in the spirit of the event by decorating its ships with multicoloured leaves and branches in the fall. Unfortunately, the boats were entirely shut out of Lakes Rosseau and Joseph that year, because the Provincial Government had authorized, for the third time since 1871, a complete reconstruction of the locks at Port Carling, with the aim of electrifying them. All this was fine, but work was started too soon for the Company to move the *Segwun* to the upper lakes, as it would have preferred. This meant that new schedules had to be worked out. Once more, the *Segwun* docked overnight at Bracebridge, meeting the *Sagamo* at Beaumaris, then cruising to Bala and Gravenhurst, but it was quite a problem to find places for the *Sagamo* to go on an all-day trip that was limited to Lake Muskoka, especially since Captain Leeder refused to risk running her to Port Carling, for fear of not having sufficient space to turn around below the locks.

One day that year, Leeder received a request from Thomas Walker of Whiteside to bring the *Sagamo* in to his hotel, the American House. The skipper promised to consider it. Then, while cruising on the west arm of the lake, the Captain slowly approached Whiteside. Hector Hatherley, who was now mate, looked at him in consternation. "You're not going to take her in there, are you?" He didn't like the look of the narrow approaches or the low wharf. Captain Leeder sized up the situation, and decided to try it. The Mate was scared. It took a lot of manoeuvring, half ahead on one engine, slow astern on the other and so on, but gradually the big ship eased closer. Meanwhile, every guest at the hotel was coming down to the wharf. This was something new! The excitement was mounting. Finally the '100 Mile Cruiser' gently came to dock. Everyone broke into a round of applause, while Mr. Walker, shaking his head admiringly, observed, "That was never done before!" Nor was it ever done again. Backing the ship out of such a confined space was almost as difficult, but she made it safely and resumed her cruise. Hatherley mopped his brow and said to Reg, "I never thought you'd do it!"

Captain Leeder would later recall a whimsical incident during those years. Quite frequently in the morning, the *Sagamo* met a tiny steamer (perhaps the *Johann Sebastian Bach*, from Nine Mile Island, near Walker's Point), occupied by the owner and his wife, coming from the direction of Shanty Bay to fish near the Narrows. Apparently a converted lifeboat with a canopy, the little boat always saluted the big ship with two high pitched toots of her whistle, which the big ship always acknowledged in kind. One day outside the Narrows, the little steamer again approached the *Sagamo*, but instead of the usual greeting she signalled four quick blasts, which to the boat crews meant "Request permission to come alongside." Captain Leeder was nonplussed. It seemed most unlikely that either of the little boat's occupants would want to come aboard, but he replied with four blasts himself and stopped engines, just as he would have done for the *Segwun* or *Cherokee*. While the passengers crowded over to the rail to watch, the tiny steamer puttered up to the towering cruise ship and, as Captain Leeder looked down from the bridge rail, the man passed a big fish up to the deckhands at the gangway and shouted, "Hope you enjoy this, Captain!" Then the tiny steamer drew away, using the correct whistle signals, while the *Sagamo* again responded as one steamboat to another. The passengers were delighted.

By 1954, the Navigation Company had earned enough to discharge its debts over the *Sagamo* renovations, while the steamers were once again able to cruise on all three lakes. Lockages at Port Carling, which formerly required at least half an hour, now took a mere ten minutes. A big charter cruise on June 23rd required both ships, sailing in concert. Once again, the *Segwun*'s home port was Rosseau, which could no longer supply many passengers since its last major resort, the Monteith House, fell victim to fire in 1950. (The same applied to Beaumaris, where the old Beaumaris Hotel, a landmark since 1883, was burned down by a pyromaniac in 1945.) Freighting had dropped to a mere trickle, earning a paltry $50.60 in 1954. Every year, it seemed, the Ministry of Transport came up with new requirements involving more and more expensive equipment, including night navigational aids, though the steamers did not operate overnight. Every year the inspections grew stiffer, until it was rumoured that the Ministry's real aim was to kill off all the inland passenger steamships. (That goal was actually achieved in 1965,

First cruise of the "Sagamo" through the rebuilt Port Carling Lock, 1954.
The three gentlemen in the centre of this group are : Mate Hector Hatherley (left), Captain
Reg Leeder, and Lockmaster Reg Stephen.

Steam Launch "Johann Sebastian Bach", a late-comer to Lake Muskoka.

when the last C.P. ships on the Great Lakes, plus the last Canada Steamships Line passenger carriers on the St. Lawrence and Saguenay Rivers, were forced out of service by regulations they could not hope to meet.) Also in 1954, in a blatant act of philistinism, the old records and ledger books of the Company, some dating back to the 19th century, were deliberately carted out and burned at the dockyards; an irreplaceable loss for History.

Another disheartening indication of current trends was the total lapse in passenger rail service to Muskoka Wharf. Now that there was no longer any money in summertime recreation traffic, the old friendship between the C.N.R. and the Navigation Company soured. The railway had been collecting an annual fee of $1,000 from the boat line for the use of Muskoka Wharf, which was simply a means of making the boats help pay for its upkeep. Now the C.N.R. wanted only to get rid of the wharf station. The railway also complained that the Navigation Company had neglected to pay the 1953 fees. The Wharf was even offered to the Town of Gravenhurst as an outright gift, but the town did not bite. As of 1954, the C.N.R. more or less abandoned the Wharf to the Navigation Company, which could hardly afford to maintain it. Soon portions had to be cordoned off. Only the occasional way freight, sometimes including hopper cars full of coal, made any further visits to the station. Less than a decade earlier, there had often been six trains a day during the summer months.

Yet another prime misfortune struck the tottering boat line in 1954. The precious mail contract, vital to the steamers ever since 1866 and still said to be worth about $12,000 annually, was now cancelled; allegedly because a careless deckhand managed to land a mailbag in the water at Port Carling. This meant that the last steady source of revenue was gone for ever. The Line's other earnings, according to unofficial figures, were computed at $72,148.72 in 1952 (a good season for weather), but these had dropped to a mere $50,822.85 in 1953. The following year showed a slight improvement but when salaries, supplies and insurance costs were deducted, there was only about $28,000 left, or so it was claimed at the time.

With all these matters in mind, Gordon Fairley decided that the Muskoka steamships were now a lost cause and rather than prolong the agony, he decided to sell them off in September of 1954. The man who answered his advertisement was Morgan Cyril Penhorwood, a 45 year old

Muskoka Wharf station in its last days.

S.S. "Sagamo", passing through Port Sandfield.
Photo by *Art Duckworth, Port Sandfield*

The Last Hold-Outs!
The "Sagamo" prepares to enter the Port Carling lock, while the "Segwun" (left) heads downstream for Gravenhurst.
Courtesy, *Ontario Archives*, Acc. 9481, Box 4, # 10-H-124

business executive, originally of Sault Ste. Marie. An Accountant by training, Penhorwood had just retired as Secretary-Treasurer of the McNamara Construction Company in Toronto, and was now interested in some new activity to occupy his energies. Except that his daughter had sometimes gone camping in Algonquin Park, he had no previous connections with Muskoka, but in September of 1954 he noticed Fairley's newspaper advertisement that a steamship line in Gravenhurst was up for sale. On September 30th, he met with Fairley, who explained that he owned 90% of the Company, which had grossed $55,949.49 in earnings that season; not counting the mail contract. (Fairley neglected to mention that the mail contract had just been cancelled!) The firm's assets included three ships, three trucks, the yards and the marine railway at Gravenhurst, plus a wharf and shed at Port Carling, and the Natural Park; all of which were to be included in the deal. Its operating expenses had come to about $40,000, including $22,820 in staff wages. Fairley wanted $85,000 for his 90%, with a minimum cash payment of $35,000, and added that he would consider a partnership. A few days later Mr. Penhorwood came to Gravenhurst to inspect the plant: he found the steamers laid up for the winter, but judged them to be in good condition. The blacksmith ship, carpenter shop and yards looked messy and dilapidated. He also amassed a number of facts and figures, including insurance rates, the rents at Muskoka Wharf, the availability of staff, and the capacities of the ships. The *Sagamo*, he noted, was licensed for 293 passengers, could sleep 40 and dine 65. The *Segwun* could sleep 18 and carry 100. He also talked with Harry Smith, the acting Manager for 1954, and Eric Wasley.

After a further series of negotiations, terms were gradually hammered out with Fairley. In November, however, Penhorwood found out that the *Sagamo* needed to have her boilers retubed, plus some new guard rails; all estimated to cost $5,000. This caused quite a row since the steamers were supposed to be in good condition, but in the end Fairley agreed to deduct the cost of the renovations from the purchase price, which was set lower than the amount demanded. (Eric Wasley calculated that a complete upgrading of the plant would cost about $173,000, but this included an overhaul of the *Cherokee* and sprinkler systems for the smaller ships, which were never carried out.)

By February of 1955, Mr. Penhorwood was the proud President of the new firm of Gravenhurst Steamships Limited, whose assets he evaluated at $104,150, including $4,500 for the docks and buildings, $6,150 for the lands, and a book value of $82,000 for the three steamers. Meanwhile the old Muskoka Lakes Navigation and Hotel Company, after 52 years, was effectively out of both the hotel and the navigating businesses, and retained only a paper existence, apparently to sell off portions of its property at Royal Muskoka. Legally it survived until November 16, 1970, when it was officially dissolved.

Under Morgan Penhorwood, the boats were given their last lease on life. Backers were sought for the new company and an earnest effort made to revive and improve the service. Eric Wasley was asked to help and agreed to be operating Manager, although fundamentally his spirit was broken and physically he was a dying man. He did, however, resecure the services of Captain Leeder and Captain Ariss, and also managed to persuade Alvin Saulter to come back as Chief Engineer. That spring, for the last time, the boilers of the *Sagamo* were retubed. It was arranged that the old schedules would remain intact with the *Sagamo* running the '100 Mile Cruise' from Gravenhurst, and the *Segwun* from Rosseau offering an 'Afternoon Cruise' daily from Muskoka Wharf. Penhorwood tried in vain to secure another mail contract, but with little hope of success since local operators were prepared to carry the mail by land at starvation rates.

Before the 1955 season could be launched, the new Company suffered an irreparable loss. In late May, Eric Wasley was admitted to Bracebridge hospital suffering from bronchial pneumonia, and on the 28th, aged 46, he died. Perhaps what really killed him was heartbreak: the heartbreak of a broken marriage and the impending demise of the steamship enterprise which he, like his father, had tried so hard to save. He was the only man left who had a thorough practical knowledge of steamboating on the Muskoka scene, and there was no one to fill his shoes. The news of his death sent shock waves throughout the Gravenhurst community, and many attended his funeral. Perhaps the most fitting tribute to both the Wasleys came from a former employee of the Navigation Company who averred that "I never knew better men."

Eric's death meant that a new manager was needed for Gravenhurst Steamships Ltd., and in June a promising young engineer named Frank Miller (now M.P.P. for Muskoka) accepted the position. Miller knew the boats well, having served as Purser in his younger days. He now plunged into his new tasks with great enthusiasm, lining up charters and urging local people to patronize the cruise. The response was encouraging, perhaps in part because of the searing heat waves of 1955 that brought frazzled city folk out to the lakes by the thousands. On July 21, 1955, the Gravenhurst 'Banner' remarked approvingly;

> "Making a special effort to revive trade on the boats plying the Muskoka Lakes, it is pleasing to know that so far the first year's operation of the Gravenhurst Steamships Company is proving quite satisfactory. Many favourable comments have been heard from those who have taken a cruise on the Sagamo and Segwun. This reception, aided by favourable weather conditions, is an indication that the company can look forward with optimism to any future development it is planning."

The lovely sunny weather held up almost the entire season and into the fall, encouraging some 'Autumn Colour Cavalcade' cruises as late as October. Just once there was a disruption caused by the elements, when the tail end of Hurricane Connie lashed the lakes on August 14th, whipping up enormous waves and knocking out the power at the Port Carling locks. As a result, the steamers were delayed five hours until the locks could be operated manually. The *Sagamo* did not get out of Port Carling until 10:00 p.m., and between the pitch black night and the driving rain, it was impossible to see anything without lowering the pilothouse windows. Captain Leeder and the

S.S. "Segwun" gets a Police escort, 1955.

mate were drenched to the skin and to be on the safe side, they put in at Beaumaris for the night, while the passengers were bussed back to Gravenhurst. The *Segwun* spent the night at Port Carling.

Unhappily, after this promising start, the momentum of Gravenhurst Steamships began to die down and things again started to go wrong. In 1956, Mervin Firth of Gravenhurst, popularly known as "Tiny" because of his enormous waistline, succeeded as Manager. Firth was an amiable fellow but he knew absolutely nothing about steamboating, and his sole qualifications for his job were an ability to type and compute figures. He expected Captain Leeder to take the *Sagamo* on Moonlight Cruises, despite the lack of lights at Muskoka Wharf. To remedy that deficiency he suggested that a deckhand with a lantern should jump out onto the wharf from the ship's bow! According to another account, Firth casually gave away the poles used for pushing the steamers into drydock, not knowing what they were for. Soon the symptoms of decline were rampant again. Supplies would run short at critical times. The fares went up while the service went down. In an effort to cut costs, the once immaculate steamers were left largely unpainted and grew shabbier every year. Everything was being done on a shoestring. The old, experienced officers were dying off, and there were no younger men trained to take their places. Towards the end, the *Sagamo* was crewed mostly by high school students, who might have been enthusiastic, but lacked experience. One time the firemen on the *Segwun* got drunk at Port Carling. A boy dishwasher in the galley was abruptly reassigned to the stoke hold, while Mrs. Penhorwood and her daughter Carol had to take over in the galley. Another time, Mr. Penhorwood had to rush to Port Carling to drive another crew member to Bracebridge for an appendectomy; happily he arrived in time. In sharp contrast to 1955, most of the weather in 1956 was so cool and wet that street paving in Gravenhurst had to be cancelled. During the last few seasons the *Segwun* began docking overnight at Bala, dropping Rosseau as a stop, but all too often she left port in the morning with almost empty decks.

By now, the *Sagamo* and the *Segwun* were the only excursion steamships left on any of the inland lakes of Canada. The handwriting was on the wall. That the boats were able to keep going at all during those last years was due almost solely to the dedication of the officers and engineers. As long as men like Reg Leeder, Jack Ariss and Alvin Saulter were in charge, the ships at least were safely and competently run. In 1957 Harry Croucher, late owner of the little tug *Niska* (which had ceased operation in 1954), joined the *Segwun* as Engineer. He, too, was a veteran boatman, but both he and Captain Ariss were growing old.

On Labour Day 1956, a regrettable incident occurred at Muskoka Wharf. Captain Ariss was bringing in the *Segwun* around noon as usual, with a strong wind blowing behind him. No one was ready at the wharf to catch and secure the lines and as a result, the *Segwun* could not be stopped until she grounded her bow in the sand at the head of the cove. Captain Ariss was furious that no one had made any move to help, and refused to have lunch when he went home. He returned for the afternoon trip, still livid. It proved too much for a man of 69 and soon after the ship reached the open lake, the skipper suddenly collapsed at the wheel from a stroke. Jim Poast, the Mate, at once took over, blowing the whistle to bring men to the bridge. They carried the Captain to his cabin, then called at Walker's Point to have an ambulance meet the steamer at Beaumaris. Captain Ariss never recovered. He returned as nominal skipper in 1957, but remained partially paralysed. Such was his love for his ship, though, that the old man offered to come back for the first few trips of 1958 to help the new Captain learn the ropes, only to be informed that his assistance was not desired.

As things turned out, it would have been helpful. Scarcely any of the old officers were left. Captain Hatherley died in 1957. Captain Hill was now on the *Bigwin*, up on the Lake of Bays. There was nothing to do but to import a captain from other waters, and "Tiny" Firth engaged a Great Lakes skipper from Hamilton who made a good impression on him, despite the fact that the man was known to have a bad record for accidents. On his first trip, the new Captain managed to bump the ship into the swing bridge at Port Carling, almost knocking it off its base. As if that were not enough, while returning from Lake Rosseau, he drove the bow of the *Segwun* into the wooden dock and the Lockmaster's house. The vessel rebounded and struck the concrete portion of the dock, leaving behind a trail of destruction and giving the ship a badly bent forepeak. Mercifully, there were no passengers aboard: the vessel's mission had ironically been to repair the dock at the Natural Park. Accidents now became a regular routine.

Near the end of July, the Captain brought the *Segwun* alongside the floating dock below the Port Carling locks, and while turning around, managed to get one of the chains securing the dock wrapped around one of the propeller shafts. Some of the men ashore saw what was happening and shouted a warning, and the vessel was resecured. The Captain demanded that the Lockmaster provide divers to untangle the chain, but they very sensibly refused to go near it unless the engines were shut down. The Captain refused to shut off his engines and in the resulting standoff, the *Segwun* remained chained up at Port Carling all night. Finally the chain was cut and the ship headed back to Gravenhurst on one screw, where a couple of divers were able to untwine it. That proved the final disservice by the new Captain, who quit or was fired soon afterwards.

To finish the season, a new and better skipper for the *Segwun* was hired from Cobourg, but his tenure proved brief. Barely a week later, on August 5, 1958, the ship again left Gravenhurst for her usual afternoon cruise. The weather was lovely and there were quite a few passengers aboard. Once out on the open lake, the Mate, who apparently had a touch of asthma, decided to lie down in his cabin for a short nap. He left a young deckhand at the wheel, unsupervised, and gave him strict instructions to go on a curved course, avoiding the centre of the channel between Point Montcalm and Browning Island. The young fellow, however, saw no reason not to take a direct course, midway between the two shores.

He soon found out why. The ship suddenly grounded on the unmarked Gull Rocks shoal, heaved up, slid over the reef, then heaved up on another submerged ridge and slipped off again. People lost their balance and some screamed in panic. The deck officers dashed to the wheel — too late! Down in the engine room young John Coulter of Toronto, then an engineering student acting as assistant to Croucher, instinctively shut off both engines at first impact.

As the steamer drifted clear of the rocks, a hasty inspection was made down below. To everyone's relief, there was no sign of a leak. However, when the engines were again set in motion, the vessel began to vibrate alarmingly. It was then realized that she had sheared some of the blades off both her iron propellers. There was enough left of them to allow her to move, but the only thing to do now was turn around and head for home at dead slow; with the ship humping her way along through the water. Inspection revealed that two blades had been snapped off one propeller and three off the other. Alvin Saulter was quickly despatched to Owen Sound to see about replacements, only to learn that the plans had just been burned and that new plans would cost more than the propellers themselves. It was now clear that the season was over for the *Segwun*, but worse, as the yardmen were preparing to put her on the marine railway, a chilling message was received from Penhorwood: Don't do it. The men looked at one another, and shook their heads. Afterwards, there was a brief flurry of activity around the *Cherokee* (then at Muskoka Wharf), which had been idle for eight years and had been extensively cannibalized for spare parts, but upon boarding her the crews found that vandals had beaten them to it, and had mutilated the woodwork and smashed all the china on board. There was no longer the slightest possibility that the *Cherokee* could be reactivated to finish the *Segwun*'s season.

For the first time in 90 years, the Muskoka steamship enterprise was reduced to a single ship. The dignified *Sagamo* was now left to cruise alone. On August 22nd a leak appeared in one of her steam lines and the cruise was cancelled, but by the following day she was running again, now under a somewhat modified schedule. She carried on until Labour Day and was then tied up. Plans had been made to run further cruises during the 'Cavalcade of Colour', but the weather turned dismal in early September and Mr. Penhorwood, who had apparently been losing money on the steamers for quite some time, agreed with "Tiny" Firth that there was little point in carrying on any longer. As the crew of the 'Big Chief' correctly surmised, "that was it for the Muskoka steamships." All was over now. The proud ships that had long been an institution on the Muskoka Lakes would evidently never sail again. After 1958, there was probably not a single steam-driven vessel of any kind in commission anywhere in the District. What had started in 1866 with the crude little paddle wheeler *Wenonah*, amid the silent forests around the shores of Muskoka Bay, had ended at the same place with the *Sagamo*, 92 years and two months later.

S.S. "Cherokee", awaiting the end behind the coal ramp at Muskoka Wharf, 1960.

Girls of the dining room staff, S.S. "Sagamo".
Courtesy, *Mr. Brian Westhouse*, Parry Sound

"There She Goes, Ma! There Goes the "Sag!".

"Long Live Steamboating!"
Courtesy, *Canadian National Corporate Archives*, # 52327

CHAPTER 10
Epilogue
(1959-1983)

The day of the steamboat, it seemed, was over in Muskoka. Nothing remained but to bury all the remaining traces.

In 1959 it was announced that two Gravenhurst gentlemen, George Morrison and Jack Vincent, had purchased the last assets of Gravenhurst Steamships Ltd. from Mr. Penhorwood. This made them the proud owners of the *Sagamo*, *Segwun* and *Cherokee*, but as generally expected they had no intention of running them. Instead, they proposed to turn the Gravenhurst shipyard into a marina, and the *Sagamo* into a floating nightclub and entertainment centre, complete with dinner and dancing. The *Segwun* and *Cherokee* they proposed to scrap.

The marina was developed at the foot of Bay Street and early in July 1960, the *Segwun* was towed over from Muskoka Wharf. A few weeks later it was announced that the *Sagamo* would soon follow. The public was invited to tour the famous old ship beforehand, and a few were even allowed on board for that "last cruise" across the Bay. It was a melancholy trip. The vessel looked forelorn and empty, with all the furniture removed except a few deck chairs and Charlie Musgrave's dusty old piano, which stood forsaken at the aft end of "B" deck. There were no longer any boilers, and the motive power for moving her came from four outboard motors attached to makeshift outriggers welded to the hull. Within a year or two the old ship had been repainted and handsomely fitted out with tasteful nautical decor and tables arranged cabaret style in the upper lounge. Nearly $12,000 worth of restaurant equipment was installed, and it was hoped that she could look forward to a gracious retirement as the Sagamo Floating Restaurant.

Those hopes were soon dashed. The ship's wharf was a considerable walk from downtown Gravenhurst, and soon there were also rumours about unsanitary conditions aboard. The restaurant was closed after 1963, and for the next several years the old "Sag" sat at her wharf at Gravenhurst Marina, looking more and more dismal all the time while the owners wondered what to do with her.

In the case of the *Cherokee*, that question had already been settled. In 1960, the ex-Sunset Cruiser, along with the *Segwun*, was offered for sale for scrap, and the following spring her engines, rated by some as the finest in the fleet, were sold and removed. Later they were installed in an American Great Lakes tug called the *Bayport*. To simplify the process of extracting the engines, the wreckers went in with ball and chain and smashed the vessel's wooden superstructure to matchwood at Muskoka Wharf. Only the pilothouse and officers' cabin from the bridge were spared, and after decorating the premises at Gravenhurst Marina for several years, they found their way into the custody of the Muskoka Steamship and Historical Society in 1973. The steel hull of the *Cherokee*, after a brief ineffectual stint salvaging sunken logs on Muskoka Bay, was sold to Francis Fowler of Milford Bay who proposed to convert it into a scow.

After Fowler's death in 1979, the old hull was fitted out with steel cabins and a diesel engine, and was used for a few charter cruises in 1980, but the following year it was more or less abandoned in shallow water by the shores of West Gravenhurst. Finally the hulk was scuttled near the delta of the Muskoka River.

In the same year that the *Cherokee* was demolished, disaster also overtook the ex-steamer *Mildred*. Dieselized in 1954, the old launch had still been offering excursion cruises down the Muskoka River from Bracebridge as in Captain Archer's time. On July 19, 1961 while returning upstream past the Beaumont farm, the vessel's engine malfunctioned, blowing a gasket and setting the oil on fire. Her owner and master, Captain Ralph J. MacPherson, immediately ran her ashore, giving the passengers a chance to get off safely. The only one hurt was the Captain himself, who received a few burns fighting the fire and was the last to leave his vessel. The 58 year old *Mildred* burned to the waterline, leaving only her bottom and steel frame. The vessel was not insured, but Captain MacPherson was definitely not a quitter. He promptly had the wreck taken to the shops

The retired steamers "Segwun" (left) and "Sagamo", awaiting an uncertain destiny at the Gravenhurst dockyards, about 1960.

Last voyage of the S.S. "Sagamo".
The 54 year old '100 Mile Cruiser' is helped across Muskoka Bay using two outboard motors at either end, mounted on makeshift outriggers, in July 1960.
Photo by *Henry Fry*, Gravenhurst.

M.V. "Mildred", departing on a cruise from Bracebridge.
The vessel's appearance has been changed considerably since her days as a steam yacht.
Courtesy, *Mr. Alldyn Clark*, Bracebridge

at Bracebridge and rebuilt with safe new steel plating. Today the *Mildred*, now a private yacht, continues to run cruises on Lake Muskoka. Her new cabins have a boxy look and are strictly utilitarian, but one can still see some of her original beauty in the lines of her hull.

Along with the cruise ships have disappeared many of the local wharves that used to service them, as well as the old railway wharf stations at Bala Park, Bala, Barnesdale and Muskoka Wharf. What was once the site of Lake Joseph Station is now a summer camp run by the Canadian National Institute for the Blind. Old Muskoka Wharf, which had been a landmark since 1896, succumbed to the blows of the wreckers in 1959. Nobody had any further use for it.

Today the site of the old Wharf is crammed with aluminum-studded boat-houses clinging like barnacles to the edges of the crib work. In viewing this desolate spot, it is almost impossible to visualize the fine, trim station that served the District for so long.

Adjacent to the old station site lie the twisted, rusting remains of the *Sagamo*. In 1968, the unkempt old steamer seemed to gain a new lease on life at the marina, when she was sold for $5,000 to be reopened as a restaurant. Once again she was the scene of bustle and activity, as meals and refreshments were served in her lounges and dining room. But it was not to last. The following winter, history depressingly repeated itself. On January 10th, 1969, while the new owner and his wife were repainting her for the next season, the heater being used to warm the paints in the dining room exploded and set her ablaze. Almost the first item to go was the carved wooden phoenix which had decorated her pilothouse since the previous fire: it happened to be lying in the dining room at the time. The Gravenhurst Fire Brigade answered the call, but all of the ship's wooden superstructure was destroyed. The hulk was sold and towed over to West Gravenhurst, where it soon inspired the new owner with the hopeless dream of restoring it. By 1980, though, it was back at Muskoka Wharf, where it was partly cut up and then abandoned. The half-sunk wreck is slowly disappearing under land fill, next to the spot where she was launched in 1906.

The demise of the *Sagamo* in 1969 meant that all the old inland passenger steamers in Eastern Canada were gone, except one. The S.S. *Segwun* still survived. This little propeller had been destined for the chopping block in 1960, along with the *Cherokee*, and to all appearances she seemed doomed to share the fate of her sister ships. But at this critical moment, fortune smiled on her. A group of Gravenhurst citizens, shocked at the thought of losing all the old steamships that had been an integral part of the Muskoka mosaic for so long, now rallied to the vessel's

Gravenhurst waterfront, around 1964.

S.S. "Segwun", now a museum, is docked at the government concrete wharf, which is still her home today. The "Sagamo", also retired, is at the marina docks. In the background are Highway 169, the (former) Greavette Boat Works, and the concrete towers of the former Gravenhurst Potash Works.

The end of the "Sagamo", January 10, 1969.

defence. They pleaded with the town to buy the *Segwun* as a floating Marine Museum, commemorating the long, proud era of the Muskoka steamboats. The idea aroused the imagination of the townspeople and many supported the appeal. Messrs. Vincent and Morrison, who could have collected a tidy sum by selling the ship for scrap, generously offered to give her to the town for the sum of $1.00, provided that the town would preserve and maintain her as a memorial to the age of steam on the Muskoka Lakes. The offer was accepted and a public campaign launched to raise funds to convert the vessel. The appeal netted $1,200, a sum matched by the town.

The result, in the summer of 1962, was the formation of a new Museum Committee and a rush of activity around the *Segwun*. Citizens volunteered to clean up and paint the ship, or to polish the brass or repair broken windows. Local firms such as the Rubberset Brush Company contributed free brushes and supplies. Soon the shabby old steamer was starting to brighten up into something very like her former self. Down in the hold, Mr. Alvin Saulter, the retired former Chief Engineer with the Navigation Company, went to work on the engines just as if he were getting ready to sail again, and afterwards graciously agreed to act as Curator. No better choice could have been made, since few could match Mr. Saulter for diligence, devotion, and many memories from the lakes which he was always ready to share with anyone interested.

Historical Plaque unveiling at Gravenhurst.
The saga of Steamboating in Muskoka gets official recognition from the Archaeological and Historic Sites Board of Ontario. Present for the unveiling are (left to right): Robert J. Boyer, M.P.P., Hugh A. Bishop, Mayor of Gravenhurst, Ken McPherson, representing the Board, Alvin H. Saulter, Curator of the new Segwun Steamboat Museum, and Peter Stuart, Chairman of the Museum Board.
Photo by *Henry Fry*, Gravenhurst

A museum implies a collection of artifacts on exhibition, and that was soon in hand as well. The ship still retained her anchor, compass, engine room bells, electric telegraphs, flags and lifeboats, and soon other items of historic interest began to appear, such as axes, saws, tongs and chains from the lumber era, old tickets and baggage manifests for the purser's office, old maps and charts of the lakes showing the steamers' routes, old costumes and uniforms, and plenty of historic photographs of the steamers in their glory.

The opening ceremonies were held on August 4, 1962, under cloudy skies, but this did not dampen the enthusiasm. The event was climaxed when the Honourable Bryan Cathcart, Minister of Travel and Publicity in the Ontario Government, cut the tartan ribbon suspended between the *Segwun* and the *Sagamo*, then docked side by side, and proclaimed the Segwun Steamboat Museum officially opened.

Supported by a small grant from the Ontario Government and another from the Town of Gravenhurst, the Segwun Museum carried on for nearly eleven years. Despite severely restricted space and funds, the exhibits were gradually refined and improved. Portions of the forward freight deck were devoted to displays from the lumbering and railway eras; the latter featuring numerous relics rescued from Muskoka Wharf station. The dining room and galley were left essentially as they were, and the engine room was an exhibit in itself. On the upper deck, the stateroom section was largely converted into picture galleries, although one stateroom was left as it was in the days of the Navigation Company. It was never forgotten that the ship itself was the main artifact. In 1968, Mr. Saulter retired as Curator, to be succeeded by George Harvey of Gravenhurst. Mr. Harvey served until 1972. Occasionally the retired Captain Hill, who lived nearby in Gravenhurst, would come down for a chat, until his death in 1970.

Despite the *Segwun*'s displays as a museum, it was difficult for visitors to form a clear idea of her past, particularly if they had not shared it. Space on the vessel was cramped and fundamentally she did not make a suitable habitat for exhibits. With her engines still and the whistle mute, she had turned into a static, lifeless thing, brooding silently at her dock. It was as if the soul had gone out of her.

Segwun Steamboat Museum, 1968.
Note the crumpled forepeak, a result of mishandling of the vessel during the 1958 season.

Meanwhile, the excursion cruise tradition on the Muskoka Lakes did not die out. Both before and after the fire, the *Mildred* continued to ply from Bracebridge. A diesel cruiser, the *Britannia* still follows the *Algonquin's* old route between Huntsville and the Portage while a similar craft, the *Miss Port Carling*, plies from that port. In 1964, Captain Robert Cockburn of Agincourt, said to be a great nephew of A.P. Cockburn, and his neighbour Captain Tom Oake, a former New-foundland shipmaster, founded the firm of Muskoka Excursions Ltd. and brought in a modern, steel cruise boat, diesel powered, which they called the *Miss Muskoka*. Despite a discouraging start, the pair enjoyed a good season in 1965 and the following year ordered a second, similar cruise boat called the *Lady Muskoka*. (Both vessels went to Montreal to serve as ferries during the Expo celebrations of 1967, but only the *Lady Muskoka* was brought back.) Owned and com-manded by Captain Oake until 1981, the *Lady Muskoka* ran regular cruises from Gravenhurst, connecting with buses from Toronto until 1982, when she moved to Bracebridge. She displaces 116 tons and can carry about 300 passengers.

Today the Muskoka Lakes belong to the sailboat, the speedboat and the aluminum punt, and indeed boat traffic has never been heavier. Handsome mahogany, inboard runabouts are still to be found but they are generally being superseded by racing fiberglass outboards, which may go faster but do not reflect the same class. Lately the activities of the gas boats seem to be levelling off a bit, as the price of gasoline keeps going up. Perhaps the gas motorboats, too, have seen their best days.

The era of the steamboats, meanwhile, is not quite over. In recent years there has even been a modest revival. Here and there, devoted buffs are gradually discovering and restoring old hulls and refurbishing steam engines which only a few years ago would have been written off as so much scrap metal. The most sensational private restoration to date has been that of the *Wanda III*, Lady Eaton's former yacht, which was rescued in deplorable condition by Mr. Sandy Thompson of Hamilton, who has been restoring her by degrees. By 1971, the elegant *Wanda III* was back cruising occasionally on the Lake of Bays, and apparently she is now the only steam vessel on the lake.

The Muskoka Lakes themselves are becoming quite a mecca for steamboat owners. The first of the new steamers was apparently the *Cara Mia*, a little 31 foot vessel with a fiberglass hull originally designed for a gas engine. Fitted out in 1962, the *Cara Mia* is berthed near Elgin House on Lake Joseph, but has recently reverted to gas power. In 1970 Mr. Paul Dodington of Port Carling, after a meticulous restoration, launched a little 20 foot steamer called the *Constance*, whose oak and cedar hull was first built in 1898. The *Constance* has a two horsepower engine and a wood-fired boiler built by Mr. Dodington himself. She can go about ten miles per hour. In 1967 a larger, 25 foot craft with a five horsepower engine, known only as 60E 7474, from her license number, was restored by Norman Stripp of Windermere. In 1971, two more steam launches were introduced: the *Geraldine*, a 28 foot coal burning craft built originally in 1885 and now based at Pewabic Island on Bala Bay; and the *Nipissing*, first built around the turn of the century and found in derelict condition on Georgian Bay. With a length of 25 feet and a two cylinder engine, the *Nipissing* is owned by Mr. John Coulter of Toronto. She is an oil burner, and can carry seven passengers at ten miles per hour.

Other steamers arrived in the 1970s, some temporarily, others permanently. The *African Queen*, adapted from a lifeboat from the S.S. *Athabaska* of Montreal, was completed at Oakville in 1973 and brought to Bracebridge in 1974. Powered by a double-acting steam engine and a boiler from an old Stanley Steamer, the *African Queen* is 24 feet long and has a galvanized iron hull and a wooden frame. In 1977, she was sold and taken to Merrickville, on the Rideau Canal. That same year a steam launch called the *Patricia*, rebuilt with a fiberglass hull patterned after a wooden original, was launched on Lake Rosseau. Another steamer, the *Hiawatha*, utilizes an old Ditchburn motorboat hull and is berthed at Cliff Island, Lake Joseph. In 1980, the little steamer *Pen Queen*, another adapted lifeboat, was imported from Peninsula Lake to Rosseau, while the little woodburner *Tioga* ("beautiful wife"), owned by a couple from London, Ontario, paid a visit to Lake Muskoka .

A much larger vessel is the *Clarion* (10 tons), a 35 foot oil burner with a high pressure engine and a hull patterned from a Mackinaw type sailboat at Grand Bend, Ontario, in 1961. Rebuilt in 1975, the *Clarion* spent several seasons cruising on Georgian Bay and the Trent Waterway, until

Steam Launch "Constance".
This little craft, often seen at Port Carling, is attending the 1973 Antique Boat Show at the
Muskoka Lakes Golf and Country Club on Lake Rosseau. Mr. Paul Dodington is at the
controls!
Courtesy, *Mr. Harley Scott*

Steam Launch No 60E 7474, at the Antique Boat Show of 1973.
Courtesy, *Mr. Harley Scott*

Steam Launch "Nipissing"
Courtesy, *Mr. John Coulter*, Toronto

Str. "Clarion" at Gravenhurst.
Author's Photograph

Str. "Nottingham Castle".
This vessel, unique to Canada, now serves as a hotel yacht for Paignton House, Lake Rosseau.
Courtesy, *Mr. John Coulter*, Toronto

she was brought to Gravenhurst in 1979. She can carry about fifteen people, and has bunks for the captain and engineer.

By far the largest new arrival in Muskoka of late is the *Nottingham Castle* (40 tons), a former Royal Navy steam yacht built in 1943 and still registered in Southampton, England. Imported to Canada by a group of steam buffs in 1975, the *Nottingham Castle* served as Ontario Government flagship during the yachting Olympics held at Kingston in 1979. She was brought to Gravenhurst in 1981, and has been fitted out as a hotel yacht to run charters from Paignton House, Lake Rosseau. The *Nottingham Castle* is 56 feet long and powered by a reciprocating engine and an oil-fired boiler.

While the buffs were collecting their miniature steamers, the aging *Segwun* remained docked at Gravenhurst, year after year. Supposedly, her future was assured by her role as a museum, but still there were undercurrents of doubt. Despite the best efforts of the Museum Committee, close inspections revealed subtle signs of decay. Parts of the hurricane deck were growing spongy and leaked in rainy weather. The scuppers were corroding badly. Fire was an ever present threat, especially with the thick incrustations of paint that had been building up over the years. More ominously, the ship's old iron hull had not been out of the water since 1955 and was becoming badly pitted. It was clear that short of major refit, the vessel's days were numbered after all.

In the meantime, the ship's very survival fanned a faint hope that was simmering in a number of peoples' minds: the idea that perhaps her days of active service were not irretrievably at an end. Could the *Segwun* ever sail again? Under steam? Carrying passengers? It seemed like a very long shot; yet there she was, still intact, and substantially in good condition. Since a major overhaul was becoming crucial, some were asking why spend large sums of money on the old ship, just to let it continue to rust and rot at her dock? In fact, it seemed very doubtful that a restoration could ever be financed on that assumption. To some observers, the vessel's potential was largely being wasted as a museum. If restored to complete operating condition, the *Segwun* would obviously have far more to offer the public. Practical demonstrations of her machinery in action would be possible. Occasional trips up the lakes and visits to some of her old ports of call could be conducted. Certainly the Muskoka District, which relies so heavily on tourism, would again have something to offer that no other region had. The possibilities seemed almost limitless.

It is said that the hour sometimes finds the man, and in this case it did. Mr. John W.B. Coulter, a young marine Engineer, had spent several years at sea on ocean-going ships since his student days on the *Segwun* in 1958. However, he had never forgotten the *Segwun*, and after his return to Toronto he vowed that the old steamer would indeed sail again. Ambitious, single-minded and determined, Coulter believed that the job could be done and that he could do it. He paid a visit to Gravenhurst on the Victoria Day weekend of 1969, met the late Mayor Hugh A. Bishop and his family, and readily won them over to his plan. Out of that meeting was born the *Segwun* restoration project. Within a few weeks other interested persons, including history buffs and steam enthusiasts, also came forward, and the project gained momentum. Two of the restorationists, including Mr. Coulter, were admitted to the Museum Committee, and feasibility studies were conducted. One of the main concerns was whether a ship with wooden superstructure would ever again be permitted to carry passengers in Canada. Such regulations had recently forced the C.P. steamships *Assiniboia* and *Keewatin* off the Great Lakes. But the *Segwun* was very definitely an historic vessel, built before the modern regulations came into effect. In fact, there were no rules governing the possible operation of historic vessels. After a long, critical look, the Ministry of Transport agreed in principle to give the *Segwun* a new certificate of approval, provided that extensive safety precautions were met, especially against fire.

Work was then started. Hundreds of pounds of dirt and debris were removed from the bilges in preparation for inspections. Labouriously, the deckheads and interior sidewalls were stripped of years of accumulated paint, both to get rid of a fire hazard and to inspect the timbers beneath. And appeals were made for funds.

It was a strenuous and seemingly hopeless task. Little money was forthcoming at first, and willing hands were few. Nonetheless, some headway was made. New members joined the Committee. News releases poured out. Donations trickled in, and were made tax exempt. With the help of volunteers from the Beaver Creek Correctional Camp near Gravenhurst, all the remaining interior paint was removed. The saddles supporting the boiler were repaired. The prestigious firm of German and Milne, Naval Architects of Montreal, very kindly drew up a complete set of plans for the ship, at nominal charge, and also agreed to act as intermediaries with the Ministry. The publicity helped

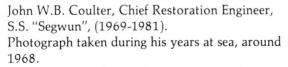
John W.B. Coulter, Chief Restoration Engineer, S.S. "Segwun", (1969-1981).
Photograph taken during his years at sea, around 1968.
Courtesy, *Mr. John Coulter*, Toronto

to remind people of what the district, and the country, stood to lose if the *Segwun* could not be saved.

It was still a race against time, and by 1972 it was obvious that time was winning. Pinhole leaks were spreading in the hull, especially around the waterline; a clear indication that the old ship could not be expected to hold out much longer. The Committee redoubled its efforts. Hitherto the plan had been to dry-dock the vessel in the Port Carling lock chamber, but in September, following a consultation with the chief engineer responsible, the idea was abandoned as impractical. It was decided instead to use the old Navigation Company marine railway at Gravenhurst, which was reported to be in excellent condition in its underwater sections. With a feeling of desperation, the Committee, whose assets were then about $8,000, now turned to the Ontario Government, which responded by promising a grant of $12,000 to help restore the railway, pending an inspection of the steamer's hull in drydock. The Committee was now in a position to negotiate with various construction companies to have the work done.

At this point, deliverance for the ship came from an unexpected quarter. The executives of the Ontario Road Builders Association (O.R.B.A.), some of whom had cottages in the Muskoka District, had learned of the *Segwun*'s plight. They invited the Committee to a special meeting at Gravenhurst in March 1973 and laid a generous set of proposals on the table: nothing less than an offer to sponsor a complete refit of the *Segwun* to operating condition, with funds and technical assistance to come primarily from the O.R.B.A. which represents roughly 130 road construction and related companies all over Ontario. The Road Builders explained their reasons for making the offer: a desire for better public relations, the wish to assist an unusual kind of project that embodied both historic and cultural significance, and which would benefit a widespread portion of the province, and finally, a certain desire to make amends for having helped to put excursion steamers like the *Segwun* out of business by building better roads. The O.R.B.A. proposed to obtain title to the ship, and to set up a new society in which the O.R.B.A. would for the time being, have a controlling interest. Later, as the project neared completion, they would gradually relinquish control of the society to competent local parties.

Needless to say, the O.R.B.A.'s offer was gratefully and enthusiastically accepted by the Segwun Committee, and was shortly afterwards ratified by the Town of Gravenhurst. A new group called the Muskoka Steamship and Historical Society was organized, with Mr. Bill Cole of Toronto, a Vice-President of the firm of C.A. Pitts Ltd., as President. The Road Builders kicked off the fund raising campaign by lending the Society $25,000. Steadily funds flowed in and soon the results showed. Arrangements were concluded with the Pawlett brothers of Gravenhurst, who now owned the marina, to reconstruct the railway (which afterwards reverted to them). Plans were drawn up and three new carriages built. Most of the actual reconstruction work was done by Fowler Construction Company Ltd. of Bracebridge, an O.R.B.A. member. By midsummer, all was ready.

On July 31, 1973, the *Segwun*, now emptied of its collection (which went into storage until such time as the Museum might be re-established) was towed by the *Lady Muskoka* from her wharf to the slip entrance. The following day, for the first time in eighteen years, she was very gingerly pulled out on the carriages; an adapted crane providing the necessary power. Several hundred people were on hand to cheer as the old ship finally completed her ascent.

To no one's surprise, all of the vessel's hull plating below the waterline was condemned by the inspectors, as well as the rudder and the outer propeller shafts. The contract to replate the bottom was awarded jointly to the firms of Collingwood Shipyards Ltd. and Herb Fraser & Associates of Port Colborne, for the sum of $70,000; not including the rudder and shaft work, which cost an additional $7,000. Within weeks Gravenhurst was again turning into a ship-building centre, as the Fraser firm undertook to remove the old plating, section by section, and truck it off to Collingwood. New plating was pressed into shape and sent back to Gravenhurst, there to be riveted to the ship's frame by the Fraser crews. The crumpled forepeak was the first section to be renewed. Two new propellers, this time made of bronze rather than cast iron, were manufactured at Iberville, P.Q., at a cost of $5,000 apiece. The inside stack, too, had to be replaced, at further cost of $2,250. Concurrently, superstructure repairs were proceeding under the expert hand and supervision of Mr. Fred Kruger of Severn Bridge, a skilled cabinet maker.

S.S. "Segwun" in drydock, May 1974.
The old ship now has a whole new bottom. The two propeller shafts have yet to be installed.
Author's Photograph

Off and Away!
The ship's damaged forepeak is removed in drydock, as the first step in a complete replating of the vessel's hull below the waterline, August 1973.
Author's Photograph

Starboard propeller installation, S.S. "Segwun".
Courtesy, *Mr. Alldyn Clark*, Bracebridge

The work took three months and by then it was too late to put the *Segwun* back in the water, especially considering that the new shafts were not yet installed. They were added the following spring and the hull repainting was completed at the same time. The most urgent phase of the refit was finished.

The date for the relaunching ceremony was set for June 1, 1974. The Prime Minister of Canada, the Right Honourable Pierre Elliott Trudeau, came to Gravenhurst to do the honours. What followed was one of the greatest days in the town's history. The weather was windy but otherwise magnificent as an estimated 6,000 people flocked to Muskoka Bay by boat and car to witness the great event. The platform and the ship itself were gaily decorated with bunting. A few people were given the privilege of riding the ship into the waves, including two veterans of the old Navigation Company, Gerald Leeder and Alvin Saulter, both in uniform.

The ceremony started at 2:00 pm. Speeches were made by the Society's new President, Mr. Glen Coates of Bracebridge, Mayor Bishop and the Prime Minister. Then the traditional bottle of champagne was smashed, a resounding cheer went up and the R.M.S. *Segwun*, just awarded the status of "honourary mail ship", slid triumphantly down the ways with a big splash. Two steamers, the *Constance* and the *African Queen*, were on hand to welcome her with their whistles. Once again, Captain Oake came over with the *Lady Muskoka* to tow the steamer back to her regular dock. It had been a big day.

Unluckily, the Society now had little money left. The O.R.B.A. and their allies, the Association of Equipment Dealers of Ontario, launched another fund raising drive. In time, further assistance was forthcoming from Federal Government grants for winter work on the ship, and from the Ontario Ministry of Culture and Recreation, through its Wintario programme, which in July 1976 approved a grant of $155,000 to help the project.

Other phases of the refit continued apace. All of the ship's unsightly exterior paint was removed (it proved necessary to burn it off—very carefully!), and gradually the vessel was repainted, using Ministry-approved fire-retardant paints. In 1976, the boiler was retubed by the

Old-Timers' Reunion on relaunch day, June 1, 1974.
Messrs. Gerald Leeder (left), Alvin Saulter and former Purser Edgar White of Toronto pose in front of the "Segwun".

The Moment of Truth.
Prime Minister Trudeau releases the bottle of champagne, minutes before the rebuilt "Segwun"
hits the waves on June 1, 1974.
Courtesy, *Mr. Alldyn Clark*, Bracebridge

firm of Automatic Boiler Ltd. of Toronto, which generously did all the work at cost. That same fall, all of the interior piping, now substandard in any case and partially corroded on the inside, was removed, though happily it proved possible to salvage the pumps and most of the boiler valves. The ship's generator was overhauled and an extra one obtained, to provide additional power when the vessel is sailing. In 1976, the engines were first tackled seriously. Both were dismantled, inspected and rebedded in accordance with modern methods. They were overhauled and repainted, and all defective components such as bushings, linkage-pins and piston rings, were replaced. Much of this work was carried out by dedicated volunteers. No changes or alterations were made except as required for safety, operating efficiency, or compliance with modern regulations.

At this point, the Steamship Society received the news that massive changes in the ship's hold, in particular the addition of four new watertight steel bulkheads, would be required if the *Segwun* was to certified for more than 49 passengers. This forced a return to the drawing boards and little actual physical work was accomplished in 1977. Finally, the revised plans were refined and approved by the Ministry of Transport, and in 1978 the Ontario Ministry of Industry and Tourism gave the project a tremendous boost in the form of a grant of $400,000. At last the final push could begin.

Four contracts were let in the spring of 1979. The firm of Craftwood Industries Ltd. of Toronto took on the remaining carpentry and interior panelling, while another Toronto company, Lumb and Scotland, agreed to finish the painting. Canal Electric Ltd. of St. Catharines carried out the piping work, auxiliary mechanical work, and the insulation of the boiler room. Construction of the new bulkheads, platework and deck gratings for the engine room was assigned to Automatic Boiler. Almost all of this work was completed by the beginning of 1980, except the painting, which was persistently frustrated by wet weather conditions in 1979. This phase was completed in the spring of 1980, and the *Segwun* ceased to look like an eyesore.

Pilothouse, S.S. "Segwun", during restoration.
Courtesy, *Mr. Alldyn Clark*, Bracebridge

Master Carpenter Fred Kruger of Severn Bridge at work on the ship's dining room (1976).
Courtesy, *Mr. Alldyn Clark*, Bracebridge

Engine room reassembly underway 1976.
Prominent in this picture are the inner port and starboard propeller shafts, the feed pump and an electric generator. The wooden stairwell will be replaced by a new steel structure.
Courtesy, *Mr. Alldyn Clark*, Bracebridge

All this left only two more phases: the electrical system and the ship's stores. Plans called for a double power system, one for emergency use, with a switchboard that could be plugged in to shore power when the vessel is not under steam, an electronic fire-detection system, and a complete public address system. So involved were the requirements that nearly one and a half miles of very expensive marine wiring was demanded, costing a staggering $124,000 to install. All this exceeded the Society's resources, but the Board of Directors, refusing to be stopped with the end so near at hand, resolved to borrow the monies needed to complete the work in time for the sea trials, which were set for 1980.

As the painting progressed and the ship's interior began to assume a finished appearance, new efforts were made to find the funds. A lottery, launched by the Road Builders in 1980 and offering four new automobiles and fifteen cash prizes, netted $65,000, which was augmented by a local fund-raising drive and a generous grant from the Bernard Sunley Foundation of the Blackwood Hodge Company Ltd. in England. As a result, the Steamship Society was able to liquidate most of its debts.

It had been expected that the steamer would be ready to sail on her shakedown cruises around Labour Day, 1980, but at the last moment a hairline crack was discovered in one of the safety valves on the boiler. This setback was soon rectified by obtaining an identical valve from the retired steam tug *Ned Hanlan* of Toronto, now on permanent exhibit at the Marine Museum of Upper Canada, which accepted the *Segwun's* defective valve in exchange. Finally, Mr. Coulter announced that the *Segwun* would begin her docking trials on Monday, October 6th, with sea-trials on the next two days.

It was a cool, overcast morning as the old steamer, for the first time in 22 years, backed dubiously away from her wharf and swung her bow north on Muskoka Bay. She was commanded by Captain Richard Farley of Chatsworth, Ontario, a veteran from the steam ferry *Trillium*, also recently restored for service in Toronto harbour. Assisting the Captain was Frank Freeman, the Mate, and a local pilot. Down below, a team of engineers swarmed over the machinery in the engine room, under the watchful eye of the inspectors. Also present in the pilothouse was Gerald Leeder, now of Kearney, who had agreed to act as advisory wheelsman. Gerald's thorough knowledge of the lakes and his personal familiarity with the *Segwun* and her eccentricities were to prove invaluable to the new officers.

The old ship accomplished little on her first day of tests beyond a few manoeuvres on Lake Muskoka. Problems developed with her port engine, and within a few hours she had to return to Gravenhurst on one propeller.

The *Segwun* left port again the next day under largely sunny skies. She again passed through the Narrows safely, and began an endurance run up the lake. More problems, however, kept surfacing in the engine room, and again she was reduced to a single engine. It was decided to make an unscheduled stop at Beaumaris to effect repairs, and a motorboat raced ahead to make certain the wharf was cleared of small boats. Though the cottagers had all left for the season, the ship caused quite a stir as she docked. She remained at Beaumaris for about three hours, but was then able to return to Gravenhurst by sunset. A cluster of people were on hand to welcome her back, wondering what was taking her so long.

The trials had not been completed in full, but they showed clearly that more work was needed on the engines and that the cabins needed radiators for cold days. The Society had no more funds available. While it was still debating its next move, Mr. J. Ross Raymond, a Gravenhurst engineer and planner who had been a Director since 1979, stepped into the breach. Hitherto the Chairman of an operating committee set up by the Society to work out plans for the vessel once the refit was completed, Mr. Raymond now put forward a plan for the formation of a private company which would lease and operate the ship, and endeavour to raise the necessary capital. He also offered to organize the company himself, and to assume the responsibility for completing the remaining work. The management of the venture would be undertaken by Mr. S. Gordon Phillips of Scarborough, an expert tourism planning consultant who had already spent seven years managing the cruise ship *Lord Selkirk* on Lake Winnipeg. The proposal, set forth in detail by Raymond and Phillips, was accepted by the Steamship Society Directors in March of 1981.

What followed was three months of frantic activity. At the suggestion of Mr. Raymond, the charter of the old Muskoka Lakes Navigation and Hotel Company Ltd., with all its attendant rights and privileges, was revived by the new firm, which thus adopted the same name as its predecessor. (By coincidence, this happened a century after the original Muskoka and Nipissing Navigation Company received its charter in 1881!) Meanwhile, schedules were evolved, brochures designed, tickets printed, and a thousand urgent details tackled, including the problems of furnishing and carpeting the ship and arranging a food and beverage service with a leading Gravenhurst restauranteur. All this, despite the exasperating hesitations of the banks in lending any money to cover preseason expenses, and without absolute assurance that the ship could even be certified and ready on time for the beginning of July! Not surprisingly, the Manager advised waiting until 1982, but Mr. Raymond was adamant that there be no further delays: there had been too many already.

Early on the morning of June 21, 1981, the *Segwun*, now under Captain Jack Allen, former Master of the *Lord Selkirk*, quietly steamed out of Gravenhurst and carried out a series of manoeuvres on Lake Muskoka, including figure eights and crash stops. She then proceeded to the Indian River. By now she had an escort, and a small boat raced ahead to alert the Lockmaster at Port Carling. The villagers were incredulous at the news that she was coming, and most refused to believe it: her return had been promised for years now, but with no results. Then her whistle was heard downstream. Many still figured that she would go aground in the river, but the whistles became progressively louder. People were even more amazed when she finally rounded the last bend without incident, and arrived for her first lockage in 23 years. She was back at last!

Part of "Segwun's" crew

Within a few more days, she had her precious certificate, and on June 27th the Honourable Frank Miller, former Company Manager but now representing the Provincial Government, joined Mr. Raymond in the official ribbon-cutting ceremony at Gravenhurst. On that day, her first public cruises began.

During the maiden season of her fourth career, the *Segwun* was commanded by Captain Clyde Mock of Owen Sound, a veteran Great Lakes officer, with young John Odell, one of Mr. Coulter's colleagues, running the engines. She ran six days a week, usually on short cruises from Gravenhurst, but with two all-day trips per week to Windermere or Paignton House, near Clevelands House. In August, she made a special visit to Rosseau, where the villagers were so glad to see her that they welcomed her at the wharf with a choir and a band playing 'See the Conquering Hero Comes'. The all-day '100 Mile Cruise' proved so popular that during the following seasons they were scheduled three times a week. Occasionally the old dowager balked at having to go back to work, but she soon settled graciously into her new routine and its attendant acclaim.

Her second season proceeded as planned, although without the services of Mr. Phillips, who was succeeded as Manager jointly by John Coulter and Mrs. Shelley Lowrey of Gravenhurst. In

In 1983 Mr. Russ Brown of Gravenhurst succeeded as manager; a post he still holds. In May the vessel, now overdue for an inspection, was again dry-docked and repainted: a heavy burden for a fledgling operation. Now commanded by the genial Captain Ratch Wallace of Toronto (with the First Mate, Mr. Patric Ryan of Kemble, in charge on Mr. Wallace's days off), the *Segwun* reopened service on May 24th. Under her new officers, she became more venturesome, varying her routes with cruises among the islands near Glen Echo, Browning Island and Muskoka Sands Inn. On the all-day runs, Clevelands House, like Paignton and Windermere, now became a weekly calling place. She also conducted five trips to Rosseau in 1982, but her proudest moment came on June 27th, when for the first time in 29 years she completed a triumphal trip up the Muskoka River to Bracebridge. About 75 motorboats escorted the grand old lady up the river, while at least 1,200 people lined the shores of the harbour below the falls to welcome her in. The *Segwun* repeated this feat five more times that year, but despite all the fanfare, the Bracebridge Town Council voted to proceed with a fixed low-level bridge across the river below the turning basin, thus shutting the old ship out of her former home port forever.

As a consolation, the vessel returned to Lake Joseph. She received another royal welcome at Port Sandfield and ran a total of three cruises on the upper lake in 1982; once to Sherwood Inn for an afternoon tea, once to the former Natural Park, and once even to old Port Cockburn, something she had never done since her days as the *Nipissing*. On October 6, 1984, she laid a wreath on the wreck of her lost sister, the *Waome*, and on August 3rd, 1986, she likewise commemorated the fate of the *Nipissing* (I) at Port Cockburn a century earlier. On the occasion of her centennial year (1987), a gala birthday party for the old ship was held at Gravenhurst on July 4th: over 10,000 people swarmed into town by boat and car for the festivities, which were climaxed by the biggest fireworks display ever seen in Muskoka. How many ships have ever inspired so much affection?

She arouses a similar sentiment from her crews. Various officers, including Captain John Manner of Sudbury and Captain Tom Oake of Gravenhurst (who retired from the *Lady Muskoka* in 1981) have taken her wheel in recent years, but since 1984 she has been entrusted to the genial Captain Jim Caldwell of Owen Sound; alternating with Captain Lee Werner of Peterborough. Her two mates, Bill Simcoe and Terry Morrison, have likewise been with her for many seasons, along with her devoted engineers, Bill Cripps and Ken Spring, and more recently Jack Stewart and John Philp. Since 1984 the ship has sailed into solvency and refuted the experts who kept insisting that she could never pay her operating costs. The Steamship Society, which still owns the vessel, has worked with the Navigation Company to create a new ticket-office and visitor-interpretation centre, styled after old Muskoka Wharf, and in 1993 they also acquired the *Wanda III* and brought her back from Dwight to Gravenhurst, where she is soon expected to run charter-cruises of her own, along with the *Segwun*.

Thus far, the S.S. *Segwun* has been a lucky ship. Physically, she is now stronger, safer and more elaborate than ever before, without sacrificing any of her essential character. She no longer has staterooms (overnight trips have been banned because of the fire risk), but she still retains her gumwood panelled dining room and oak panelled forward lounge, restored almost exactly as they used to be, and she now has two updated washrooms and a lovely new lounge and bar. Her new safety equipment includes radar, a depth sounder, several new life rafts, and ship-to-shore radio, plus several new fire stations. Today she is unquestionably the "Queen of the Muskoka Lakes".

It is not often that a reminiscence history of this kind can be closed on a happy note. Canada once had hundreds of fine steamships. Perhaps 140 steamers plied the Muskoka Lakes alone, not counting another 50 on the Huntsville lakes and the Lake of Bays, and more still on the Magnetawan and Lake Nipissing. All of them are gone today, except the *Wanda III* and the *Segwun*, and with them has vanished a charming, gracious portion of our heritage. When the steamers plied, life was sometimes harsh and obviously lacking in modern conveniences, but at least it was a quieter, less mobile age; less assailed by novelty and computer technology, and consequently a little more poised and serene. Perhaps in future, people will get tired of all their new electronic toys and plastic gadgets that are supposed to guarantee the good life, but for some reason don't. Perhaps in time, the exhaustion of our petroleum resources will force us back to a slower pace of life. Perhaps then, trains and steamships will come back into their own.

At least in Muskoka, thanks to the foresight, dedication, hard work and sacrifices of many agencies and individuals, Canadians have been given a second chance to enjoy a priceless portion of their past. Long may the fine old steamer *Segwun* continue to run, with honour and dignity, on the lakes that have known her so well, perpetuating the memory of the proud era of the lake steamers on the waterways of Ontario—The Steamboat Era in the Muskokas.

On a mild September evening in 1983, the majestically restored "Segwun" boards passengers at Gravenhurst for a Moonlight Cruise on Lake Muskoka.
Courtesy, *Ralph Beaumont*, The Boston Mills Press

A nostalgic scene from the past, yet very much a part of today, the S.S. "Segwun" pays a visit to stately Windermere House in June of 1984.
Courtesy, *Ralph Beaumont*, The Boston Mills Press

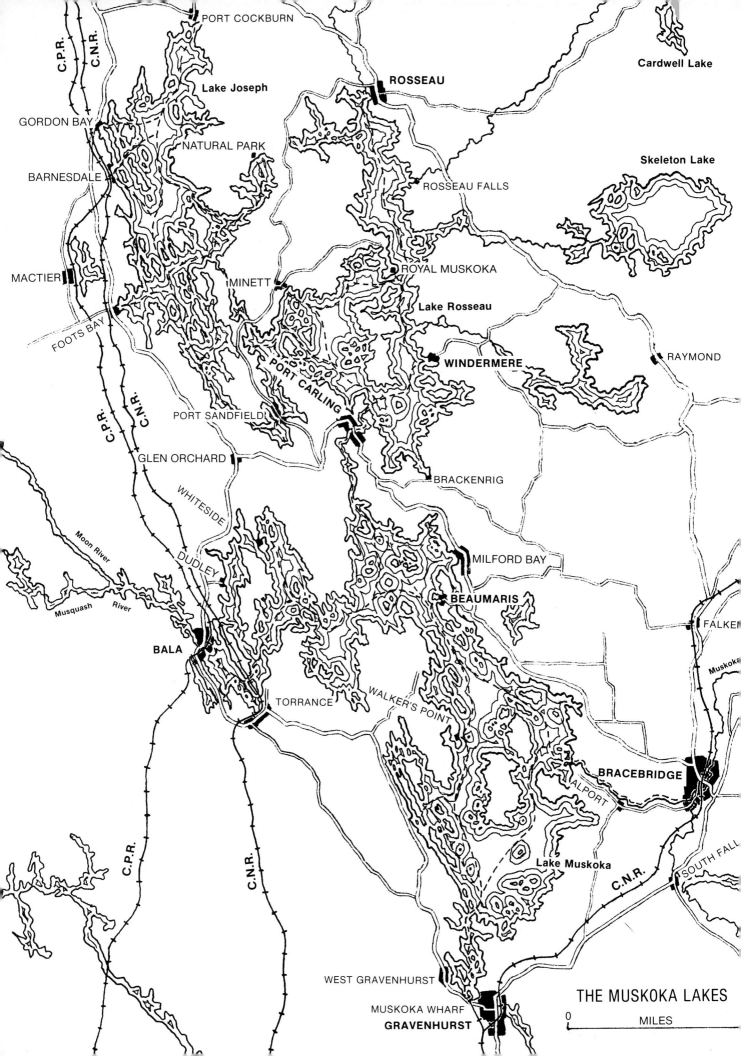

PORT COCKBURN

C.P.R.

C.N.R.

ROSSEAU

Cardwell Lake

Lake Joseph

GORDON BAY

NATURAL PARK

Skeleton Lake

BARNESDALE

ROSSEAU FALLS

ROYAL MUSKOKA

MACTIER

MINETT

Lake Rosseau

FOOTS BAY

WINDERMERE

RAYMOND

PORT CARLING

C.P.R.

C.N.R.

PORT SANDFIELD

GLEN ORCHARD

BRACKENRIG

WHITESIDE

Moon River

DUDLEY

MILFORD BAY

Musquash River

BEAUMARIS

FALKE

Muskok

BALA

WALKER'S POINT

TORRANCE

BRACEBRIDGE

ALPORT

C.P.R.

Lake Muskoka

SOUTH FALL

C.N.R.

C.N.R.

WEST GRAVENHURST

THE MUSKOKA LAKES

MUSKOKA WHARF

0

GRAVENHURST

MILES

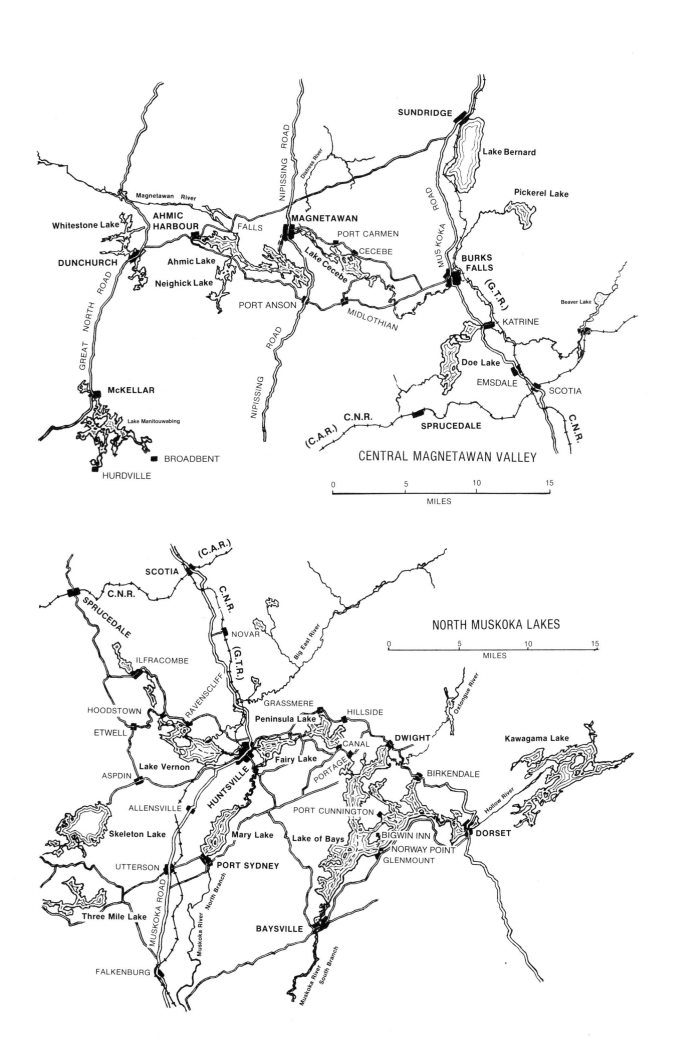

SUNDRIDGE

Lake Bernard

Pickerel Lake

Magnetawan River

Whitestone Lake

AHMIC HARBOUR

FALLS

MAGNETAWAN

PORT CARMEN

CECEBE

Distress River

NIPISSING ROAD

MUSKOKA ROAD

BURKS FALLS

DUNCHURCH

Ahmic Lake

Lake Cecebe

Neighick Lake

PORT ANSON

MIDLOTHIAN

(G.T.R.)

Beaver Lake

KATRINE

GREAT NORTH ROAD

NIPISSING ROAD

Doe Lake

EMSDALE

SCOTIA

McKELLAR

Lake Manitouwabing

NIPISSING ROAD

C.N.R.

SPRUCEDALE

C.N.R.

(C.A.R.)

BROADBENT

HURDVILLE

CENTRAL MAGNETAWAN VALLEY

0   5   10   15

MILES

(C.A.R.)

SCOTIA

C.N.R.

SPRUCEDALE

C.N.R.

NOVAR

Big East River

NORTH MUSKOKA LAKES

0   5   10   15

MILES

ILFRACOMBE

(G.T.R.)

RAVENSCLIFF

GRASSMERE

HILLSIDE

Oxtongue River

HOODSTOWN

Peninsula Lake

CANAL

DWIGHT

Kawagama Lake

ETWELL

Lake Vernon

HUNTSVILLE

Fairy Lake

PORTAGE

BIRKENDALE

ASPDIN

ALLENSVILLE

PORT CUNNINGTON

Hollow River

Skeleton Lake

Mary Lake

Lake of Bays

BIGWIN INN

DORSET

NORWAY POINT

GLENMOUNT

UTTERSON

PORT SYDNEY

MUSKOKA ROAD

Muskoka River North Branch

Three Mile Lake

BAYSVILLE

FALKENBURG

Muskoka River South Branch

BIBLIOGRAPHY

PRIMARY SOURCES:

Government Reports:
Canada:
Census, 1981
Department of Marine and Fisheries:
  Steamship Inspection Reports, 1910, 1920
Department of Marine and Fisheries:
  List of Vessels on the Registry Books of the
  Dominion of Canada, Volumes for 1903, 1907,
  1908
Department of Railways and Canals:
  Shipping Registers (Hamilton, Kingston,
  Toronto etc.)
Rowell-Sirois Report: Economic Background on
  Dominion-Provincial Relations, Volume 1, 1939
Post Office Department Annual Reports:
  1866-1917
Postmaster General's Annual Reports: 1947-1954

Ontario:
Office of the Provincial Secretary: *Annual*
  Statements Huntsville & Lake of Bays
  Navigation Company Ltd Muskoka Lakes
  Navigation & Hotel Company Ltd.
District of Muskoka: *Land Patent Books*
District of Parry Sound: *Land Patent Books*

Manuscripts:
Mills, John M.: World Ship Society *Compilation*
Muskoka Papers (Collection of Mr. Harry Linney)
Morgan C. Penhorwood *Papers*
Redmond Thomas *Papers*
Tweedsmuir Women's Institute: *History of*
  McKellar Township

Newspapers:
Bracebridge: *Herald*
Bracebridge: *Herald-Gazette*
Bracebridge: *Muskoka Sandpiper*
Bracebridge: *Muskoka Sun*
Burks Falls: *Almaguin News*
Burks Falls: *Arrow & Echo*
Gravenhurst: *Banner*
Gravenhurst: *Muskoka News Magazine*
Huntsville: *Forester*
Orillia: *Packet & Times*
Orillia: *Times*
Toronto: *Daily Star*
Toronto: *Globe & Mail*
Toronto: *Mail & Empire*
Toronto: *Telegram*

Published Diaries, Journals, Reminiscences etc.:
Cockburn, Alexander Peter: *To the Shareholders*
  of the Muskoka and Georgian Bay Navigation
  Company, 1902
Courtney, Clarence C.: *The Story of Ka-wig-a-Mog*
  Lodge Pittsburgh 1922
Cullen, Thomas S.: *Memories of Camp Ojibway*
  1952
Muskoka & Nipissing Navigation Company: *Guide*
  to Muskoka Lakes, Upper Magnetawan Channel
  & Inside Channel of the Georgian Bay 1888
Walton, W.W.: *"Kawigamog"—Pickerel River*
  Tales Cobalt, 1976

Periodicals and Brochures:
Lloyd's Register of Shipping London (U.K.), 1940
Muskoka Lakes: Highlands of Ontario (brochures)
  1903, 1906, 1909, 1916 editions
Muskoka Lakes Navigation Company: Brochures
  1911-1919, 1922-1925, 1935, 1939-1940, 1944,
  1946-1947, 1950, 1953
Official Guide: Huntsville & Lake of Bays
  Navigation Company Ltd. 1905
Railroad Magazine 1953
Silver Anniversary: Bigwin Inn, Lake of Bays,
  Muskoka, Canada 1944

SECONDARY SOURCES:
Avery, Sid: *Reflections, Muskoka and Lake of Bays*
  Yesteryears Bracebridge, 1974
Barry, Larry J. (editor): *Memories of Burks Falls*
  and District, 1835-1978 Burks Falls, 1978
Bice, Ralph: *Semi Centennial—Town of Kearney—*
  Incorporated 1908—District of Parry Sound,
  Ont. 1958
Boyer, Robert J.: *A Good Town Grew Here*
  Bracebridge, 1978
Brown, Ron: *Ghost Towns of Ontario*, Volume 2:
  Northern Ontario & Cottage Country Toronto,
  1983
Conway, Abbott: *The Tanning Industry in*
  Muskoka 1974
Cope, Mrs. Leila M.: *A History of the Village of*
  Port Carling Bracebridge, 1956
Fraser, Captain Levi R.: *History of Muskoka*
  Bracebridge, 1946
Higginson, T.B.: *A Sportsman's Paradise: Historical*
  Notes on the Burk's Falls District, 1835-1890,
  and the Village of Burks Falls, 1890-1965 Burks
  Falls, 1965
Jestin, Mrs. G.R.: *The Early History of Torrance*
  Bracebridge, 1938
Johnson, George H.: *Port Sydney Past* Boston
  Mills, 1980
Lavallée, Omer: *Narrow Gauge Railways of Canada*
  Montreal, 1972
Porter, Cecil: *The Light of Other Days* Gravenhurst,
  1967
Rice, Harmon E.: *A Brief Centennial History of*
  Huntsville, Muskoka, Canada (Second Edition)
  Huntsville, 1964
Scarfe, W. Lucien (editor): *John A. Brashear, the*
  Autobiography of a Man Who Loved the Stars
  New York, 1924
Schell, Mrs. Joyce I.: *The Years Gone By: A History*
  of Walker's Point and Barlochan, Muskoka,
  1870-1970 Bracebridge, 1970
Schell, Mrs. Joyce I.: *Through the Narrows of Lake*
  Muskoka Bracebridge, 1974
Scott, Harley E.: *Steam Yachts of Muskoka*
  Bracebridge, 1975
Stevens, G.R.: *The Canadian National Railways,*
  Volume 2 Toronto, 1960
Sutton, Frederick W.: *Early History of Bala*
  Bracebridge, 1970
Wolfe, Roy I.: *Recreational Land Use in Ontario*
  Toronto, 1954

The Author is also enormously indebted to a great many private persons who very kindly supplied him with a host of valuable pictures and priceless information. In particular, he wishes to acknowledge the assistance and co-operation of the following people, all of whom helped make this volume possible:

Miss Mary Elizabeth Aitken of Windermere
Mr. Charles Allair of Katrine
Mr. Carl Ames of Gregory
Mrs. M. Anderson of Woodington
Mr. Wilbur Archer of Muskoka Township
Mrs. Eva Ariss of Gravenhurst
Mrs. Jean Ariss of Rosseau

Mr. John Baker of Rockwynn and Toronto
Mr. Ken Beaumont of Toronto
Mr. Max Beaumont of Alport
Mr. Lorne Bell of Spence
Mr. Heamon Bennett of Hamlet
Mr. Alfred William Berry of Walker's Point
Mr. Ralph Bice of Kearney
Mrs. Mildred Bird of Huntsville
Mrs. Edith Blackmore of Magnetawan
Mr. Jim Blackmore of Midlothian
Mr. Bill Boettger of Magnetawan
Mr. and Mrs. Charles Bonnis of Gravenhurst
Mrs. May Boothby of South Portage
Mr. Irwin Boyd of Beaumaris
Mr. William C. Bradshaw of Toronto
Mr. Les Brandt of Burks Falls
Mr. George Brodie of Bracebridge
Mr. Hilton Brown of Port Sydney
Mr. Ted Bunt of Burks Falls
Mr. George Burk of Dorset

Mr. Joe Calverley of Toronto
Mr. Dan Campbell of Milford Bay
Mr. Norman Campbell of Huntsville
Mr. Peter B. Campbell of Campbell's Landing
   (near Gravenhurst)
Mr. Ray Campbell of Campbell's Landing
Ms. E. Casselman of Port Sydney
Mr. Norman Chevalier of Dwight
Mr. Fred Clairmont of Gravenhurst
Mr. Victor Clarke of Port Sydney
Mr. Wilfred Clarke of Port Sydney
Miss Dorothy Coate of Rosseau
Captain Robert Cockburn of Agincourt
Ms. Ellen Conelly of Baysville
Mr. Morgan Conroy of Huntsville
Mr. Abbott Conway of Guelph
Mr. Raymond Cooke of Orillia
Mr. Joe Cookson of Grassmere
Mr. Clarence Coons of Kemptville
Mrs. Leila Cope of Port Carling
Mr. Ted Corbett of Bala
Mr. Robert E. Cornell of Minett
Mr. Frank Cottrill of The Locks
Mr. George Cottrill of The Locks
Mr. Jim Cottrill of The Locks
Mr. John W.B. Coulter of Toronto
Mr. Fred Courvoisier of Poverty Bay
Mr. Sid Cowan of Port Carling

Mr. Enoch Buell Cox of Port Sandfield
Mr. Guy Croswell of Burks Falls
Mr. and Mrs. J. Harry Croucher of Bracebridge
Mr. Robert Crozier of Cecebe

Mr. Gordon Dean of Sprucedale
Miss Marjorie Demaine of Hoodstown
Mrs. Irene Wasley Dickson of Willowdale
Mr. Charles Dillon of Birkendale
Mrs. Albert Dixon of Monck Township
Mr. Dan Dobbs of Dunchurch
Mr. Paul Dodington of Port Carling
Mrs. Dorothy Duke of Port Carling
Mr. Merrill Dunbar of Sundridge
Mr. Bill John Duncan of Gravenhurst

Mr. Bill Edwards of Burks Falls

Mr. Gordon D. Fairley of Toronto
Mr. William Ray Fife of Windermere
Mr. Rod Fleming of Huntsville
Mr. Bill Foley of Gravenhurst
Mr. Francis Fowler of Milford Bay
Mrs. Mary Fowler of Beaverton
Mrs. Allan Fraser of Bracebridge
Miss Edna Fraser of Port Cockburn and Toronto
Captain Charles Fullerton of Barrie

Mr. Thomas Norman Giles of Peterborough
Mr. Cecil Goodwin of Gravenhurst
Mr. Bill Gray of Port Sandfield and Toronto
Mr. Arnold Groh of Gravenhurst
Mr. Godfrey Grunig of Magnetawan

Mr. Albert Hallett of Magnetawan
Mr. Rufus Harris of McKellar Township
Mr. George Harvey of Gravenhurst
Mr. Peter Harvey of McKellar
Mr. A. Ernest Hatherley of Gordon Bay
Miss Marie Henry of Huntsville
Captain Wesley D. Hill of Gravenhurst
Mr. Frank Hutcheson of Huntsville
Mr. George Hutcheson of Huntsville

Mr. Floyd Ireland of Bala
Mr. Robert Ireland of London

Mr. Claude Jackson of McKellar Township
Mr. Harry Jackson of Monck Township
Mr. Harwell Jackson of Bracebridge
Mr. John Jackson of Gravenhurst
Mr. Rod Jenkins of Ahmic Harbour
Ms. Margaret and Tillie Jestin of Torrance
Mr. Lorne Jewell of Port Credit
Mr. George Johnson of Port Sydney
Mr. Bernie Judd of Juddhaven
Mrs. Mary Kennedy of South River
Mr. Colin Keppy of Spence Township
Mr. Everett Kirton of Powassan

Mr. John Laking of Kearney
Mrs. Martha Langford of Magnetawan
Mr. Ronald Langford of Stephenson
   Township
Mrs. A. P. Larson of Gravenhurst

Mrs. Doris Lawrence of Milford Bay
Mr. John Laycock of Huntsville
Mr. Gerald Leeder of Kearney
Captain and Mrs. Reg. F. Leeder of Orillia
Mr. Henry Lennox of Magnetawan
Mr. Henry Longhurst of Windermere
Mr. J. Lydan of Pinelands

Mr. Andrew D. MacLean of Gravenhurst
Mrs. Pearl MacLennan of Dunchurch
Mr. Gilbert MacLennan of McKellar
Captain Neil MacNaughton of
    Parry Sound
Mr. Joe Marks of Scotia
Ms. Pearl May of Huntsville
Mr. Ernest J. McCulley of St. Catharines
Mr. William McEwen of McKellar
Mrs. Dick McGibbon of Mimico
Mrs. Alec McLachlan of Magnetawan
Mr. Norman McNeice of Bala
Mrs. Barbara Mills of Georgetown
Mr. Fred Mills of Milford Bay
Mr. Luther Mills of Parkersville
Mr. Gordon Morris of Port Carmen
Mr. Norman Morris of Magnetawan
Mr. and Mrs. Eddy Mortimer of
    Mortimer's Point
Mr. Bernie Moulton of Parry Sound
Mr. D. Murdoch of Orono
Mrs. Flora Murray of Burks Falls
Mrs. Anna Myers of Gravenhurst

Mr. Murray Neal of Torrance
Mr. Bill Norton of Huntsville

Mr. Ben Olan of Orillia
Mr. Edgar Olan of Huntsville
Mr. Fred Oldfield of Severn Bridge
Mr. Charles Orgill of Bracebridge
Mr. Murray Osborne of Magnetawan

Mr. Ross Paget of Sundridge
Mrs. Bert Parsons of Burks Falls
Mr. and Mrs. Morgan C. Penhorwood
    of Bracebridge
Mr. Harry Phillips of Burks Falls
Messrs. Cecil and Levi Porter
    of Gravenhurst
Mr. Cecil Proudfoot of Huntsville
Mrs. Elsie Proudfoot of South River
Miss Winnifred Prowse of Bracebridge

Mr. Bill Raaflaub of Bracebridge
Mr. Gordon Raaflaub of Magnetawan
Mr. William Ralston of Huntsville
Messrs. Charles and Lloyd Readman of
    West Gravenhurst
Mrs. Dorothy Robson of Fox Point
Mr. Enoch Rogers of Port Sandfield

Mr. and Mrs. Alvin H. Saulter of
    Gravenhurst
Mrs. Joyce Schell of Barlochan
Mr. Peter Schell of Muskoka Township
Mr. Harley E. Scott of Minett
Mrs. Edythe Scriver of Huntsville

Professor Gordon C. Shaw of Thornhill
Mrs. Vera Sherwood of Gravenhurst
Mr. Arthur Silverwood of Huntsville
Mr. Robert Sleeth of Gravenhurst
Mr. Gordon Sloan of Gravenhurst
Mr. Adam Snider of Magnetawan
Mr. Claude Snider Gravenhurst
Mr. Thomas Stanton of Port Stanton
Mr. Ralph Stephen of Port Carling
Mr. Reg Stephen of Port Carling
Mrs. Frank Stephenson of Huntsville
Mr. David Stewart of Burks Falls
Mr. Fred W. Sutton of Bala
Mr. Owen Swann of Huntsville

Mr. Paul Tapley of Fox Point
Mr. Redmond Thomas of Bracebridge
Rev. Bill Thompson of Gravenhurst
Mr. Gilbert Thompson of South Portage
Mr. Sandy Thompson of Burlington
Miss Ruth Tinkiss of Bracebridge
Mr. Wilfred E. Tipper of Etwell
Mr. Ronald Tomlinson of Oakville
Mrs. Marie Tryon of Scarborough
Mr. Lester Turnbull of Dundas

Mrs. Viola Van Clief of Baysville

Mr. Austin Wait of Barrie
Mr. Aubrey Walton of Christian Valley
Mrs. Edgar Walton of Port Loring
Mr. Merrill Walton of Burks Falls
Mr. Claude Wardell of Huntsville
Mr. James St. Clair Wardell of Huntsville
Mr. Dan Watson of Baysville
Mr. Brian Westhouse of Parry Sound
Mr. Hector Whitehead of Gravenhurst
Mr. John Whitehead of Parker's Point
Mrs. Dorothy Wilmot of Midlothian
Mrs. M. Wittick of Burks Falls
Mr. Victor Woodcock of Huntsville

MUSKOKA
L. N.
& H. CO.

S. Playfair, Toronto, Ont.
PRESIDENT

W. F. Wasley, Gravenhurst, Ont.
ACTING MANAGER AND TREASURER

Muskoka Lakes Navigation and Hotel Company, Limited

Gravenhurst, Ont.

Officers of the S.S. "Sagamo", August 1909.
Commodore Bailey and Chief Engineer MacKenzie are seated together on the bench, front centre.

Index "A"
of the Steamboats that Appear in this book

Asterisk (*) Indicates Photograph

Iroquois II (m.v.) - 233, 234*, 236
Islander - rear endpaper*, 15, 19*, 23, 24,
    28*, 39, 45, 46*, 51, 52*, 53, 54*-58*, 146,
    148, 150*, 154, 162, 163*, 182, 203, 205*,
    211, 215-217, 243, 244*, 245, 246*,
    249-251, 253*
Izaak Walton - 208

J

Jennie C. - 89, 91*, 94
Jennie Willson - 19, 46
Joe - 64*, 65, 66*, 68, 69, 71, 72*, 74, 78,
    79*, 81, 82*, 94, 97
Johann Sebastian Bach - 256, 257*
John Bull (alligator) - 92*, 93, 96, 228
Juanita - 36

K

Kacymo - 26*, 32*, 33
Kate Murray - 162
Kawigamog - 137*-142* passim
Keewatin - 276
Kenozha - 5*, 13, 18, 19*, 45, 51, 52*, 53,
    54*, 58*, 59, 60*, 146, 154
Kestrel - 47
Kingston - 249
Kola - 36

L

Lady Muskoka (m.v.) - 273, 277, 280
Lady of the Lake - 18, 69, 74, 78
Lake Joseph - 46
Lena - 33
Lillian M. - 89, 91*, 97
Linden - 33, 46, 121
Linnia - 45
Lizzie - 69
Llano - 21, 100, 146, 147*
Lord Selkirk (m.v.) - 284, 285
Lotus - 31*, 33, 208
Louisa Lee - 36

M

Mabel M. - 87
Maggie Main - 46, 47
Manitoba - 249
Manitoulin - 249
Manolia - 41
Maple Leaf - 69, 78
Margaret - 36
Margaret S. - 91
Marion F. - 101, 125
Martha - 120, 121*
Mary Caroline - 43
Mary Louise - 68, 69, 74, 77*
Mattie - 33
Mayflower - 88
Medora - 5*, 13, 15, 18, 51, 55, 58, 146, 148,
    151*, 154, 164*, 180*, 186, 187*, 188,
    189*, 212, 240
Midland City - 249
Mike - 122, 124*, 128, 129*
Mildred - 146, 147*, 208, 209*, 267, 269*, 273
Mineta - 19, 20*, 21, 33
Minga - 36•
Mink (first) - 37
Mink (second) - 37*, 38, 41, 148, 154, 162,
    196 (see Waome)

Minnie C. - 36
Minota - 87
Miss Kingston (m.v.) - 236
Miss Muskoka (m.v.) - 273
Miss Port Carling (m.v.) - 273
Miss White Pines (m.v.) - 273
Modello - 211
Mohawk Belle - 79*-81, 83*, 85*, 97-99,
    104*, 105*, 194, 208, 221, 223*, 225*,
    226, 229
Morinus - 27, 29*
Muskoka - 15, 16*, 18, 44, 180*
Muskokalite - 41*, 209
Mystic - 132

N

Naiad - 162, 194, 208, 209*, 228
Naniwa - 27
Ned Hanlan - 283
Nellie Bly - 142
Newminko - 37*-39*, 41*, 148, 149*, 162,
    194, 208-210*, 211, 215, 253
Nipissing (steam launch) - 273, 274*
Nipissing - 12, 13, 18, 51, 53, 55-57*, 58*,
    60*, 146, 154, (see Segwun) 155*, 160, 286
Nishka - 35*, 91, 93, (see Niska)
Niska - 73*, 91, 92*, 93, 208, 215, 216*,
    246*, 263
Norcross - 142
Noronic - 249
Nottingham Castle -274*
Nubertha - 47, 48*
Nymoca - 24, 33, 39, 41, 42*
Nymph - 19, 20*, 21, 49, 50*, 148

O

Onaganoh - 39, 41, 42*
Ontario - 27, 49
Opeongo - 85, 86*
Oriole - 5*, 9*, 18, 45, 51, 52*, 146, 160,
    161*, 162
Oriska - 27, 29*
Osso (first & second) - 35*, 36

P

Pagan (gas tender) - 122
Patricia - 273
Peerless II - 44*
Pen Queen - 273
Phoebe - 33
Phoebe II - 33, 34*, 208, 227*, 228
Phoenix - 68*-70*, 78, 80, 87, 97, 100
Pinta - 87
Pocahontas - 125
Priscilla - 162
Ptarmigan - 36
Pukwana - 27, 120, 121*
Puritan - 33

Q

Queen Anne - 131
Queen of the Isles - 46, 47*, 148, 182, 208, 209

R

Rambler - 5*, 208
Ramona - 71, 73*, 76, 78, 80, 97-100, 104,
    221-223*, 224*, 226, 229
Rhoda - 36
Rob Roy - 62

The S.S. "Segwun" is greeted by hotel guests at Windermere in the summer of 1984.
Courtesy, *Ralph Beaumont*, The Boston Mills Press

Index "B"
of the People, Places and Enterprises that Appear in this book

Asterisk (*) Indicates Photograph

S.S. "Islander" at Bala station wharf.
Courtesy, *Tweedsmuir Women's Institute, Bala*

S.S. "Islander", near season's end, Port Carling, 1929.

S.S. "Islander", dry-docked at Gravenhurst.

S.S. "Florence Main" (Third Version), docked near Baysville.
Courtesy, *Tweedsmuir Women's Institute*, Baysville